2·00

The things that are Caesar's

A.D.P. Heeney

ARNOLD HEENEY

The things that are Caesar's
Memoirs of a
Canadian public servant

Edited by Brian D. Heeney

Foreword by John W. Holmes

University of Toronto Press

© University of Toronto Press 1972
Toronto and Buffalo
Printed in Canada
ISBN 0-8020-1930-7
ISBN Microfiche 0-8020-0268-4
LC 72-90745

Contents

To

my wife Peggy

and for

my children and grandchildren

Foreword

If you knew Arnold Heeney in only one or other of his official roles or from press reports, you could have missed the Irish in him. But that would not have happened if you had known him better. His assurance, his utter competence, his grace and style, and his unassuming air of distinction seemed far removed from the Gatineau hills where he had his roots. But one of the many joys of this recollection of his life is his romantic account of his Irish family background and his own growing up in Winnipeg and at Oxford. It is a remarkably happy history, full of wonder and excitement, yet it is saved from sentimentality by his sense of irony – a quality which is essential to a successful civil servant and diplomat.

Out of such a combination of characteristics great mandarins are made. Here is a lucid, modest, illuminating, and entertaining account of value to historians, political scientists, and others. He recalls his life as creator of the post of secretary to the cabinet, as ambassador to Washington, and in the various other capacities in which he, more than any other individual, established a sound and effective structure within which the Canadian Public Service could grow. One might have feared that a rigid devotion to the principles of Civil Service confidentiality would make this a dull record. Arnold Heeney was always firm; but he was never rigid. This book is properly discreet but never unduly so. Without betraying secrets, he sheds light on the development of some government policies over thirty years, as well as on a large cast of Canadian and foreign characters. He might seem too generous in his judgments, but he was a Christian who understood human weakness and looked for and brought out the best qualities in those with whom he dealt. We might hope that his accomplishments will serve to convince a cynical generation (the older one, that is) that the philanthrope succeeds better than the misanthrope in public life and diplomacy.

This is the story of a man who deserved good fortune and fashioned a career with which he had every right to feel satisfied. His father was an acquaintance of Mackenzie King and there was, he says, 'no damned nonsense of merit about my entry into the Public Service of Canada.' A deep attachment to his native country, a sense of duty which was the product of his inheritance and the education of his times, a zest for the noble and exhilarating game of government, as well as honest ambition led him from a more profitable profession in Montreal to public service in Ottawa. His prompt resistance to Mr King's assumption that service to the Liberal party was included in the new job strengthened a new generation of public servants. His intellectual and moral integrity, the granite in him, radiated confidence.

He was always a passionate Canadian, but his nationalism was of the large-spirited kind which enabled him to glory in the whole Canadian inheritance. As his accounts of his days in diplomacy reveal, the respect and affection he felt spontaneously for his foreign colleagues never got in the way of his arguing toughly the Canadian case. The modest irony with which he tells this story does not fully reveal his quality as a diplomat. Arnold Heeney, well briefed, articulate, master of a terse and muscular prose, and always in control, was not a man to whom the representatives of great powers readily said no, partly because they respected his argument, but also because they liked him.

Heeney's attitude to the United States, too often misunderstood, was that in dealing with a giant whom we cannot exorcise and who could crush us if he were so disposed, we are more likely to protect our interests if we preserve a spirit of mutual good will and of give and take. There are times for loud diplomacy and tough talk, but preferably after sweet reasonableness has been tried. In recognizing that Canada was locked on a continent with the United States and that Canadians had to keep their wits about them to survive, he was a 'continentalist.' One purpose this book will serve, however, is to make clear that he was no continentalist in the pejorative sense in which the term is now often used. He was alarmed by talk of customs union after the war, and in his term with the International Joint Commission he strengthened a principle of international association which, in his view, guaranteed Canadian independence and Canadian interests by providing for equal membership in continental associations and also preserving the sovereign right of the Canadian government to take the final decisions. At a gathering of powerful Canadian industrialists and financiers several years ago someone ventured to suggest that because Canada depended on the United States for defence, investment, and markets it should associate itself unequivocally with American foreign policy. 'I could not disagree with you more,' said Arnold Heeney from a height of about eight feet, his conviction by no means diminished by his smile. During his terms in Washington, as he reports here, he defended Canadian contributions to continental defence not as tribute but as the means by which an ally which had freely committed itself to defence by alliance maintained its independence and self-respect. His explanation of the report prepared with Living-ston Merchant on the principles of Canada-United States relations will, it is to be hoped, remove the misinterpretations to which the report was subjected at the time. Typically he blames himself for wording that was open to mis-understanding.

He retained to the end his capacity to adapt and adjust his ideas to chang-ing conditions. This scion of Irish Protestants not only defended the exten-sion of French in the Public Service, he insisted on using that language him-self – and before it was fashionable or expedient to do so. He never ceased pondering on the United States-Canadian relationship, and his last testament on that subject at the end of this book shows a heightened awareness of the Canadian dilemma. He knew that times and the balance of forces had shifted. He was an optimist not only by nature but by discipline. Whatever the odds against the Canadian interest, he knew that when one is engaged in the strug-gle, defeatism is inadmissible. If, as he admits in the end, the Americans too often marshalled superior resources and outmanoeuvred the Canadians, the weakness was usually the government's, not that of this public servant.

To call this a heroic account would have gravely offended the author's sense of proportion. And yet it is the gratifying story of a young man with a heroic view of life who grew to do his country service. He was a generous man to work for and with, precise, encouraging, and fair, rarely downcast. Nothing was more courageous in his life than the ending. It had taken some persuasion to get him to write a memoir, as he deprecated both the significance of his experience and his literary capacity. Most of this account, so full of the joy of life, was composed during his last year as he weakened from a mortal illness. All his life he had carried out his assignments. He finished this one by the deadline he had set himself. Three days later he died.

Toronto 1972   JOHN W. HOLMES

Preface

The first draft of this book was completed by my father less than a week before he died in December 1970. For two years he had worked at it spasmodically on holidays and weekends, and during the last few months of his life he devoted an ever increasing proportion of his declining energy to its completion. His original intention was to work through the first draft with care, to reconsider its proportions, to check his recollections against available evidence, and to revise the whole work. Had he been able to do these things this would have been a better book.

As it is, the final result is a team effort. The Canada Council generously allowed me to make use of a research grant originally awarded to my father. Supported from that source, John Bryson undertook the arduous task of checking references, names, and dates, and identifying quotations whenever he could do so. He also offered me very helpful literary advice. Nerta Lacharity, my father's secretary, assisted him at every stage. The editorial skill of Diane Nelles of the University of Toronto Press greatly improved my draft version. I am grateful to King and Ruth Gordon who made valuable practical suggestions and, along with Rik Davidson and many others, gave me encouragement and moral support. Two people deserve special recognition. John Holmes helped both my father and myself in many ways. His warmth and affection, as well as his advice and aid, were invaluable. My mother's contribution has been incalculable. She reassured my father that the project was worthwhile; she raised his morale by keeping him at it when he was mortally ill; she has supported me firmly and lovingly since I took over.

Although a great deal of the substance of this book is based on the author's recollections and not any written records, references are made to a small collection of letters and fragments of diaries which form Arnold Heeney's personal papers. The letters quoted in this volume, including the correspondence between Mackenzie King and Bertal Heeney and the short selections from the author's very sketchy and occasional journal, are in this collection. This material is now deposited in the National Archives of Canada. The only source materials referred to in this book which are still retained by our family are the diaries and journals of the author's father, William Bertal Heeney.

Champlain College   BRIAN HEENEY
Trent University
Peterborough, Ontario
August 1972

The things that are Caesar's

1

A long way from Tipperary

I begin with William, my paternal greatgrandfather, for it was due to him that our family became Canadian in the first place. He was born in County Meath, Ireland, on 10 April 1811. His father died when he was very small, and when his mother remarried young William was packed off to school in Dublin. There he remained, apparently until he graduated. Little else is known about William's early life except that in 1834, at the age of twenty-three, he married Sarah Howard. Ten years later, perhaps because, as family legend would have it, he had been involved in some troubles in which he had probably killed some one, William and Sarah sailed for Canada. With them were their five children, including my grandfather, Henry, who was then six weeks' old. They were going to join a number of Sarah's relatives and friends from Tipperary who had emigrated some years earlier and settled in the Ottawa valley.

The Heeneys first established themselves at Fitzroy in the western part of Carleton county, an area largely settled by Protestant Irish and English emigrants many of whom had served in Wellington's armies. Nearby were miscellaneous and interrelated Howards and Greenes and Carrys so that while there was much that was strange and forbidding about the new surroundings there was much too that was warm and familiar. Above all, there was new hope for the young, free of the dark anxieties of the old land. William seems to have settled quickly into teaching, first at the 9th Line school and later in nearby Huntley, and soon a second daughter and two more boys were born. Here, for the next two decades the family shared in the life of a pioneer Canadian community, and with their fellow Irish contributed to the speech and customs, the standards and prejudices, the strengths and weaknesses characteristic of that region.

To participate in the emerging lumber trade, the family moved in 1861 to Danford Lake in the Gatineau north of Ottawa. Luke, the oldest son, had taken the initiative and built a house there for himself and for his father's family. Soon after, Henry acquired a considerable tract of crown land in the neighbouring township of Alleyne at what later became known as Danford Corners. Then followed the building of a barn and necessary outbuildings and, finally, the grand house to which he brought his young bride Eleanor Jane Walsh of Bearbrook, Ontario, in the spring of 1867. My father was born here on 18 February 1873, the third of eight children, six of whom were boys. He was christened 'William' after his grandfather and 'Bertal' by some undisclosed fancy of his mother's.

As Bertal and his brothers and sisters grew up, the problem of educating them became increasingly worrisome to their parents. To his own regret in later years, Henry's schooling had been brief and rudimentary. As a youth in Huntley he had preferred to go north to the shanty with the men rather than to stay the winter at home under the severe hand of a father who was also his teacher. What had appealed to him then was the life of the woods and the rivers and the freedom and companionship that went with it. As a youngster he had chafed under the discipline at home, but he never had been afraid of hard work and, in the company of men who exalted physical strength and skill in the demanding lumbering trade, 'Harry' Heeney had acquired something of a reputation. The vitality and wit which had made him popular along the river in the early days was matched by a sharp intelligence and voracious curiosity about all manner of things in the wider world. So, for his children, he was almost as anxious as their mother – who, despite the cares of a growing family and the never-ending labours of the household, would snatch whatever time she could to refresh her mind and imagination in poetry and fiction – that they should have schooling. Both father's parents went to great pains to provide the best they could for the education of their children.

Father's first school was a crude one-room log building near Luke's farm, presided over by a veteran of the Crimea and the United States civil war who had a wooden leg and a terrible temper. An attempt to establish a school in Danford Corners failed after father had spent only one year there, so in 1887 James Senior, the local Church of England clergyman, was prevailed upon to provide regular lessons to the older Heeney children in return for room and board. For two years my father and the others gathered daily around the diningroom table with the textbooks on which Senior insisted, while this 'red-headed Englishman and scholar,' as Henry later described him, attempted to acquaint them with the traditional disciplines. A year or so later, when father was sixteen or seventeen Senior returned to his former lodging by the lake. Then father had to make daily journeys through the bush in order to have the old parson's continued guidance and some beginnings in the study of Latin and Greek. After a short stay at a school in Shawville, in the fall of 1891 father was accepted at the Lachute Academy, a high school which at that time enjoyed one of the best reputations in the province of Quebec.

For the eighteen-year-old boy from the Gatineau, the little town of Lachute, a mostly English-speaking rural community, must have been a new world. By comparison with what he had known it was modern and comfortable. His first problem was to arrange for his lodging and board, for the family could provide little more than moral support. He was taken on as the night operator at the telephone office, a job which had the important advantage that the calls were infrequent so that he was able to study or to sleep. By the time father had passed the University School Examination and was certified as an Associate in the Arts in 1893 his decision of several years earlier to devote his life to the Christian ministry was confirmed.

That fall father entered the Diocesan College in Montreal and registered in the Arts Faculty at McGill, for he was determined to obtain a bachelor's degree before embarking on his theological training. During the years which followed he continually struggled to secure the means to provide university and college fees and personal living expenses at the most modest level. He spasmodically received small sums from home, although these were more an indication of the family's moral support than a serious contribution to his budget. But his life at McGill was not all grim. The whole academic community of that university at the end of the century, generously nourished by the prosperous mercantile element of English-speaking Montreal, was stimulating and optimistic. Among his McGill friends was Lemuel Robertson, later professor of classics at the University of British Columbia and the father of my own close friend and colleague, Norman. At McGill father expanded his horizons and tastes by reading outside the limits of his formal curriculum, and by the time he left college in 1899 he was steeped in the Victorian literature to which as the years went by he returned for refreshment and release. Two years later he graduated in theology. When he walked out of the Diocesan College for the last time, at the age of twenty-eight, his emergence from the Gatineau was complete.

On 1 June 1901, after father had been ordained and appointed curate of Christ Church in Belleville, Ontario, father and mother were married. They had met when father was in his final year at McGill at what was then known as a 'conversazione,' an evening gathering in the home of a Montreal family at which out-of-town students were received for coffee, cake, music, and talk. Mother was Eva Marjorie Holland, a tall, slim, dark-haired girl with beautiful violet eyes. From the beginning it was a romance in the Victorian manner, and as their friendship developed into love, mother came to embody for him an ideal of Christian beauty and refinement which set her apart from all other women. She was the daughter of one of the large group of merchants who in the latter part of the nineteenth century and in the early years of the twentieth gave to English-speaking Montreal its special flavour of commercialism and evangelical Christianity. Though not wealthy by the standards of some of his contemporaries, her father was able to maintain his family in comfort and some style. Both he and his wife were Methodists, and his considerable energies were expended with equal zeal on his import business, his church, and on the work of the YMCA. The young couple was married in the old Holland house on Sherbrooke Street West and set off at once for Belleville.

The life of the young Heeneys at Belleville was taken up immediately with the establishment of a new home and the many church and community duties. And then on 5 April 1902, I was born and christened Arnold Danford. Father recorded in his diary that it took 'some time to realize I am a father,' but even at this early stage my primitive hibernian appearance led him to nickname me 'Paddy.' That first summer of my life father took us back to Danford, for him the 'dearest place on earth,' where he could find refreshment and renew himself so that he could return to his parish to deal with the poor, the old, and the sick, whose wretched conditions always depressed him.

After four years at Christ Church, father accepted appointment as rector of St George's Church, Newport, Rhode Island. It was a difficult decision for the young parson, not least because it meant leaving his own country. But it was a new challenge and we moved there in the summer of 1905. It is not difficult to imagine the contrast of the new surroundings to the familiar environment of the small Ontario town on the Bay of Quinte. St George's parish was by no means the part of the Newport of the 'cottages' where the fashionable and wealthy from New York and Boston spent their lavish summers. Nevertheless father and mother did have some contact with that other strange and glittering society which was then near the height of its fame – or at least with some of its less ungodly members. But despite the compensations of their life in Rhode Island, it was not long before the longing for home became irresistible to both mother and father. In fact father had come to realize that from the time of their arrival there had been a feeling of strangeness, a transitory element, in the new surroundings. Perhaps that was because he had expected it to be so. He had always intended to return to Canada, but before a year had gone by he became determined that his son should be 'brought up under the British Flag.' When he had an opportunity to return to Canada, less than two years after he had gone to Newport, father had no doubt as to where his duty as well as his inclination lay. By the end of 1906 the family was installed in Barrie, Ontario, which a newspaper account of my father's appointment described as consisting 'mostly of retired Englishmen, officers and gentlemen of culture and refinement.' Father became the vicar-in-charge of Holy Trinity Church, I attended my first school, and my sister Marjorie Eleanor was born.

Father's sentiments and loyalties meant that from the very first I was surrounded by British influences. The earliest stories which I read were of British heroes from Alfred of the Cakes to Kitchener of Khartoum; a cousin of mother's had won the Victoria Cross in South Africa for 'saving the guns.' By the time I was seven I knew every line of a book, *Deeds that Won the Empire,* by an unremembered author, and when I arrived in Winnipeg I was ready for the spate of G.A. Henty to roll over me. Most of my companions at that first school had the same influences working on them; it was the time of the British empire.

In the spring of 1909 our family moved to Winnipeg, which was to remain our home for the next quarter century and more. These were important, critical, and exciting years for all of us. Father was at his most vigorous and productive, and though he continued to love and often to visit eastern Canada, he became caught up from the very beginning in the new and stimulating environment of the prairies; indeed so much so that to the end of his life he was to think of himself as a westerner. For my sister and me it was natural that the years of school and college should have a lasting influence and leave an enduring bias on our later attitudes.

In the first years of the twentieth century Winnipeg was an exciting self-confident community only recently emerged from the pioneer period. With some reason, Winnipeggers regarded their rapidly spreading city as the capital of the prairies, the hub of the west between the Lakehead and the Rockies, for which a prosperous future lay round a brief corner in time. Manitoba school children knew of Laurier's prophecy for the Canadian twentieth century and we felt in our bones that a special destiny was intended for Winnipeg. When the visiting Bishop of London described our city as the logical capital of the British empire, we were not one bit surprised but took it as our due. These were also the years of the great annual waves of European immigration which followed the railways and changed the face and spirit of the settlement community. It was the time of the wheat boom which turned Winnipeg from a remote prairie railway town into a centre of international trade. Except for the immigrant labourers whose wretched conditions were soon to arouse the righteous indignation and social conscience of J.S. Woodsworth, prosperity and confidence in the future were virtually universal. The community into which the young Anglican clergyman and his wife and children came was boisterous, self-assured, and exhilarating.

As I recall prewar Fort Rouge, the south Winnipeg suburb where the still-to-be completed St Luke's Church stood, it was a community of wide, flat streets bordered by comfortable but undistinguished frame houses and garnished rather surprisingly by respectable trees and grass boulevards. Most of our neighbours seemed well-to-do, at least by my standards, although I was conscious that within father's parish there was less affluence south of the inevitable tracks. St Luke's drew its support from all quarters of Fort Rouge and included all the variations of economic circumstances as existed among the essentially English and Scottish inhabitants.

Our own means remained modest enough. I cannot remember a time during my childhood or youth when my parents did not have to exercise caution and ingenuity in their household budgeting. One way or another, however, they were able to establish a comfortable home at the rectory and also to provide my sister and me with the conventional advantages of environment and education.

In 1911 I was sent to St John's College School from which I matriculated in the last year of the war. It was an unusual establishment by any measure. Located near the then city limits in what was known as the North End, the old grey building with its mansarded towers stood along Main Street in an enclave of grounds and playing fields. It was a tough school morally and physically. Here I first experienced the anxiety and satisfaction of taking part in the organized games which our elders then considered essential in preparing the young for the exertions and temptations of adult life. Fair or foul, hot or cold, a goodly portion of our days was devoted to rugby and hockey under the stern supervision of our seniors. There were also various informal but no less violent varieties of physical competition to occupy our few unscheduled hours. As the terms went by, my endurance increased with my stature, and my fear of exhibiting embarrassing incompetence diminished with experience. Like most of my schoolmates, I came to regard regular physical effort as an integral and at least relatively enjoyable part of normal life. Trophies and photographs of championship teams were displayed at the school and for years St John's was a recruiting ground for major hockey teams.

From the lower first form to the fifth and sixth, the school population included boys from all over the Canadian west and northwest, the sons of Hudson's Bay Company factors and missionary Anglican clergy and settlers, some from as far away as the Rockies and the Arctic circle, a number of whom were unable to return home even for the long summer holiday. In my time there were still a few boys of Indian blood; earlier there had been many more. Many boys came from the burgeoning towns and cities of Saskatchewan and Alberta as well as from Manitoba. Most of us came from Anglican homes, but there was a healthy minority of 'dissenters' and always a few Roman Catholics.

The school's origins were frankly English. They had derived in some vague way and in part from the Westminister School, but I think we owed more to Rugby and the tradition of Thomas Arnold than to any other source. Discipline was harsh but on the whole governed by a rough justice. Morning and evening chapel were compulsory, and I can still recapture the special savour of our school assemblies as I hear the familiar phrases of the *Book of Common Prayer*. The British aspect was reinforced by the fact that many of our masters came from the United Kingdom. My first headmaster was Eric Hamber, a Cambridge man of intellectual quality but of somewhat unpredictable and violent temper. Doubtless he had been tried beyond endurance by his barbarian constituency.

But although its origins were trans-Atlantic, there was never any doubt that an important element in St John's was that it was unmistakably indigenous to western Canada. My second headmaster was Walter Burman, himself a Johnian and vibrantly Canadian in every sinew. He too could be driven to savage outbursts, but 'Old Walt' – he was in his forties – was an inspired and relentless teacher, especially of Latin and English syntax, a sound knowledge of which he believed to be essential to an ordered mind. His whole being was devoted to the school and its grubby inhabitants who, needless to say, did not appreciate their good fortune. It was only many years later while serving briefly as a junior master that I came to realize Walter Burman's rare gifts of mind and spirit.

Inevitably the school is among the strongest memories of my boyhood. And although the accepted values of the school were impressive and influential, I have no doubt that the chief inspiration of those years was the family in which my father reigned but my mother governed in her own unobtrusive way. Our home provided the warmth and love which nurtured our growth and development. For each one of us, especially father, it was an unfailing source of encouragement and reassurance when the going was rough, a refuge from the harshness and exhaustion of life outside. We were a close, affectionate, rather demonstrative family, and our emotions were never very far from the surface. School, like church, was important, but there was never any doubt that home and family loyalties were first in our hearts.

Two years before the first world war we managed a family visit to England, the first for all of us. It was a memorable summer. As we moved among the enduring evidence of the history we had read and revered, father was entranced. For me, London was the living centre of the great post-Victorian legend of Empire. My appetite for Henty and Kipling and the others was sharpened by the sights and sounds of Britain. From the day I spent in Cambridge with father, it was my ambition to get to Oxford or Cambridge myself. This was the country which seemed to me, at the age of ten, to stand for everything that was noble and exciting.

When the war came in 1914 father endured a long struggle of conscience. Should he respond to the call of 'God and Empire' and go overseas? Or did his superior duty lie with the people of his growing parish so soon to be drawn into the deep personal tragedies of the war? Before it was over St Luke's would send no fewer than two hundred and fifty volunteers, and its roll of honour bore witness to the scores of families to whom he would bring comfort in their bereavement. If his own emotional nature, his physical vigour, and his Irish unionist background impelled him strongly to the more active role, his judgment and his conscience directed him to stay. His decision was to remain at home to nourish and sustain those left behind, though to the end he regretted that it could not have been otherwise.

For me the war was all excitement and glamour, or nearly so. Like others of my age my anxiety was that it would not go on long enough for me to get into it somehow. I thrilled to watch the 27th City of Winnipeg Battalion, soon to endure the horror and glory of Vimy, as they swung past the rectory gate to the strains of *Soldiers of the Queen*. When the 61st Battalion won hockey's Allan Cup before going overseas, it seemed to me a matter of national importance, an augury of victory in a bigger league. Only in the final year, months even, when the names of some of the eighteen- and nineteen-year-old boys I had known at school began to appear in the long casualty lists did I become conscious of the tragedy of war. But in spite of that in the autumn of 1918 I was disappointed to learn that the Main Street recruiting office for the Royal Naval Air Service could not take anyone before his seventeenth birthday.

The bands, the marching troops, the heroism at Second Ypres, the Somme, and Vimy, the growing legend of Canadian airmen, even the familiar names in the casualty lists, the whole impact of the war served to emphasize and to exaggerate the British element in my experience. At the same time, my reading outside as well as inside the schoolroom was mostly British. Every year before Christmas my friends and I would walk downtown in our mocassins, pea-jackets, and toques through the cold winter streets to identify as preferred Christmas gifts the volumes of Henty which we had not yet read: *With Clive in India, With Moore at Coronna,* yes, and *With Wolfe at Quebec* and all the rest of that amazing series. With *Chums, The Scout, The Boys Own Annual,* and *The Captain*, these were our favourite reading and our staple diet.

Until after the first world war there was little that I recall to balance this dominant British element in our 'cultural' environment. There was certainly nothing of equal weight on the 'American' side. True, we read Horatio Alger's stories and doubtless appreciated in them the already familiar western doctrine of the triumph of virtue and industry. There were James Fenimore Cooper and Mark Twain, of course, though to my discredit I never warmed to Tom Sawyer or Huck Finn. The movies, too, with their strange new flavours of Hollywood, were beginning to impinge on our minds before I had left school. Douglas Fairbanks – senior, of course – combining his engaging and continual smile with splendid athletic accomplishments was an early favourite. I also remember my attempts to adjust my limited wardrobe to the style of Jack Pickford. But these were later and less enduring idols.

And then at the age of eleven or perhaps twelve, I encountered the French language outside the schoolroom and in sympathetic circumstances. Through what particular chance I do not recall, an attractive young French woman whose name I quite forget somehow presented herself at the rectory, with the result that my sister and I became pupils of hers. I was taking French at school, taught much the same as Latin though less efficiently, but with Mademoiselle it was at once totally different. The language came alive. We would go for walks through Fort Rouge, the three of us, and as we walked we heard for the first time the precise and exquisite music of perfectly spoken French. Unhappily for us this interlude did not last long, for I suppose our friend found more profitable employment elsewhere. But from that brief experience I derived my first interest in the language and literature which was to mean a great deal to me as time went on.

Throughout my years of school and college, our family retained its close connection with eastern Canada. Every summer, until I left school and began to take jobs during the holidays like most Manitoba undergraduates, father took us to Danford Lake. Each year as well, we would pay an extended visit to Montreal where the hospitality of mother's only sister and my Ross cousins made us feel like members of their own household. Danford was for all of us 'the old place' which we loved; English Montreal – I have no recollection of French-Canadian friends – was an infinitely exciting and sophisticated community which we vastly enjoyed and to which somehow we seemed also to belong.

In 1918 I moved out of the familiar environment of St John's into the wider freedom of undergraduate life. My arrival at the University of Manitoba coincided with the end of the war. The fact that by the next year many of my classmates were veterans of the Canadian Expeditionary Force and the Royal Flying Corps added to my impression that, though only sixteen myself, I had moved into an adult world. In those postwar years the University of Manitoba was much like the other prairie universities, though older and less homogeneous, for at that time it was mostly a conglomeration of widely separated and loosely affiliated colleges. I believe that it did possess something beyond the primitive vigour and elementary enthusiasm one might have expected. Perhaps I was especially fortunate in my teachers, a number of whom were personally stimulating as well as eminent scholars. Perhaps it was that in my final two years, I shifted my attention to the study of English and French language and literature. The head of the French Department was the conscientious and scholarly Professor William Fredrick Osborne who had a wide knowledge and, even better, a deep love of France and French literature. To him and to his colleague Madamoiselle Cèline Ballu I owe great debts, the one for opening to me the doors to the French classics, the other for reviving my sense of the written and spoken language. Whatever the combination of reasons my memories of Manitoba are of a community of some intellectual excitement. But it might have been that I had just glimpsed the vast frontiers of knowledge for the first time.

I was not a particularly good student, no better than somewhat above average. Nor were my energies by any means wholly concentrated on my studies. In the tradition in which I had been reared I expended a large proportion of my time and energy on games. Football, or 'rugby' as it was still called, was in its early days at Manitoba. From the beginning it stood high on my list of priorities and I was quite disproportionately proud to become captain of the university team in my final year. There were other games too. But the new and even more absorbing element was my extramural life, the social and cultural activities and the campus politics which then as now – if a good deal less earnestly – occupied the energies of undergraduates. In such things I spent much time and made many new friends. University arts was agreeably coeducational, and for the first time my circle included young ladies.

During these years Canadians, inspired by the accomplishments of the Canadian Corps, developed a new spirit of nationalism. While we were proud of the British connection, we became determined, nonetheless, to achieve autonomy of status under the crown. Spurred on by John W. Dafoe, we had applauded when Sir Robert Borden had insisted that Canada should sign the peace treaty in her own right. It was natural that student thinking should be attracted by the new nationalism, and talk of liberation from Downing Street was common among undergraduates. We were impatient too of Ottawa. When Chester Martin, then head of the History Department, introduced us to the idea of the undoubted right of the western provinces to their natural resources, we responded instinctively. As Canada had come to maturity among the nations, so the prairie provinces had come of age and must have the means by which to pursue their own destinies within confederation. It would be some years yet before a fully sovereign Canada had its own representatives abroad, but by the early twenties we in the west had no doubt that this was the direction in which our politicians must steer. Our essays and our debates and our conversation at Manitoba in those years were loaded with such opinions.

As students we also used to spend hours thinking and talking about what we would do when we left the university. Many of us expected that in some way we would ultimately find a 'vocation,' the old-fashioned term employed to mean something rather more than an occupation suitable to our capabilities and circumstances. By inheritance and upbringing we had been led to feel that we had a responsibility to be of use in the world. I know that I used to worry about this a good deal. No doubt the environment of the rectory had a lot to do with this in my case, but I am quite sure that I was not alone and that many of my contemporaries felt the same way for the same reasons. I continued, however, to feel no recognizable call either in my father's footsteps or to the mission field or, indeed, anywhere else. Nevertheless I certainly did not question what seemed the conventional standard of my time that it was a normal responsibility of those of us who enjoyed the advantages of a good home and education to choose a career which, as well as providing for our livelihood, would enable us to serve our community and our country according to our abilities.

In this frame of mind, in doubt as to whether I should choose the law, or perhaps teaching, I decided that I should have some postgraduate training outside of Manitoba. To do so I would need substantial help. At that time one of the very few avenues available for such ambitions was the Rhodes Scholarship. Oxford would fit in admirably with my own tastes, while an Oxford degree would provide the initial equipment either for the Bar or for the beginning of an academic life. In my third year I made my first application for the scholarship; not surprisingly I was beaten. In my final year I tried again with the same result. Since I could see no other way out I determined to make one more attempt after graduation and to take some temporary employment meantime.

In 1921 I graduated, registered in a master's degree program in English, and obtained an appointment as a junior master at my old school. For eighteen months I combined the duties of master of the third form with work for my degree. For my thesis I had chosen 'Rupert Brooke and his Poetry,' and in due course I produced a pedestrian and sentimental piece of work which fortunately proved sufficient to the examiners. Meantime the Selection Committee met again and to my inexpressible relief, and no doubt to theirs, I was awarded the Rhodes Scholarship from Manitoba for 1923. No scholar-elect had more cause to rise up and bless his benefactor. The next stage of my life had been determined, and my most cherished hopes seemed assured of realization. As the summer of that year wore on, I found no reason to doubt the truth of what one of my history professors, Daniel Harvey, had prophesied would be 'the three happiest years of my life.'

2

Oxford and beyond

By September 1923 the therapy of lively anticipation had effectively relieved the heartbreak of two years' hopes deferred. What I had read and 'dreamed of was about to be realized so that the weeks of preparation for my departure for England were pure pleasure. After a family holiday up the Gatineau and a few happy days with my Ross cousins, I made my farewells and sailed on the old steamship *Montrose* from Montreal.

In April I had had my twenty-first birthday. In most respects I suppose that I remained relatively immature; certainly I was unsophisticated both intellectually and emotionally. Conventional and uncomplicated, my attitudes reflected my upbringing and my environment. I was physically robust and vigorous, romantic and given to enthusiasms in the late-Victorian manner, and confident but not I think insensitive in my relations with people. My intellectual capabilities were good but unremarkable. I approached this new chapter in my life without diffidence or anxiety.

Although I had been nurtured in affection and respect for things British, by the time I left for Oxford I shared fully with most of my generation what we conceived to be a thoroughgoing Canadian nationalism. Of this gospel John W. Dafoe was the prophet and the *Manitoba Free Press* the inspired word. The role that both had played in the development of a worthy and independent place for Canada among the nations of the world was one in which all Manitobans could take pride. Although we remained loyal to the crown and attached to the old country, we were determined to be free of the vestiges of colonialism. As I set out down the St Lawrence that bright autumn day I was eager to know Britain better, and prepared to love her. At the same time I was consciously, and I suspect rather tiresomely, Canadian, assuming innocently that the British would accept me as such and not as another sort of American. There were other students on the *Montrose* bound for British universities. Among them was that year's Rhodes Scholar from British Columbia, Norman A. Robertson. We were to be together often and long during the next forty-

14

five years, first as Oxford undergraduates and later as the closest of colleagues in the affairs of government. Throughout my life no friendship has meant more to me.

My first days and weeks in England were filled with new and varied pleasures. Even the Duchess of Connaught Hostel in London, a somewhat shabby relic of noble charity from the war years at which I put up, seemed endowed with an imperial grandeur. There I encountered other colonial undergraduates including George V. Ferguson, later editor of the *Winnipeg Free Press*[1] and of the *Montreal Star*. Already wise in the ways of the British, he guided my first steps around many of the London landmarks and introduced me to the mysteries of the English banking system.

My first sortie from London was to Winchester where I was to spend the weekend before going up to Oxford. Before leaving Canada I had been invited there by the dean of the cathedral, W.H. Hutton, whom father had met in England the previous summer. Hutton, an elderly bachelor of ascetic appearance and courtly manner, had been a fellow of St John's College and it was on his advice and recommendations that I had applied there. Having acquired my first tailor-made dinner jacket in London, I set out for Winchester on Friday and duly presented myself at the deanery. During the following three years Winchester was to become for me a serene and familiar sanctuary, but on that first weekend it was new and special and had about it a dreamlike quality. To find myself residing in that ancient close, under the shadow and the sounds of the cathedral, was an experience that I shall never forget. As if by some magic I had been translated into the living core of British history. The newest part of the large and rambling deanery was the wing overlooking the garden built to accommodate Charles II and Nell Gwynne on some forgotten royal progress; the oldest was the residue of tiling in the porch which dated from Roman times. As I looked through the deep and high embrasured window of my bedroom that evening, the canons' houses, the vast shoulder of the cathedral nave, even the trees and the soft green turf seemed to encompass me in a world undisturbed and unchanged from remote beginnings.

A few days later I arrived in Oxford and passed for the first time through the gate of the College of St John the Baptist. I had been met at the station and taken to the rooms we were to share high up in the Canterbury quadrangle that first year by an old school friend Hasted Dowker. Doubtless this diluted the strangeness of an occasion that freshmen traditionally find forlorn. Despite the novelty of my new surroundings, I recall no such feeling; from the beginning I had a sense of belonging. The severity and poise of the college porter, the resourceful care of my newly acquired scout, the remoteness and

1 *The Manitoba Free Press* became the *Winnipeg Free Press* in 1931.

the eccentricities of the dons, and the wide variety of my fellow undergraduates all contributed to make Oxford different, heaven knew, from what I had known at home in Canada, yet there was little that seemed ultimately foreign or unsympathetic.

In my time, overseas students going to Oxford were customarily warned that they would find life very different to that to which they had been accustomed at home. In particular they should not expect British undergraduates to behave like North Americans. We should bear in mind that they were by nature and upbringing diffident and reserved and would recoil from premature approaches on our part. One must bide one's time. Let them come to you was the well-meant advice. I was well-prepared for such glacial behaviour, but I do not in fact recall encountering it; indeed my memory is of rapid integration into the college community. By an easy and natural process my circle extended, and quite early in that first year I formed close friendships, a number of which endured long afterward. It seemed to me that the British were less inhibited, less severe in their judgments of us from abroad, and more prepared to give us the benefit of any doubt, than in their attitudes towards each other. We might be expected to have rather odd clothes and queer manners and our speech was bound to be strange, nevertheless we were more likely to be judged on our merits than their own compatriots who had the wrong accent or wore the wrong tie.

Like most undergraduates, however, I was mystified by some of my initial encounters, especially with senior members of the college. For example, the shy classicist, who as my moral tutor was to bear some undefined responsibility for my behaviour, received me graciously enough, but I saw little of him after that first meeting and felt certain that he never recognized me again. At first my academic tutor, Austin Poole, the senior history don, seemed equally baffling. Pale and remote, he proved to be incredibly learned. I was entered in the Honours School of Modern History and as we sat in front of the fireplace Poole talked at me about Anglo-Saxon institutions in a discursive and embarrassed sort of way, evidently as relieved as I was when the hour had passed. He assigned me an essay for the following week, referring casually to no less than eight books which 'might be helpful.' When I inquired what lectures I should follow (I had obtained the long and formidable list of those 'available' that term), he replied that I should not pay too much attention to lectures. One or two of those listed, three at the most, 'might be of some interest,' and Crutwell at Hertford was said to be amusing on Aristotle.

Such was my introduction to the tutorial system of which I had heard so much. When I left Poole that morning I was confused and rather dismayed by what he seemed to expect of me. But in the months that followed I came to appreciate his learning, the subtle method of his teaching, and more than these, his shy capacity for friendship. Slowly I adjusted to the new regime, and under the patient guidance and stimulus of my tutors – Poole and later W.C. Costin – my intellectual appetites were sharpened and my capabilities began to develop. Costin, later president of the college, laboured hard over me and I owe him a great deal; he has also remained my good friend over the long years since.

The mid-twenties were not, I suppose, especially notable years in the long life of the university. In general I imagine Oxford reflected the superficial character of western bourgeois society, which was not overly concerned with the basic problems of national or international life that remained unresolved after the war. Or so I remember it. Of course there were exceptions and the Union debated these questions, albeit in a manner which heeded style more than substance. Perhaps the most conspicuous phenomena of undergraduate life were the re-emergence of a preoccupation with aesthetic values and the acceptance of elaborate male attire. Oxford 'bags' became ever wider until the shoes of the wearer were completely hidden, and like the ties and sweaters they appeared in the whole range of pastel shades. Within such splendid co-coons there proved to be stirrings of genuine aristry in which a few men of talent, like Harold Acton, played the chief part. But of this side of university life I saw little. Not to my credit I had more sympathy with the current popular press and the 'hearty' majority of undergraduates who deplored the decadence of the generation and mocked as mere exhibitionism any departures from the accepted mean. For me, I confess the great actors of the Oxford scene tended to be those of achievement on the river and the playing field.

Within a few days of the beginning of that first Hilary term it was made quite clear to me that, while I might be expected to spend some time and effort at study in the forenoon, the period between lunch and tea was sacred to organized outdoor exercise for which the college provided a wide variety of facilities. Any number could play, and most did, whatever their level of proficiency. This suited me well and I forthwith joined the college boat club. Day in and out over the three ensuing years I spent many hours and expended much energy in slogging up and down the Isis in different kinds of craft under various instructors. I cannot even now regret those long afternoons passed in strain and discomfort, often in penetrating damp and cold, for they provided me with easy and immediate companionship. More than that, such employment fitted well into my accustomed, if adolescent, pattern. For two years I nourished the ambition to be selected for the Oxford boat; in those days I would rather have returned to Canada with a rowing blue than with a first class in the Schools. But the first events in which I took part provided no happy omen: the St John's boat in the Torpids that winter foundered ingloriously in that part of the river known as the 'Gut,' and our record in the next summer's eights was hardly more distinguished. Consequently, the polite daily invitations for me to row in the university trials petered out. In the end I left Oxford with neither the blue nor the first.

My first visit to the Continent was a consequence of my addiction to games. Ice hockey at Oxford was then almost exclusively a Canadian sport, although there were a few obstinate British adherents. Since there was not a sufficiently large ice surface nearer than Manchester (which seemed to offer few other attractions), the annual trials for the university team were usually combined with the first game of a cross-Channel tour early in the Christmas vacation. In 1923 the first competition prior to the match against Cambridge was against the Belgian national team. Those were the days when European hockey was in its infancy and made no great demands upon either players or spectators. The fact that I admitted to some schoolboy experience, possessed or could assemble the bare essentials of equipment, and was willing to pay the minimum fare to Antwerp was sufficient. 'Les Canadiens d'Oxford' scrambled to a narrow victory before the British ambassador and an excited crowd. A local newspaper in its account of the event reported that, during a heated mixup around the Oxford goal, Heeney had been injured and collapsed to the ice, but 'heureusement plus de peu que de mal.' It was an inauspicious start to my European hockey career, but I had survived the less than severe selection process and went on from there to Switzerland with the team. There, as I remember, the Cambridge game at Mürren was our sole athletic obligation over a whole fortnight's indoor as well as outdoor gaiety under the auspices of Arnold Lunn and the British Public Schools Alpine Sports Club. In Mürren, the home of the Kandahar, I was introduced to the glorious world of skiing. Mürren then was also the centre of British enthusiasm and activity, and our days and evenings were full as the Oxford and Cambridge hockey teams were welcomed by everyone. At the Christmas Eve dance I was not even surprised to receive a silver cup for my performance in a strenuous competition known as the balloon dance. When the snow finally stopped falling and the Palace Hotel rink could be cleared, we beat Cambridge handily.

On my way back to England that first Christmas vacation I saw Paris for the first time. It was then that I fell in love with that incomparable city, an affair which has endured undiminished over the years. I put up at a modest hotel which had been recommended to me by an Oxford friend. It was in the rue de Fleurus close by the Luxembourg Gardens and must have been within hailing distance of where Gertrude Stein had recently established her salon. But I was then quite unaware of her existence; indeed I had little way of knowing of the literary and artistic life going on about me, for I was young and unsophisticated. It seems unlikely that I would have been greatly impressed in passing Shakespeare's bookshop had I actually encountered Hemingway or Scott Fitzgerald or Joyce himself. Yet they must all have been about. Later, when Norman Robertson showed me a copy of the just pub-lished *Ulysses* he was taking back to England, I was more interested in his encounter with the British customs than in his having secured a first edition of an already notorious work. Norman had spent the vacation in another small hotel near the Odeon, and while I was playing hockey and frolicking in Swit-zerland, he had been rummaging in the bookshops of the Left Bank, already sensitive to the intellectual environment we were sharing. But it was Paris out-doors that appealed to me, and from morning until nightfall, and much later, I wandered the city until I could walk no further.

During the two following years I spent other memorable vacations from Oxford on the Continent and elsewhere in the British Isles. The first summer, loaded down with the books to which I had been told I must address myself if I were to take a 'decent' degree, I met John A. Wilson, an American, in Edinburgh and set out for the Highlands. Repulsed at Pitlochry by the cost of available lodging, we negotiated acceptable terms with the innkeeper at the little village of Weem close by Aberfeldy where we had been directed by a somewhat mystified station agent. We passed the next six weeks happily in the heart of Scotland. The mornings were reserved for reading and study but during the rest of our days we explored the splendours of the Perthshire coun-tryside. We tramped over miles of heather, we climbed Schiehallion, we swam in the frigid Tay, and we followed history through the pass of Killiecrankie. In the evenings we drank Scottish beer and talked with each other and with locals and other visitors. We even made some effort to learn the reels. It was a happy and profitable time. I did a lot of hard reading that summer, primarily in Brit-ish history and what was then called political science. Of the many volumes I read I remember best T.H. Green's *Principles of Political Obligation*, for it made on my awakening mind an impression of order and wisdom which still persists.

Later that summer, with two companions this time (Wilson and I had been joined by my friend Philip Bell), I set out in August for Brittany. Having sur-vived the discomfort of third-class passage, we made directly for the Côtes du Nord where we had found lodging in the little village of Treveneuc. In a little stone cottage on the cliffs overlooking the grey seas we were received by its owner, a retired petty officer of the French Navy, and his wife who had, dur-ing his service afloat, been a cook in Paris. The Thouément-Macés were a dear old couple, and they welcomed us warmly. We lived on thick soups of fish and vegetables, splendid fresh bread, and locally produced cider, which may well be a scientifically balanced diet. When we felt the need of additional protein we had but to reach up and pluck a dried anchovy from the bundle hanging from the beam above the table. On weekdays the cider came from a cask; on

Sundays, when we also enjoyed our only meat of the week, from a bottle. For the three of us it was a novel month. The walks for miles along the rugged Breton coast, the expeditions to other villages inland, the swimming, the encompassing charm of a genuine French environment, and the developing friendship of the old couple combined with the discoveries and excitement of hours of reading and talk with friends to enshrine that first summer abroad in a special place in my memory.

When I returned to Oxford in the fall of 1924 for my second year it became evident that I would have to pay more systematic attention to the looming prospect of my Schools. At the turn of the year my tutor told me that, unless I took advantage of the senior status accorded me as a graduate of an approved colonial university and opted to take my final examinations the following June, I would most certainly 'drop a class.' If, on the other hand, I addressed myself to my work I would get a second. It was clear that he gave me little chance of a first. With some reluctance, for I had come to enjoy Oxford's extra curricular freedom, I set to and managed to work fairly hard for the balance of the winter. In the Easter vacation I took my books to the Lake Country for a fortnight with a reading party led by Costin. We lived close by Derwent Water and I remember our sojourn mostly as mist and rain and study under pressure. The remainder of the holidays I spent in Bruges with Phil Whiting, a fellow candidate for the History Schools. There in a modest pension beside a canal we were able to combine academic work with long walks, and one grey afternoon we managed to make Zeebrugge from the end of the tram line at Knokke and on to Blankenberge, talking and arguing European history all the way.

I confess that I found the Schools a heavy ordeal. It was desperately hot in Oxford that year, all the more so when accoutred in cap and gown, *subfusc* suiting, and white tie. Each day of that stifling week we wrote two papers and when each afternoon's effort was over I would go down to the river for a strenuous workout. A St John's eight had been entered in the Thames Cup at Henley and I was bound that I would not miss that opportunity. All went well enough with the exams. Weeks later when the results were out I found I had achieved a sound second. Nothing that had transpired in my *viva* had given any indication that I'd had a chance for a first nor indeed that I had been in danger of falling to a third.

Henley proved a welcome contrast. It was a combination of savage effort on the river and gaiety ashore in the simmering English sunshine. Our boat did respectably and we were eliminated only by a few feet, and then by a crew that went on to the finals. When the regatta was over I was weary and happy to leave for the long vacation at home. That voyage was a happy one chiefly because of the company of two quite remarkable fellow Canadians: John

Lowe, later dean of Christ Church; and my old Manitoba friend, Norman Young, who was killed in the Dieppe raid.

My third and final year at Oxford was virtually free from academic responsibility. I had taken my degree and was required to follow no regular course of study. During the summer I had decided to read for the Quebec Bar and, since for that purpose no credit could be obtained at Oxford, my time was my own. Generously and without close inquiry of my intentions, the Rhodes trustees were persuaded to permit me a year of what had become known euphemistically as consolidation. During the first term I tried to acquaint myself with Roman law. I bought Gaius and Justinian and for some weeks met at All Souls with the venerable and distinguished Vinerian Professor of English Law, Sir William Holdsworth. But 'the Hogger' had little interest in a legal system he regarded as clearly inferior to that in which he had made his reputation, and when I discovered that I need have no tutor at all, and that by doing without I could save money, I terminated my brief academic relationship with him. He put up no resistance. Happily, however, we had become and remained friends, and I recall with affection that grand old man, his vast moustache, the black ribbon flying from his glasses as he followed the fortunes of the St John's eight from the towing path.

For my last two terms I was thus at liberty to devote myself to more general and less demanding pursuits. Looking back now through the mists of over forty years I see that it was a golden period. I shared 'unlicensed' lodgings in one of the less salubrious quarters of Oxford with Norman Robertson. Norman spent his days with the books which attracted his catholic taste and fed his capacious mind, at the game of bridge in which he delighted and excelled even then, and in walking and talking with Balliol friends. He was never one to limit himself to the curriculum even when he was reading for his Schools; had he done so there is little doubt that he would have taken a distinguished first class for he was certainly one of the ablest undergraduates of his time. As it was he followed his own tastes and was content with a second. Though Norman and I remained good friends and naturally, living in the same house, saw a good deal of one another, there were interests and friends we did not share. Since then I have sometimes thought that I missed opportunities that last year to know him better. But I had no taste or talent for cards, my reading was for the most part quite different from his and much less extensive, and I had little of his facility in the contemplation and discussion of ideas.

I continued to spend my time largely at games, in travel, and in the many frivolities of student life. Each morning I read *The Times* thoroughly, then went out to the Cadena for coffee. I took little or no part in the activities of the graver societies of the university and college. I lunched and dined with a different people at a variety of college clubs both solemn and bibulous. The afternoons I spent either in vigorous exercise or watching cricket in the parks. I went to parties and attended the theatre in London as well as Oxford. Occasionally I spent weekends away at the homes of English friends. Oxford University in the twenties was an even more masculine community than it is now, and we saw little of the occupants of the women's colleges. Yet, especially in the summer term when the sisters, cousins, and assorted female friends of undergraduates from far and near added spice and colour to the scene, it seemed wholly natural to be constantly falling in or out of love.

For Christmas in 1925 I travelled as far as Pau in the Pyrennees where I spent the holidays with my Ross relatives from Montreal. From there we made the pilgrimage to Lourdes; later we were off to Carcassonne. Then, on an urgent wire from Henry Borden calling for reinforcements, I journeyed through Lyons and on to St Moritz to join the university hockey team for one last game against Cambridge. There, in the special sunshine of that glamourous centre of winter sports, I basked in the luxury of a cosmopolitan and opulent society.

In that last year, too, I saw Italy for the first time. I heard Toscanini conduct at La Scala and went on from Milan to an unforgettable spring in Florence. With my close friend at St John's, Thomas A. Wilson, later director of the Harvard University Press, I lodged in a small pensione across the Arno. Like generations of students before us, we both succumbed to the beauty and antique wonder of that daughter of Rome. There too we had a first sensation of fascism in action one night when we experienced the frightening tremors of a crowd harangued from a Florentine balcony. Later as we set out on our return journey we got some taste of the minor unpleasantness of the regime when a black-shirted militiaman brusquely turned us back to pay an arbitrary and excessive charge upon the load of books we were carrying. Our funds reduced below the bare and normal minimum and confirmed in our opinion of Mussolini, we sustained ourselves on the long journey to Paris on a diet of cold pasta and green chartreuse bought at the monastery of Certosa for more festive occasions.

The life of the university in that summer of 1926, like that of the rest of the country, was shocked and interrupted by the general strike. It is difficult now to recall the intensity of the anxiety of the British people. There was little violence, and on both sides of the dispute, citizens rallied to a wide variety of unaccustomed occupations so that life might go on, or at least so that the essential services could be maintained. Oxford was soon involved. Dons drove the London buses and manned the Underground, curiously and miraculously without serious incident. Norman Robertson volunteered his services to a newspaper and went to London. With no compelling ideological bias, I found myself, with other Oxford and Cambridge undergraduates, a 'Special' in the Southampton Dock Police. There, quartered in a Channel steamer for the duration, we patrolled the gloomy docks with armband and baton, our only real danger being that during the night we might stumble into the harbour.

As I sailed from Liverpool at the end of June, the sorrow of leaving the places and people that had been part of me over three years was lightened by a sense of gratitude. As we pulled out into the Mersey I realized that what I had received had been something much more fundamental and enduring than the fulfilment of an adolescent dream. My academic accomplishment had been modest but respectable. I had little reason to believe that with greater effort it would have been much better. But I had had some vision of the broad and rich geography of scholarship. I had learned how to learn and gained some idea of how to formulate the product of my study directly and succinctly. I had made many and varied friends who had taught me much. I had come to know England and the English. I had lived in France enough to have some understanding of that country and its people and to develop warm affection for both. I had made many North American friends from widely different parts of our own continent. It had been a rich and rewarding three years. More than most I knew I had reason to be grateful to the memory of Cecil Rhodes who, whatever his shortcomings, had found a worthy means of ensuring that his memory would be revered through the generations.

3

Montreal and the law

If I felt a certain sadness at the ending of my Oxford years, I also experienced a pleasurable feeling of relief and anticipation as I embarked on the long voyage home. I was returning to my own country and was about to get on with the business of living. The previous summer I had abandoned any idea of a permanent teaching career, and inquiries in Ottawa had led me to conclude that there was little prospect for me in the Canadian Civil Service. Moved by the need to make some decision and complying with father's oft-repeated injunction that the first duty of the responsible male was to learn a trade, I had decided to enroll in the Faculty of Law at McGill. I felt no great attraction to the legal profession, yet the Bar offered a life of some interest and an occupation not unsuited to my abilities, and at any rate a law degree was a recognized marketable commodity of which I remained sadly deficient.

In the summer of 1926 father and mother had already come east to Danford to prepare my welcome home. It was a happy reunion and a happy summer, the family circle complete again. As if there had been no break, we spent our days as we had in years past for as far back as I could remember: the picnics with various cousins and aunts, the swimming expeditions to Danford Lake, fishing for trout from the red canoe on the Kazabazua creek, long walks through the woods over the old school path, the 12th of July celebrations and, each Sunday, the simple country service in the little church on the rising hill behind the house. For me it was a salutary as well as happy re-entry into the life of my own people and my own country. Three years abroad had surely worked changes in me. To an extent doubtless unrealized at the time my attitudes like my tastes had altered in many ways. So much had happened since I had left that Winnipeg seemed far away and long ago. Yet that summer at Danford I recall no doubt that it was in Canada that I would make my life.

The considerations which had led to my settling in Montreal were mixed. In the first place I had been satisfied that there were at the Quebec Bar good opportunities for young lawyers. The profession was not then especially crowded compared with the other provinces, and Montreal was the head office for most of the large commercial and financial corporations in the country. McGill had a law school of good reputation, and the arts faculty might afford opportunity for me to exploit my Oxford degree by teaching history on the side, for during the next three years I would have to find new sources of income to provide for university fees and minimum subsistence and to pay off the modest debts that remained from my last uninhibited year at Oxford. A third and by no means unpersuasive factor was that through a cousin of my mother's, then a justice of the Court of Appeals, I had been introduced to a prospective patron, Arthur Holden, KC, who was willing to accept me in articles. He was the active head of Meredith, Holden, Heward, and Holden, a long-established and respected firm in St James Street with which I was associated for the next twelve years. Finally, Montreal meant family ties.

My McGill existence was a marked contrast to my Oxford life. Yet it was at once stimulating and agreeable to be in my own country in a situation which was quite new to me. True, my circumstances and scale of living were necessarily modest but there was certainly no hardship. I was able to find lodging in the Montreal Diocesan College, in the same room in fact that father had occupied as a student thirty years before. As always my aunt and her family gave me comfort and support, and I made friends among my fellow students, a number of whom remain to this day among my closest acquaintances. That first year I worked hard and systematically at my books and began attending the office as an indentured student-at-law. The History Department also took me on to conduct weekly seminars in American history. Since I knew little of the subject, the resulting benefit to my budget was at some cost to my available leisure.

As the weeks and months of reading and lectures succeeded one another I found that my interest in the law developed steadily. At that time the Law Faculty was fortunate in having a number of distinguished scholars on its staff. First among them was Dean P.E. Corbett, one of the earlier Canadian Rhodes Scholars. He had had a brilliant record at Oxford after the first war and was reputed on one occasion to have hung by his toes in the Senior Common Room of All Souls after being named a fellow. I have never sat under a better teacher. His lectures in Roman law were models of clarity and precision. Of the others, a few were of high quality, others were passable, and some, especially among those borrowed part time from Bench and Bar, were at best pedestrian. In the office my seniors were uniformly friendly and helpful as I went about my apprenticeship. I especially recall the generosity of that grand old dandy, F.E. Meredith, the senior partner, who would quite often have me home with him for lunch and test me with the largest, strongest martinis I had ever known. As time went on I began to enjoy the routines of the office and the surroundings of the courts and to understand the disciplines necessary to practice of the law.

That first year I did well in my examinations. In the new environment my mettle was untried and the diversions at hand were relatively few. In the second year my resolution faltered and my academic record was less creditable. I had moved from the austerity of the Diocesan College up the street to my fraternity house where the atmosphere was rather less conducive to a severe schedule of study. Furthermore I had allowed myself to be caught up more in the life of the university and in the current gaieties of the English community which was in the full flood of prosperity and extravagance. In my final year, however, not without some effort I pulled myself together, rationed my diversions, and managed to take a good degree. The BCL behind me, I then went on to survive the incredible physical and nervous twenty-four hour ordeal which constituted the Quebec Bar examinations; in August 1929 I took the advocates' oath and was duly called.

That year would long be remembered by more than the new barristers admitted that day. The crash came within weeks of my joining my firm as a junior partner at the beginning of September, and it struck St James Street at every level with the force of a physical convulsion. Within days of its first main shock many prominent members of the Montreal financial community whose names had been synonymous with material and social stability were known to be confronted with disaster. Ordinary people in every occupation – clerks, stenographers, elevator operators and office boys, merchants and professional men, all of whom had come to believe that the stock market moved only one way – found themselves faced with ruin. Among my very first experiences were to attend for some client those doleful proceedings known as meetings of creditors. By the late autumn of that my first year, the force of events impelled me into the role of instant expert on bankruptcy, winding-up, and the law of negotiable instruments. I spent much of my time and energy in and out of court in efforts to collect debts which clients, notably the Bank of Montreal, had given up as hopeless. It was not perhaps a very glittering area of practice. Nevertheless it taught me a good deal about many sorts of people in many walks of life, and it rapidly provided me with a practical grasp of one branch of the law.

As time went on and my seniors felt able to play out the line of my responsibility, the work allotted to me became more demanding and more interesting. From the beginning I enjoyed my time in court. In my very first case I defended, unsuccessfully, the old Montreal Tramways against a claimant in damages who was represented by one of my Bar examiners. Office work too had its compensations, especially the preparation of pleadings and the formulation of opinions. While searching titles to property and estates left me cold,

I derived increasing satisfaction in the drafting of instruments which called for precision and order. Even company law, which in one form or another provided the principal revenue of firms such as ours, had its points; I enjoyed devising the procedures for the organization and the conduct of meetings (experience which was to stand me in good stead later on), but I had little taste for the financial side, even though I went to some pains at one stage to master the mysteries of double entry.

Of the court cases I recall, perhaps the most entertaining was an action on behalf of my friend, Professor F.R. Scott of McGill Law Faculty, taken jointly and severally against the City of Westmount and a local building contractor. Returning home from a party late one night in his ancient Franklin, Scott struck an unguarded and unlighted pile of gravel at the side of a city street. On the dubious ground that I was lecturing in municipal law, Scott retained me with instructions to seek recovery for the damages incurred to his car. Although I was uncertain as to the liability of the city, I agreed to proceed on condition that we limit the risk by confining the claim within the limited jurisdiction of the Circuit Court (at that time under one hundred dollars). The writ was issued, the pleadings were completed, and we went to trial. The plaintiff proved an unruffled and eloquent witness in his own cause. The fact that he was a well-known radical and his brother a well-known conservative, an alderman of the City of Westmount (later chief justice of the Court of King's Bench) added piquancy to the event. The trial before the late Judge Stackhouse occupied an entire day. Our opponents sought unsuccessfully to introduce evidence of the circumstances immediately preceding Scott's collision with the gravel pile, but to no avail. The facts admitted no real doubt, and cross-examination failed to shake my client. Finally, agreeing that the issue of municipal responsibility was important, Stackhouse took the case under advisement. When his judgment appeared, Scott was awarded his hundred dollars in damages and we had added to the body of law. *Scott* vs *The City of Westmount and A.N. Other* still stands, I believe, as a leading case. More than that, it was good fun, and my lectureship seemed safe for another year.

One occasion during my years at the Bar is worth recalling because of the light which it cast upon the personality of one whom I was to serve later on. The Quebec government had asserted a large claim for succession duties against the estate of an Ontario resident bank president. Our firm was acting for the estate. The case turned upon the situation of shares owned by the deceased and registered in Montreal. I had done all the preliminary work and had prepared the case for trial which was to take place in Quebec City. The week before the date fixed I was summoned by the two senior partners and informed, albeit with some delicacy, that, since the issue in law as well as the sum involved was of such importance, they had concluded that it would be wise to retain senior local counsel in Quebec. They had in fact just spoken to Louis S. St Laurent and he was willing to be consulted and to act at the trial; of course I would be with him throughout. My disappointment that I was not to carry the trial through on my own was mitigated by the prospect of being associated with a man acknowledged as one of the most distinguished advocates in the country. When I called upon him a few days later in Quebec City, however, I found myself tense, uncertain, and anxious. With that sensitive courtesy which I later learned to be characteristic, he promptly put me at ease, inviting my opinion on the points of law at issue and on the tactics we should employ at the trial. When we had finished our discussion of the case he suggested, if I had nothing to do that evening, that I drop in at his house on Grand Allée. Naturally I was delighted and it was then I met for the first time Madame St Laurent and other members of his family.

When our case was called the following Monday morning St Laurent made it clear to all in court that he regarded me as a serious colleague in the conduct of the case. After he had completed his succinct and brilliant opening he leaned over pointedly to confer with me, then turned over to me the examination of all the witnesses. After the evidence was in and we came to argument he deliberately left part of the case for me to make. It was a notable lesson and one that I have never forgotten of how an older man can give confidence to a younger and thereby not only perform an act of kindness but evoke the best efforts of another in a common endeavour. With St Laurent, as I came to know in quite different circumstances later on, such demeanour was normal and instinctive, deriving from a natural gentility and generosity of character. Years later, as Ernest Lapointe's funeral train was pulling out of Quebec City, Mackenzie King asked my opinion of St Laurent. I recounted this incident because there was no better way for me to convey what I felt about St Laurent.

At about the same period I had a quite different experience with I suppose an equally eminent counsel, though on this occasion from the Bar of Ontario. Our firm was acting for the underwriters in the first railway equipment trust contracted in Quebec. The amount of the financing involved was large and the precedents were few. With the lawyers for the railway, I had been assigned the task of settling the text of the agreement and arranging the procedure for its conclusion. When the documents had been settled to the satisfaction of both sides, the question arose whether there was a requirement to register the trust deed under the law of Quebec. As there was no direct precedent, the railway was naturally anxious to avoid such a complication. However, after studying the situation I gave my opinion that the provincial statute was applicable and that our clients should require registration. Shortly afterwards, when I was in the middle of a conference with officials of the railway, W. Norman Tilley, at that time the company's most senior legal adviser, stormed into the room bringing our meeting to an abrupt halt. Who and where was 'the young man' who was proposing to have his clients subject themselves to complicating and damaging procedures for which there was no basis in law? When I identified myself, Tilley promptly put on an act of bad temper and bad manners which was quite obviously designed to blast me out of the position I had taken. Shaken though I was by the eminence as well as the conduct of my critic I felt I had no option but to stand firm. I said, however, that in view of his own adverse opinion, I would refer the question to my seniors. They stood by me; Tilley was bluffing, and they knew it.

I was only before the Supreme Court of Canada once. The occasion was an appeal arising out of the collision of a Royal Navy cruiser with a Canadian tanker in Montreal harbour. We had lost at the inquiry and in the trial court. The argument was long and interventions from the Bench were frequent. My senior had taken the whole morning session; after lunch I rose nervously behind the bar to cite and comment upon the authorities on which we relied. I had barely begun when I was interrupted by the Chief Justice and upbraided for not having provided to our opponents an advance copy of the document to which I was referring. Nevertheless we won the appeal. A few years later the same judge, Sir Lyman Duff, as administrator of the government, swore me to my first permanent post in the Public Service of Canada.

The Montreal Bar in those days was a fraternal association characterized by relations of friendliness and good manners. The division between the English and French sections was real enough in a functional way; with few exceptions my contacts with French-Canadian colleagues and the largely French-speaking Bench tended to be formal, even perfunctory. Our firm's clients, naturally enough, were predominantly English speaking, drawn from the city's commercial and financial community and from elsewhere in Canada, Britain, and the United States. Certainly all of us had some knowledge of the French language, for it was necessary for most lawyers to be able to read the authorities and to examine French-speaking witnesses. Only a handful of English-speaking advocates was really bilingual, although we all agreed that bilingualism was professionally desirable. The fact was, however, that we worked in an English atmosphere and in our own tongue. Professional and personal relationships were always correct, usually amicable, and sometimes very close. During my whole time at the Bar I remember no incident of prejudice, discourtesy, or even unpleasantness which could be attributed to bad feeling between French-speaking and English-speaking colleagues. Yet we lived, and in large part worked, in separate worlds. The quiet revolution was long in the future and our insulation from the life of the majority of our fellows disturbed us little or not at all. English-speaking clients retained English-speaking lawyers; and, since the financial, industrial, and commercial life of the province was predominantly in English hands, this meant that, with a few exceptions like St Laurent, Aimé, and Geoffrion, the legal business was concentrated in the hands of a few large English firms like our own.

Altogether it was an agreeable and civilized existence in the practice of a profession with traditions of scholarship and good behaviour. I continued as well to teach at McGill and at evening classes in commercial law. At a time when many of my contemporaries were having great difficulty in making ends meet I knew I was very fortunate. My income in those years was modest enough but I felt secure in work that I liked and surroundings that I enjoyed. Certainly I had little reason to regret that some years before I had declined a surprising offer from Sir Herbert Marler, the newly appointed head of the first Canadian diplomatic mission to Japan, to join his staff and forego my legal ambitions. Nor was I sorry that I had not yielded to the temptation of the much larger material rewards available in a large New York law firm.

Until my marriage, my social life was in most respects an extension of my time at McGill. I enjoyed rather more leisure and was subjected to rather less pressure after the long period of recurring examinations, to which I never really became accustomed, came to an end. I was also more independent than ever before. For a time I lived in the home of my Ross relatives as a member of the family. Later I moved into a small flat of my own where my sister Marjorie, who was taking graduate work at McGill, joined me to my domestic comfort. But our joint menage did not survive long for she met and in August 1930 married Frederick Mott.

Soon after, one September evening that same year, I proposed marriage to Margaret Yuile. Our wedding took place on 27 June at St Mary's Church, Como. It would be an absurd understatement to describe that event the most important of all my years in Montreal. From the moment that Peggy Yuile agreed to marry me my life took on a new dimension. That she was prepared to commit herself to me then, when for the first time I was in a position to consider marriage, will continue to be for me a near miracle. I had known her before; but it was only when I met her in the place she loved best beside the Lake of Two Mountains on the Ottawa river that I realized that I wanted to be with her always. When the ceremony was over and we had 'given our troth to each other' before my father in the solemn and beautiful words of the marriage service, there began for us both a benediction which has continued and multiplied with the years.

Our first home together was a small flat on the side of the Westmount escarpment looking westward across a municipal reservoir – not especially poetic fancy perhaps, but the glow of those Laurentian sunsets lives in our memories. While we lived there, our son was born on 17 January 1933 and christened –

appropriately, we thought – William Brian Danford. The summers we spent largely at my father-in-law's farm near the Yuile's own place at Como, and I commuted daily to the office. It was a pleasant life, busy enough especially after our son and later our daughter Tish were born; yet there was enough leisure time to enjoy family and friends. Without fully realizing it I was developing new and strangely satisfying routines.

The society in which my wife and I moved was that of English Montreal. Not really very numerous in relation to the total population of the metropolis, it continued to possess, nearly two centuries after the conquest, many of the characteristics of a garrison separated in almost every way from the larger community which surrounded it. The inner bastion of this society was a relatively small and well-defined area running west from McGill University into Westmount and north from Dominion Square up the slopes of Mount Royal. Its leading members were pleasant, well-to-do, self-satisfied, and, in their chosen causes, charitable and generous. With notable and honourable exceptions, their horizons and their interests were limited to their own affairs, and their relations with other parts of Canada were often closer than those with the rest of Quebec. Willing to leave to the French-Canadian politicians the governance of the province and the city, they reserved only their right to criticize and complain. Few were prepared to participate directly in provincial or civic affairs. Yet these people were by no means lacking in local patriotism. Nor did they find it inconsistent to count themselves genuine Quebeckers and to compare their position favourably with that of their contemporaries in other parts of Canada and the United States. If their own isolated situation was, in fact, anomalous and narrow, they did not think it so. They believed themselves responsible citizens and were proud of their record of community accomplishment of which McGill, two widely renowned hospitals, and other institutions were living and substantial proof.

There were others among our friends who were more prescient and more involved. Nowhere were the human evidences of the depression sadder or more widespread than in the Montreal area. Even those who were normally insensitive to their political and social environment could not ignore the implications of the economic cataclysm which threatened to engulf the whole Canadian society. In those dark days I counted among my close friends a number of particularly responsive and concerned Montrealers, notably a small and remarkable company which came to be known to its members simply as 'the Group.' Of fluctuating composition and totally without organization, it consisted originally of a handful of friends who, after the war, had been at McGill together; some had also known each other at Oxford. The Group's heart and soul was G.R. McCall, whose home in the city and house in the Laurentians provided warm and hospitable surroundings for the combination of fun and talk which were the accepted objectives. Of the others I had known several before: Frank Scott already launched on his career as a lawyer, poet, and champion of social-ist solutions; and Terry MacDermot, the gadfly whose curiosity like his heart was as wide as humanity. MacDermot became an increasingly close friend and later a colleague in the foreign service. Then there was Brooke Claxton with his immense vitality, his knowledge of, and concern for, all areas of public affairs. He and I were closely involved with one another through our work in Ottawa a few years later when he emerged as a strong, sane force in Canadian politics during and after the second world war. Included as well were Jack Farthing, the massive, worried, intellectual son of the then Bishop of Mont-real, and Victor Wansbrough, then headmaster of Lower Canada College. There were others too who came and went, each with his own contribution to our long, stimulating, and irreverent discussions which never suffered from the inhibitions of organized dialogue. The talk would range without form or order over every sort of topic, frivolous and grave, social, philosophic, political, eco-nomic, and artistic. But most of all, as the good Quebec beer flowed, we would discuss the public problems of our country.

In these years many concerned Canadians sought in organized socialism solutions for the agonizing national problems which traditional policies seemed unable to provide. They were the early days of the Co-operative Common-wealth Federation and the League for Social Reconstruction, the heyday of the *Canadian Forum*, the columns of which provided the ablest and most pro-vocative prose of the decade. As the thirties wore on grave developments on the international scene began to disturb the lethargy and indifference which had settled over Canadians preoccupied with domestic issues. Mussolini's at-tack on Ethiopia and Canada's undistinguished role in the failure of sanctions, the Spanish civil war, and finally the rise of Hitler sharpened divisions within Canada as elsewhere. During this period the nightmare of totalitarianism in one ugly form or another seriously began to disturb our dreams of a peaceful ordered world and our hopes for the security and prosperity of a united Can-ada. The attitudes one encountered in quite ordinary people, even in Montreal, gave rise to anxiety. I remember on one occasion attending a meeting in a downtown office (at whose instance I do not recall) which turned out to have been arranged for the purpose of organizing some sort of vigilante group, allegedly at the request of the Commissioner of the Royal Canadian Mounted Police. The object was to deal with the local 'communist menace.' Fortunately common sense prevailed and that particular folly came to naught.

An event which served to quicken my interest in public affairs was the Lib-eral Summer School at Port Hope which my wife and I attended in the sum-mer of 1933. Organized by Vincent Massey this was, I suppose, the first of the celebrated 'thinkers conferences' which have since become common. Then, as in later years, the object was to provide stimulus to political discussion in the country and inspiration to the Liberal party. Guests of greater and lesser distinction from Britain and the United States, as well as from Canada, were invited to read papers and to participate, irrespective of political affiliation. In the company of a number of our friends we decided to go along. I heard later that many of the active politicians, including Mackenzie King himself, were somewhat less than enthusiastic about the project and more than sceptical about its probable value to the Liberal cause. There is no doubt, however, that it did engender a quickening and broadening of the party in the years which followed. I believe, for example, that Brooke Claxton's subsequent entry into active politics was precipitated by his experience at Port Hope; there were other less distinguished additions; and it cannot be questioned that the domestic and external policies of succeeding Liberal administrations were materially influenced by the proceedings.

My wife and I enjoyed ourselves thoroughly. The guest speakers brought new and provocative points of view and it was interesting to meet the leaders of the Liberal party in such informal surroundings. I encountered for the first time several of the figures that I was to come to know well not many years later: T.A. Crerar, J.L. Ralston, young Paul Martin (then at the threshold of his long career), and finally the leader of the Liberal party of Canada himself. I confess that I found King less impressive than I had somehow expected. I thought him apprehensive and evasive in discussion and uncertain of himself in an environment he seemed to find uncomfortable. Yet he was sociable and charming outside the conference sessions. I was to learn later that Mackenzie King was rarely at his best in such circumstances, and never in the company of Vincent Massey.

My increased interest in public questions during the mid-thirties did not lead to any form of partisan involvement for which I had no special opportunity and, indeed, no particular taste. I called myself a Liberal but I belonged to no party organization, and I can remember only two occasions on which I played any active political role: one when I made a speech for a friend who was a candidate in the 1935 general election; the other when I acted as scrutineer for another friend who was offering himself in Westmount. Both were defeated. On the other hand I found myself involved to a growing degree in community organization concerned with public issues. I have recollections of numerous discussion groups and evenings spent examining proposals for social legislation, constitutional reform, and other subjects of current national importance.

I was also connected with the Canadian Institute of International Affairs, the Montreal branch of which was very active in those years with a battery of exceptionally able and energetic members, including Claxton, J.M. Macdonnell,

Francis Hankin, and Frank Scott. Our meetings then were well-attended and invariably controversial, often lasting on into the small hours. Despite these associations my own views on external affairs were hardly prophetic and afford me now little reason for boasting. On 30 November 1936, for example, I wrote to father, who had apparently expressed his concern as to the adequacy of Canadian defences, that

> I notice you are concerned about defence and while I feel that Canada might do something toward bringing her present equipment up to date and developing particularly her air arm, I am not very worried about this problem though I know many people including the members of the government are.
>
> War involving us geographically is I think remote and the conduct of British foreign policy this past year and more makes me very cool toward Canadian participation in any 'Imperial' conflict which may arise in Europe. Had the U.K. stood by the principles of the League and democracy many would have felt differently. As it is there is in many quarters a growing conviction that our future as a nation is in the American area.

During my last two years in Montreal I was also associated with an inquiry into the school system of the province as counsel and secretary to the Quebec Protestant Education Survey, a full-scale investigation into all aspects of the English minority regime conducted by a remarkable group of men and women under the chairmanship of W.A.F. Hepburn, the director of education for Ayreshire in Scotland. In the course of our duties we travelled throughout the province visiting urban and rural schools, interviewing school boards and teachers, and hearing representations from interested organizations and individuals. It was an admirable experience, not only because it brought me into contact with the primary and secondary education systems in our bicultural society, but also because of the high quality of those people with whom I worked, in particular the chairman himself. Hepburn became a valued friend from whom I learned many important lessons. In a way the survey was my initiation into bureaucracy. For the first time I participated in investigative procedures and an organized deliberative process, and as the work progressed I had my first experience of drafting reports from voluminous records.

In many ways the work of the survey foreshadowed the revolutionary developments which have since occurred in Quebec education. It is not too much to say that our report was an important landmark in the history of the Quebec school system. It was notably prophetic on the subject of instruction in French.

The circumstances of the Province of Quebec demand that time, money and teaching skill should be freely spent to give as many as possible of the English-speaking children of the Province a speaking, reading and writing command of the French language ... There is need for marked improvement in the teaching of the French language in the Protestant schools of the Province ...

Parents should give their children every opportunity of hearing and speaking French, both within and without the home; business and industrial firms should join actively with educational authorities to further a knowledge of French among their employees.[1]

That our proposals took so long to be embodied in legislative and administrative reforms is another story.

Finally, my association with Hepburn and his colleagues of the Quebec Protestant Education Survey gave me my first appreciation of what can be accomplished by hammering out solutions to complex public problems with a group of individuals of varied experience and viewpoint when they are capably led and united in their devotion to a common objective. More than that, it revealed to me the unique satisfactions to be derived from participation in such undertakings. The report was signed at Montreal on 30 May 1938. By the time I had seen it through to publication I had already left the province and moved into a world where investigation and the preparation of reports and recommendations were to be my frequent and familiar lot.

During the years that followed and until father's retirement in 1942, he and mother continued to drive the long road east each summer. They normally remained a month or more at Danford where, although the great house had been burned to the ground years before, father had managed to have erected miscellaneous substitute shelters into which, with ingenuity, we could be fitted. There Marjorie and I, and soon our families with us, paid annual visits. By the mid-thirties the sounds of children had returned to the garden and the fields about the site of the old home. The presence of the young was a joy to our parents who saw us again in their children's children. Nor did their pleasure seem to be diminished by the inevitable disturbances to father's study and the additional burden to mother's housekeeping in still-primitive conditions. At the site of Henry's old home we managed to maintain and refresh the close ties of family by which both father and mother set increasing store as the years went by.

At the beginning of 1938 the course of my own life seemed clearly and firmly established. With the continuation of the good health and good luck which I had come to take for granted, the future in human terms seemed both agreeable and certain. I was happily married. We had two attractive children. Our immediate family circle in Montreal was sympathetic and generous, and

1 *Protestant Education in the Province of Quebec: Report of the Quebec Protestant Education Survey.* W.A.F. Hepburn, chairman (1938), p 304.

we had many friends whose company we enjoyed. In town and in the country we led an active and pleasant existence. Though we were far from affluent and imbalance was the normal state of our modest budget, I had no reasonable ground for serious financial anxiety. Nine years in practice had established my position in the Montreal legal profession and I could look forward with confidence to a steady improvement in seniority and income. Barring a disaster, which there seemed no reason to anticipate, I could expect in due course to rise to the top of a leading firm and to enjoy with my family the security and status in the community that such a position would naturally entail. Furthermore, my professional work was expanding and becoming increasingly responsible and interesting. I had begun to attract clients on my own and had even contemplated at one stage setting up in practice with a couple of my contemporaries. Outside of my family and business life, there were my teaching, which I found diverting and which afforded opportunities in the future, and the various community undertakings in which I was able to engage.

Despite all this, I had developed a kind of malaise, an undefined, perhaps indefinable, dissatisfaction with my own place in the scheme of things. It was not that I disliked what I was doing; rather I had come to perceive too clearly what in all probability I would be doing for years and years. It was a future too certain. Sometimes, indeed, it seemed a dull and conventional prospect, devoid of any vestige of adventure. I suppose that this mild disturbance of spirit derived partly from my early environment and the feeling that my very good fortune carried with it a responsibility. It was the old sense of vocation again, stimulated and enhanced by the ominous movement of events in Canada and abroad.

In 1938 I was increasingly moved by such musings. The chances of my breaking out of the pattern in which my life was set would from then on become progressively less frequent until I was enclosed forever in the local establishment. In the modern phrase, any options I might have would not long remain open. It was a gray and sombre thought, yet it was in this frame of mind that I left with the family on our summer holiday in 1938.

4

Principal secretary to Mackenzie King

As the thirties wore on and the human consequences of the economic collapse became pitifully manifest, particularly in western Canada, debate on the political means of dealing with the situation grew increasingly anxious and bitter. It was a time for new theories, for radical solutions to problems which had gone beyond the limits of endurance. In Alberta the Social Credit gospel of Major Douglas, as revealed by the Bible Institute of William Aberhart, attracted broad support. In the other two prairie provinces, where successive wheat failures had added a special dimension to the depression, new vigour was injected into Canadian socialism and the foundations of the CCF were consolidated and extended. Those were the years of the embattled Bennett government, the march on Ottawa and the Regina Manifesto, the work camps, the years of pathetic makeshift relief and panhandling, and of 'brother, can you spare a dime.' The anger and despair of the thirties had rudely dispelled and replaced the enthusiasm and confidence of the twenties.

Confronted daily in his pastoral duties by the poignant human evidences of economic collapse, my father became increasingly depressed and worried at the inability of government to cope with the social consequences of the crisis. Like many other Canadians he came to feel that traditional political means were wholly inadequate to provide the solutions for massive unemployment and the intolerable human miseries which it entailed. For some years he had ceased to count himself a Conservative; R.B. Bennett did not appeal to him. Without realizing it entirely, he had begun to resent the attitudes and policies of the federal government which were associated in most western minds with St James Street and industrial Ontario. He would have admitted freely that he had been influenced to an important degree by J.W. Dafoe and the *Free Press*, though he would not have been willing to accept a Liberal party label. In his view neither of the old parties were getting to the root of the problems which confronted the country.

The preaching and teaching of J.S. Woodsworth profoundly affected my father. Here was a movement which had its origins in a concern for the lowly and depressed, a social philosophy akin to the Christian gospel. Yet, for father, there were intellectual and instinctive barriers to acceptance, because he found it difficult to go along with the massive state intervention which seemed to be involved in socialist solutions. I suppose that his inherited conservatism and his own personal experience since boyhood, in which the primary and ultimate emphasis was on the individual and the family, were as responsible as anything else for his unwillingness to embrace the new party.

In 1934 he expressed his reflections and convictions on the subject in a sermon on 'Christianity and Socialism,' which was subsequently printed and led to father's meeting with Mackenzie King. I do not know whether he sent a copy to King or whether it fell into King's hands from some other source. At any rate, it made a considerable impression on the Liberal leader, for it seemed to reflect and complement his own approach to the problems of economic and social justice as set forth in *Industry and Humanity*. After reading the sermon King wrote to father and invited him to call when he was in the vicinity of Ottawa. They met at Kingsmere that summer, and so began an association and friendship which was to mean much to both men over the next ten years. For me it was to open the door to a new life.

Each summer until father retired eight years later, he saw a good deal of Mackenzie King. He would visit the prime minister (as he became in 1935) both at Moorside, the big farmhouse at Kingsmere, and Laurier House. Now and then King would drive up to Danford Lake, sometimes with friends, sometimes alone, to take tea with father and mother and occasionally, when we were about, with my sister and me as well. There, as at Kingsmere, the two men would take long leisurely walks through the woods and talk of many things, personal and public, in the environment to which both were so greatly attached.

For father the discovery and development of this friendship provided an outlet for the pastoral energies which, in his own parish at that period, seemed to be taken up so largely by recurring financial crises. 'The honour of intimacy' with the leader of the Liberal party gave him the opportunity to contribute, he felt, to spiritual strength in high places. Their talk, like their spasmodic correspondence in those prewar years, was chiefly of religion and the moral content of life. Occasionally, however, they would discuss matters of public policy and national behaviour. In one of his journal entries in the first year of their meeting father wrote:

We talked late into the night. We talked of everything. We talked of the greatest of all things, religion. We were out-of-doors. All about us was dark, the sky spotted with myriads of stars. And there the two of us alone, apart from all human beings, knelt down and prayed to the God of the stars to rule and overrule all things in this distracted nation's life to the good of our people and the glory of God.[1]

By the time the general election campaign of 1935 was underway, father's friendship with Mackenzie King had deepened. While it is clear that he regarded his role primarily as that of spiritual adviser, he did not shrink from extending his mandate to more specific matters when occasion seemed to offer. The month before the election, for example, on the eve of a Liberal campaign mass rally in Winnipeg, father wrote to King:

I should not be over-anxious as to policy but let everything you say glow with moral passion. There is call for righteous indignation ... They [the people] will elect you in trust and you may develop your policies as situations arise ... The heart of this nation is longing for deliverance. It will respond to courageous spiritual leadership. This is much more than a Liberal battle and must be much more than a party victory. The whole people are concerned and ready to try new ideals and strike for new standards. I shall pray for a great meeting.[2]

Late that night after the meeting, King took time out from partisan pressures to drive out to Fort Rouge and call at the rectory.

When the results of the election were known in the evening of 14 October father sent a message of affection and gratitude to the Prime Minister. Four days later King wrote to father:

I am glad you found the impulse to wire me so strong that it could not be resisted, for I can assure you that no message which came to me on Monday night brought with it more of pure delight. Like all communications from you, it will have its abiding place in my heart, as well as among the communications which I shall wish always to keep.[3]

The 'burdens of office,' the phrase which he was to use so often as the years of power rolled on, left the Prime Minister little time for personal affairs. Yet in the summer which followed, King had several meetings with father. On 12 July he made a visit to Danford Lake that was to be memorable for them both. Of that occasion father later wrote in his journal:

I find him very gentle this year – not at all boastful, longing for a good rest; yet ready to carry on while colleagues go on vacation – very fond of nature

1 W. Bertal Heeney, 'Journal,' 24 July 1935.
2 WBH to WLMK, 26 September 1935.
3 WLMK to WBH, 18 October 1935.

and very observant of its attractions, genuinely spiritual in outlook and conscious of his responsibility to guide. He showed great affection for myself and family. There is no question of his desire to have us spend time with him at Ottawa or Kingsmere. He lingered seeming to enjoy the bit of home life.[4]

Later that same month father spent two or three days with the Prime Minister at Moorside. Writing of their resumed conversations during another walk through the Kingsmere paths, father noted:

He [King] ... is much alive to beauty, particularly in a large way, distant views rather than birds or flowers. There is a mystical strain in him which comes often to the surface, partly induced it may be by my being a clergyman but unquestionably there is that quality ... He has with him also a volume of his specially bound Bible. He is particularly fond of the O.T. [Old Testament], a good instance of what his puritan early years have done for him ... [He is] very conscious of a presence in nature ... King is puritan without its severity. He refers often to Austin and Thos. Carlyle, who seemed to get behind the crust of things. He condemns strongly cocktail parties, women's lipstick and frivolous life ... Altogether a simple and beautiful mind set in guiding people and the country along the path of Truth.[5]

During those days at Moorside they talked also of world affairs against the deepening atmosphere of crisis in Europe:

We must not get tangled up in European squabbles [King said]. If a war comes we shall be involved in the end. He is going to the League of Nations hoping to help in reconstituting it on broad general lines. Most men talk too much. He tries to act through other men. The Cabinet is a family not a regiment. He tries to call forth the talents of each. We talked long last night under the stars and at 11:30 ended with prayer. Just the two of us in the house together and we on our knees. He draws his strength from loneliness and God, this remote and quiet place not public meetings ... He finds it unsatisfactory to speak on other men's investigations and now dreads public utterance because of a conscious lack of thoroughness. I love the man and find so much in common. He is sincere and is bent on the nation's good. He is also an astute business man. I am not sure of his generosity. Christ is the Son of God – but he [King] is foggy as to the ... redemptive effect of His work. The Holy Spirit is not much in his concept of things.[6]

King's communications to father during the summer of 1936 showed an increasing reliance on the friendship and support which father could afford

4 WBH, 'Journal,' 12 July 1936.
5 *Ibid.*, 22 July 1936.
6 *Ibid.*

free of the suspicions and importunities of politics. Remembering one brief visit to Danford Lake that summer King wrote, 'we came away singing that little hymn "Blessed be the tie that binds our hearts in Christian love, the fellowship of kindred souls is like to that above."' It was a Victorian friendship. They exchanged quotations, volumes of verse, and references from tracts and biographies. They were in many ways very different, but they nevertheless shared enthusiasms in literature and life. Both were deeply attached to Wordsworth and Tennyson and Browning and related their poetry to the world about them in the Gatineau. On one occasion King referred to a sermon he had heard at Westminster Abbey on the friendship between St Paul and St Luke. 'There was much [in it] that brought our own friendship to mind,' he wrote. To which father, touched by the reference, responded: 'I cherish your attitude toward me and look upon it as a heavenly reward for striving after the ideals of the Gospel. High church honour has not come my way. Your friendship and intimacy have more than compensated.'[7]

The friendship continued through 1937 and 1938, each birthday and anniversary being recognized by the exchange of elaborately affectionate messages. Yet there was one element in King's attitude as gradually revealed to him at this period which seems to have bothered father increasingly. He had noted in 1935 that King was 'a nature mystic,' by which he meant that he shared father's own consciousness of the presence of God in nature. So far, so good; there was plenty of respectable authority for such a view. But there was a kind of mysticism developing or being uncovered in King, as time went by, far from anything which father could share. In January 1938 King wrote: 'Like you, I have become increasingly absorbed in the mystical. Reality, to me, has never existed in material things.'[8] It was at about that time, I believe, though by what hint or reference I do not know, that father to his distress learned that King was attracted by 'spiritualism' and was dabbling in the occult. In his view, mediums, seances, and all the paraphenalia of spiritualism were anathema, the very negation of the kind of faith he prayed to see strengthened in the prime minister of his country. From that time on, although their mutual affection and friendship continued until King's death, I detected a change in their relationship.

It was not until the beginning of his friendship with my father that I had any close personal contact with Mackenzie King. In the three ensuing summers, however, I encountered him several times. The man I saw on these occasions was charming, entertaining, and considerate. His first interest and the focus of his attention was father. Yet he took obvious pleasure as well in

7 WBH to WLMK, 23 November 1936.
8 WLMK to WBH, 5 January 1938.

the circle of our family, especially when mother, my sister, or my wife were present. Surprisingly, he was very good with the children. If we were flattered by his visits to us because he was prime minister, it was equally true that all of us came to accept him as a welcome friend. Once, in 1937, he invited me to dine with him alone at Laurier House. On that occasion I remember his inquiring about my interest in the Public Service. I suppose I must have replied that, should a suitable opportunity occur, I would be greatly tempted to try my hand, and that while I was happy in the law and my prospects were good, the idea of a Civil Service career had always appealed to me. Whatever transpired at Laurier House that evening King became aware of my interest at about that time. But it was his admiration and friendship for my father which paved the way. There was, as Lord Melbourne said of the Garter, 'no damned nonsense of merit' about my entry into the Public Service of Canada.

In July 1938 father and I had spent an afternoon and evening at Kingsmere. After dinner King asked me to expand upon my interest in the Public Service, of which he already had some inkling. What I said I do not recall, nor does it matter. What was significant in the light of what followed was King's mention of his desire to have someone perform in Canada the role Maurice Hankey had discharged at the centre of government in Britain since the first world war. At that time Hankey was to me little more than a name, his place in the British scheme of things almost totally unknown.

A week later, back at my office in Montreal, I received a letter from the Prime Minister marked 'Personal and Confidential.' It was this letter that was to effect a dramatic change in the course of my life.[9] After referring to our conversation at Kingsmere on Sunday, during which I had expressed my 'desire to become engaged in some form of public service,' the letter noted that I was 'at a time and place in [my] profession which would make any change one which would require much in the way of consideration.' King then proceeded to offer me the position of 'Principal Secretary to the Prime Minister,' describing its functions as follows: '[The] position would correspond in a way to that of a Deputy Head of a Government Department ... in immediate touch with the Prime Minister, and would act as a liaison with other Ministers of the Crown and exercise a general supervision over the work of the Prime Minister's Office.' After saying that he had discussed the matter with the Under-secretary of State for External Affairs, O.D. Skelton, whom he had arranged for me to see in Ottawa after our Kingsmere conversation, King reverted to the Hankey theme:

You no doubt know what happened in England in the case of Sir Maurice Hankey, who, through his relationship with the Prime Minister of the day, be-

9 WLMK to ADPH, 13 July 1938.

came a sort of Secretary to the Cabinet, a position which he continued to hold under several different Administrations. In this position Sir Maurice has, over many years, performed a service more influential than that performed by any other man in the public service of the United Kingdom. I see no reason why a similar post might not be developed in Canada. As you well know, where work is really important, it is the man who makes the position, not the position which makes the man.

The letter then went on to cite the case of Norman Rogers who at that time was minister of labour. King attributed his immediate entry into the ministry upon his election to Parliament to Rogers' previous experience in the Prime Minister's Office. Here, as at an earlier point in the letter, King demonstrated that he had not appreciated that my interest in the Public Service was professional rather than political, a point of view he found hard to understand. Later on this was to cause some difficulty between us.

Finally, realizing that for me to accept such a position would be a leap in the dark, the letter concluded:

I recognize that, attractive as many of its features may be, there may, in your case, be obstacles which are insuperable. I shall, therefore, fully understand if you feel that the risks involved might preclude you from taking a step which, for many reasons, would be most attractive to you. I have felt, however, that not to let you know of this particular chance might be to let something go by which you might wish to consider.

Let me assure you that whatever your decision may be, I shall realize that it has been made in the light of circumstances and considerations of which you alone are in a position to take adequate account.

My immediate reaction was one of great excitement, for the Prime Minister's letter opened up a wide new vista. Here surely was a chance to be totally and professionally engaged at the centre of national affairs at a critical and fascinating time and under the best of auspices. The nature and functions of the position I would occupy were not easy for me to visualize, for I was ignorant of Ottawa and of the ways of ministers and civil servants. I needed to find out more about Hankey and the Cabinet Office in London and what the chances were that Canada could and would provide conditions favourable to the development of a similar institution. And not least important was what assurance for the future of my family could be expected of such employment. There seemed to be a curious mixture of political and Civil Service elements in King's description of the post and its incumbent's duties. Now that the choice was actually put to me, my conservative instincts combined with my legal training to warn me that there was need for definite, clearly understood conditions before acceptance should be matched to offer. I must talk with my seniors in the firm and consult a few friends whose experience was relevant and whose judgment I trusted. But before anything else, I must examine every implication of the decision with the one whose life was bound up in my own.

My wife's reactions were typical. If I wanted to change course and go into the Public Service, there would never be a better opportunity. As I knew, she loved Montreal and would stay on happily in the surroundings she knew so well. On the other hand she was quite willing to set about establishing a new home for the family in Ottawa. She confessed that for some time now she had felt that my current work was proving less than satisfying to me. If the Prime Minister's proposal appealed and on further reflection carried my judgment, she would go along, and cheerfully.

When I put the proposal to father his initial reaction proved surprisingly reserved. Would the Prime Minister's Office prove 'a cul de sac' or rob me of 'mobility of action?' Would I not be exposed to an environment in which for many 'expediency rather than honesty was the rule?' Despite these worries father made it clear that he would accept my decision. For outside advice I turned to two individuals of widely different backgrounds both of whom had had recent experience of Ottawa. Arthur Purvis, a prominent industrialist and respected member of the Montreal financial community, had just returned from chairing a royal commission on unemployment insurance. I felt that he would give me an informed objective opinion. T.W.L. MacDermot, then principal of Upper Canada College, was a close and trusted friend with many contacts across the country. Each in his own way proved valuable counsellors. Both were in favour of my accepting.

Although Purvis frankly described his own disappointments in his relations with politicians and officials and warned me that King was a strange and difficult man, he nevertheless encouraged me to accept the Prime Minister's call. One does not refuse lightly the offer of the head of the government of one's country, particularly at such a critical time.

Typically, Terry MacDermot took time and effort in formulating his judgment. He was intrigued by the proposal, at once full of ideas and eager to help. Soon after I received the Prime Minister's letter he came out to Como one evening and we had a long talk. From the outset he favoured acceptance. The offer was flattering and, in his opinion, the possibilities substantial if I were prepared to take the chance. He had gone to great pains in digging into the history of the British position and had brought with him references to and citations from a number of works on cabinet government. I should study these with care so as to be able to reply knowledgeably to the Prime Minister and to set down precisely the terms and conditions which should govern my appointment. So far as possible every eventuality should be foreseen. A few days later MacDermot wrote to me:

This kind of opportunity doesn't always knock even as often as the postman. If you ignore it, not only may you not hear the knock again, but you will have added the first layer of a thick, hard shell to your conscience which when it is fully grown – impervious to memory – and only then, will allow you to advise young men to go into the public service of their country. It is also worth considering how many younger men will be struck by the fact that you gave up a St. James Street office for harder work, less pay and probable obscurity.[10]

Another friend to whom I wrote was W.A.F. Hepburn, then back in Scotland drafting the recommendations for our report on Quebec Protestant education. His response was of a piece with MacDermot's, though not so eloquent. As a Montreal lawyer, he wrote, 'you have a prospect of 30 years of activity ... and in the end you will be a well-preserved, florid old gentleman who has a right to a seat at the best table in the St. James' Club.' On the other hand, 'to go to Ottawa ... means embarking upon an uncharted sea with a chance of storms and the possibility of being marooned on a desert island.' Yet

with the world in the state it is at the present time and with Canada's relation to it yet undetermined, a position at the heart of affairs is to my mind attractive beyond all imagining ... You see how my mind is working. I should, without hesitation, accept the Prime Minister's offer, go to Ottawa and take what fate sent me.[11]

Finally, to their credit, my seniors in the office were both understanding and helpful. Our chief, F.E. Meredith, a life-long Tory and no admirer of Mackenzie King as he reminded me, felt that such a proposal from the Prime Minister of the country could hardly be rejected; if I accepted he would quite understand and I would always be welcome to return if things went ill.

With support from all these quarters, my negotiations with King proceeded. Primed with my newly acquired and strictly limited knowledge of the situation in Britain and its development under Hankey, I drew up a 'Personal Memorandum' for my own guidance in further discussion. Going over that somewhat naive document thirty-two years later, I realize once more how great is the debt which the embryonic cabinet secretariat in this country incurred to Britain. For the points made in the memorandum and in our subsequent terms of reference for the office were derived mainly from British precedents and what I then inferred to be British practice.[12]

If any doubt of my decision remained, the final straw was added when during August I travelled to Ottawa to lunch with King and Skelton under the

10 T.W.L. MacDermot to ADPH, 21 July 1938.
11 W.A.F. Hepburn to ADPH, 11 August 1938.
12 See appendix A.

trees at the Country Club. King was genial and sympathetic to my personal requirements as I stated them. Skelton felt that the possibilities of the post were important and that reasonable conditions could be provided for its development in the manner I had described. I was encouraged and flattered and on my return to Montreal I drafted and despatched my solemn letter of acceptance. It was a strange, probably presumptuous, communication for a young man to address to the head of his government. It was only later that I learned that prime ministers did not receive many such. For, in my best legal manner, I set out in categorical terms 'my understanding of the position which I am to occupy and its intended development.' Upon appointment as principal secretary to the Prime Minister I should immediately act as his liaison with other ministers and assist him 'in general and particularly with the business of the Cabinet.' I went on to state that 'prior to any general election I will be given the alternative of regular appointment to the permanent Civil Service either as Clerk of the Privy Council or First Secretary in the Department of External Affairs,' which of these alternatives would be 'determined according to their suitability to the performance of those functions which you have in mind' – those of secretary of the cabinet à la Hankey. The letter also dealt with salary, date of assumption of office, and other administrative details.[13]

King responded favourably by telegram to my decision 'as given in your letter of August 24 received this morning' and in a subsequent written reply confirmed that his 'understanding of the position you are to occupy and its intended development is in accord with the position outlined in your letter.'[14] Two days later he wrote to me again:

You are coming into the public service at a momentous time in the world's history. Indeed I can think of no possible position which should mean as much to one with your training, abilities and purpose as the post you have accepted. To have the inside knowledge of world affairs and a directing hand in Canada's part therein is, at this particular time, an opportunity, the value of which can hardly be appreciated. I know you have made a wise choice.

Having in mind the crisis in Europe, the Prime Minister continued:

Just what may happen between now and October 1st, no one can definitely say. I feel, however, that within that period of time, the scales of the world's future will tip very decidedly either to the left or to the right. I am only sorry that we did not begin our negotiations a month sooner, that you might be entering upon your duties here to-morrow rather than a month hence. It might be well for you to have in mind the possibility of a very critical situation de-

13 ADPH to WLMK, 24 August 1938.
14 WLMK to ADPH, 29 August 1938.

veloping within a fortnight's time. Of that, however, there will be, in the interval of time, a chance for us to have a word when you come to Ottawa to see Dr. Skelton and myself.[15]

A fortnight later Neville Chamberlain announced his flight to Berchtesgaden, and by the time I arrived in Ottawa with my family the Munich settlement had been concluded and Mackenzie King had welcomed it with 'deep satisfaction.' For a brief interval Canadians were able to share the relief of their government that the suspense of the late summer was over. It was not long, however, before it became manifest that the cruel sacrifice of Czechoslovakia had bought nothing more than a little time. I was indeed going to Ottawa 'at a momentous time in the world's history.' My appointment as principal secretary to the Prime Minister was made by order-in-council on 8 September (to take effect 1 October), announcement of the fact being made from the Prime Minister's Office the same day.

For my wife and me there were moments of sadness in leaving Montreal but they were fleeting. We were not going far, and in any case once the die had been cast and we were both caught up in a pleasurable sensation of adventure. Skelton proved to be singularly thoughtful and generous with his time and advice on our personal problems, despite his crushing official preoccupations. Thanks largely to him, we decided to live in Rockcliffe where we found a little house on a quiet road lined by high elms and bordered by bright gardens. At the end of September 1938 we were installed at 1 MacKinnon Road. It was the most engaging of the Ottawa seasons, and between us my wife and I could count nearby a handful of friends, so that I recall our having no feeling of strangeness ever in those first weeks.

In contrast the surroundings of my working days were wholly novel. In the course of a personally conducted tour of the Prime Minister's suite at the north end of the East Block, King introduced me to the other members of his staff and, without notice to them, offered me my choice of accommodation. Unaccustomed to the gothic grandeur of those historic premises and somewhat put out by the obvious surprise our appearance had created, I selected what seemed a relatively modest room remote from the Prime Minister's own. Unwittingly, my choice fell on that of my fellow Manitoban Jack Pickersgill with whom I was to be long and happily associated in work and friendship. Overlooking the Rideau Canal to the east with glimpses of the Gatineau hills north through the elms, it proved to be one of the pleasantest offices in Ottawa. Later I found that, adding great insult, I had simultaneously robbed Pickersgill of his private secretary, Mae Roe, who happily was to remain with

15 WLMK to ADPH, 31 August 1938.

me over the next seventeen years. More by luck than by judgment I had made a brilliant beginning.

My new associates in the Prime Minister's Office – Pickersgill, King's veteran private secretary, Howard Henry, Walter Turnbull, and the others – could hardly have been warmer in their welcome or more helpful in every way. There was no sign that they resented, as well they might have, my being parachuted into their midst and given charge over their affairs. My surroundings might be strange and the problems of my new position unfamiliar and forbidding, but I never failed to receive help and advice from my more experienced colleagues.

From the first I worked harder and longer than ever before, partly because of my unfamiliarity with ways of doing things in government, but mostly because there was more work for me to do. It is inevitable that a prime minister's office should be like that. Every day brought its own crisis, or so it seemed; indeed crises rarely came singly and the decision as to what fell in that category belonged to one man. It is well known that Mackenzie King was a demanding master. By the time I joined his staff, his personal routine involved a late start in the morning and unpredictable hours at night. Meal times, unless he were lunching or dining out, were irregular and fitted surgically to his own occasions. Cabinet colleagues as well as officials had to accommodate their timetables to his necessities and his whims. For us in his own office, and for Skelton and a few senior officers of External Affairs, virtually no personal or family occasion was immune from King's interruption. He would usually be charming when he telephoned at some abnormal hour, but there could be no question that he was expecting immediate attention to whatever was then at the top of his mind. It might be a matter of national or international moment; it might be trifling. In either case the call was inexorable.

In the autumn I travelled with Mackenzie King to Washington for the signing of the Canada-United States Trade Agreement, and for my first view of the city where I was later to spend so many years. Soon after our arrival I accompanied King when he called on the Secretary of State, Cordell Hull. Hull was an old friend of the Prime Minister's and the conversation which ensued soon moved from the commercial occasion of their meeting to the developments in Europe which both men contemplated with foreboding. On that trip I also saw Norman Robertson, one of the three leading members of the formidable Canadian negotiating team which had laboured long on the bewildering details of the 1938 trade agreements (with the United Kingdom as well as the United States).[16]

16 The others were Dana Wilgress, of the Department of Trade and Commerce, and Hector McKinnon of the Department of Finance.

Since we had gone down from Oxford, Norman had been back to the University of British Columbia, on to Harvard, and from there to the Brookings Institution in Washington. In 1929 he had joined External Affairs and had soon become one of the small inner group around Skelton. Because of his experience of the East Block I was anxious to have his frank opinion of the feasibility of my performing a useful role in relation to cabinet business. Was there a real job to be done? If so, would I be given the chance to do it, to establish something on a permanent basis? Norman knew how King operated because he had been attached for a brief period to the Prime Minister's staff, and I valued his opinion. Never one to give a snap judgment, he heaved one of the great sighs which became his trademark. He felt bound to say that he was sceptical. There was certainly a job to be done, but the real question was whether the conditions could be created which would allow anyone to do it. This would depend almost wholly upon the Prime Minister. For example, Robertson continued, would King be willing to accommodate himself to what I regarded as the essential professional, apolitical character of the position? Perhaps, but it would go against his grain, and I should recognize this kind of difficulty from the start. It would not be easy, but he hoped I would persist and give it a good try. In the process I would have an interesting if often frustrating time. Norman's counsel was sobering; but my daily experience was soon to prove it wise.

On that same visit to Washington I entered the Canadian legation for the first time, that formidable 'mansion' at 1746 Massachusetts Avenue, every corner of which was to become so familiar to me twenty years later. The government had bought it in Vincent Massey's time, and it still endures as the Canadian chancery, though the ambassador's residence has long since been established elsewhere. In 1938 the legation was presided over by the same Sir Herbert Marler who had suggested my embarking on a diplomatic career when I was a law student. He, as minister, was at the head of our mission, but it was Hume Wrong, his second in command, who provided to Canadian representation in the United States the distinction and repute it possessed immediately before the war. He and Charles Ritchie, another legation pioneer from Massey's time, were a spirited, intelligent team. One was to precede, the other to follow me as ambassador in the same city many years later.

When King returned to the East Block, the accumulation of messages and advice made it increasingly evident that neither honour nor peace had been bought at Munich. As the weeks went by and the prospect of meeting Parliament loomed, anxiety grew and the Prime Minister and his colleagues were constrained to pay more attention to Canada's relationship to European developments and to practical questions of defence policy. There were discus-

sions in cabinet about the larger appropriations for military purposes which
the government would put to the House of Commons in January. King himself was progressively preoccupied with the international situation and the
position to be adopted by Canada. In this it seemed to me that he consulted
almost exclusively with Skelton. Ernest Lapointe was his ministerial confidante and he would have occasional private talks with a few other colleagues,
but as yet there was no sign of ministers and officials being marshalled for
systematic consideration and disposition of external issues. Not before the
summer of 1939 did the Prime Minister request my attendance at any meetings on defence matters with him and any of his colleagues. Even then I remember very few, and only the two or three ministers directly affected and
senior military officers were in attendance. On such occasions I made brief
notes of what transpired but solely for King's own use.

For many senior officials the first months of 1939 were devoted to detailed planning for the visit to Canada of the King and Queen. Inevitably I became involved. One of my early tasks was to work with Loring Christie on the
drafts for the King's speeches across the country. Christie's assignment to this
duty was not without a certain irony for it was well known to his colleagues
that his private sympathies were something short of monarchical. Nevertheless, he gave to the task the same conscientious attention and intellectual
quality that characterized everything he undertook. Given the limitations
within which we laboured the results seemed to me respectable.

King insisted on having every detail of the immensely complicated arrangements for the royal visit submitted for his personal decision. Such decisions
were not easily or quickly come by. For one thing, the multitude and importance of his other concerns made it difficult to get the Prime Minister's attention when it was needed. In the second place, the nature of many of the questions to be dealt with were such as to bring to the surface King's bachelor
fussiness and uncertainty. Who should bask in immediate proximity to the
royal guests at a particular function in Montreal or Toronto or during any of
the fifty-one other scheduled stops on the month-long tour? On such matters
King could spend long and precious time in deliberation and in consultation.
That was bad enough, but when he demanded that his personal approval be
sought for such matters as the cars to which ladies-in-waiting would be assigned, the order of presentation at various places, and other minutiae of the
long program, officials came close to their wits' end. Yet they complied. Sometimes under the pressure of events they went ahead without superior sanction
and risked the severe displeasure which was duly forthcoming if the lapse were
discovered. It was a rough time for E.H. Coleman, the undersecretary of state
who was chairman of the interdepartmental committee in charge, but he and
his associates survived and had the satisfaction of doing a most efficient job.

King also took a keen and unrelenting interest in the resolution of the delicate questions of protocol for which there were often no acceptable precedents. What were we to do with the Governor General when the Sovereign himself was on the spot? Was there any place for the agent when the principal was present? It was only with difficulty that King could be persuaded that Tweedsmuir should welcome the King and Queen to his own residence, Rideau Hall. It seemed clear to Mackenzie King that it was the Canadian Prime Minister who was host to the monarch of Canada. The Table of Precedence had to be changed, a cumbrous and delicate procedure. King insisted that federal authorities be given priority over provincial representatives (among the premiers his old enemy Mitchell Hepburn was no doubt in mind here; but neither were the lieutenant-governors going to be allowed to occupy much of the stage). What about members of the diplomatic corps? Canadian government ministers must be given precedence over foreign representatives no matter what the traditional rule elsewhere. The visit was to be a Canadian occasion with the minimum flavour of London or any lesser rival centre of authority. The Prime Minister himself would be seen to be nearest the Sovereign throughout, even for the sortie into the United States where he would be the minister in attendance upon the King. So, against the looming prospect of a second world war which would strain the foundations of the nation, the cause of unity would be served. If some of the kudos rubbed off on the Liberal party and its leader, so be it. Indefatigably and determinedly King pursued his course through the woods and thickets of the royal program. With a combination of adroitness and obstinacy he resisted and deflected the pressures which built up from every quarter for recognition and preferment in the royal presence. Finally the arrangements were completed, printed, and approved by Laurier House and by Buckingham Palace. On every page of the resulting official booklet the guiding auspices were obvious.

The story of the royal visit has been told many times, officially and otherwise. I shall add no more than a few personal memories from that extraordinary journey on which I travelled with Mackenzie King in official Car 5 from Quebec City to Victoria and back to Halifax. My responsibilities over that busy month were extensive but undefined, and they bore little resemblance to what had been discussed the previous summer. I became in fact a sort of handyman at the disposition of the Prime Minister. Not that I minded, for the experience proved as fascinating as it was novel. It was also to prove helpful to me in my new life. In the space of one month I travelled twice across Canada, visited every provincial capital, met every provincial premier and scores of local politicians, officials, and Canadians from many areas of the nation. I saw parts of my country I had never seen before. Most pertinent to the task I was about to undertake, I was constantly with Mackenzie King and had a unique opportunity to observe him in action in a wide variety of circumstances. It was a happy experience for very many people, something akin to centennial year of 1967 to which Canadians across the country responded with warmth and enthusiasm. The Royal Train was a curious caravanserai and we who made up its complement seemed to develop a group life of our own. From the Monarch and his Queen in Car 1 to the baggagemen in Car 12 we shared a common crowded timetable punctuated along the way by unscheduled incidents both grave and gay. The programmed stops with their parades, presentations, lunches and dinners, and rallies of scouts and guides became the daily pattern for the whole train's company. Our eyes and ears became accustomed to the same sights and sounds: the voices of the school children, the massed bands and orchestras, the thin strains of *The King* swelling and fading as the train passed slowly by small prairie stations, the bunting and the cheering, the fireworks and the bright uniforms, the tension of the crowds in the big cities, and the humanity and pathos of individual faces.

There were some anxious moments. Maurice Duplessis failed to come to the first major function at Quebec City, a lunch given by the government of Canada at the Chateau Frontenac. There was consternation and dark speculation at the reason for the discourtesy, but after an embarrassed delay the meal went on without him. To the surprise of nearly everyone, however, he turned up afterward in time to conduct the King and Queen to the Plains of Abraham to be seen by a great cheering gathering of school children. Later he explained that he had not been able to make lunch because a sister he had not seen for a long time had unexpectedly arrived in town. The next day at Montreal the elaborate ceremonies were presided over by Camillien Houde, the city's incredible mayor who a year later was interned as a danger to the state. In Toronto the embarrassment which had been feared because of the bitter feud between King and Hepburn was somehow avoided, and in Edmonton the Queen's magic managed to attract into the same room for tea the Premier and the Lieutenant-Governor who were not on speaking terms.

There had been a good deal of anxiety about the visit to the United States and particularly about security. Although no serious security problem emerged, the program was crowded and strenuous and the heat intense especially for those of us who bore the consequences of King's distaste for air conditioning. When the Roosevelts received the royal party at the Washington station, by an accident of protocol (as principal secretary of the minister in attendance I had become a member of the retinue) I had the strange experience of hearing the King introduce me to the President. Similarly I was included in other high occasions like the White House dinner at which, to the horror of the Daughters of the American Revolution, Marian Anderson moved the whole company with her glorious voice. At the British Embassy garden party the full weight of Washington heat and humidity gave me a foretaste of later occasions; its only cool element was the frigidity of Marler towards his British colleague, whom the Canadian Minister thought less than sympathetic towards any Canadian flavour in the royal program.

So on to New York and the World's Fair, the never-ending lines of those waiting to be presented, the vast lunch, the seemingly endless speeches, the cavalcade to Columbia University and, at long last, the arrival at Hyde Park and again the warmth and charm of the Roosevelts. Next day the four-day diversion to United States soil came to an end. The King and Queen bade goodbye to their hosts with whom they had established a genuine personal relationship. The American visit had more than justified its proponents, its critics had been confounded, and a new era of good feeling had been inaugurated. The whole party, tired but happy, gave a sigh of satisfaction and relief when the train stopped early next morning at Rouses Point. When we awoke, there were the scarlet tunics of the RCMP; British as well as Canadians felt we had come home. Finally, on 15 June 1939 the royal ship pulled out of Halifax harbour to the strains of *Will ye no' come back again.*

The royal visit was over. It was time to turn attention to graver, grimmer things. No sooner were we back in Ottawa than the Prime Minister and all of us in the East Block were caught up in the rapid succession of events which was to culminate in war in less than three months.

5

War years

For many thousands of Canadians the second world war is remembered chiefly as a period in their lives when long spells of boredom were combined with hardship, anxiety, and suffering. For others, not all of whom were sheltered from physical danger, the years are memorable for new and absorbing undertakings in which they could involve themselves cheerfully and fully in the consciousness that they were contributing to a national purpose. I was one of the lucky ones. Far removed during the whole period from the scene of battle, I was engaged in work that I liked and that stretched all my faculties. Mackenzie King believed rightly that the prime minister should be absent from 'the seat of government' as little as possible; the inference for one with my duties was obvious enough. Nevertheless it continued to irritate me that not once in the war years did King allow me to go abroad into an active zone. In the early stages, when the prospects for my doing an effective job in the East Block seemed dim, I used sometimes to feel that I was 'missing' the second war as I had missed the first. Yet it was clear that any military employment would mean no more than a change of clothing and a move down the street with less responsibility.

So I stayed on in the East Block. The pressures were heavy and constant. I have never worked so hard or so long. Those of us whose responsibility it was to support the deliberations of the Prime Minister and his principal colleagues had few hours that we could call our own. In my own case, after setbacks and frustrations, I found myself projected into cabinet business in circumstances which permitted a job to be done. From early 1940 my duties demanded constant attendance on cabinet ministers, especially when critical decisions were being taken. I became a witness of great events and observed at close quarters not only the principal national performers but many of the leading allied actors as they crossed the Canadian stage. When the guns ceased firing and there was chance to pause and look back, I would have been both insensitive and ungrateful had I failed to appreciate what good fortune had been mine during the war years.

By the end of 1938 I was convinced that Mackenzie King had come to the conclusion that war in Europe was inevitable and that Canada would be involved. Certainly any faint hopes he may have continued to cherish into 1939 were rudely and finally dispelled by Hitler's march into Prague. From early in the new year I had little doubt of the position King would take with his colleagues and the policy he would recommend to Parliament when war came, despite the emphatic reservations of O.D. Skelton, his closest adviser. Meantime, day in and out, his compelling preoccupation was to prepare the way for the acceptance of participation 'at Britain's side' without sacrificing the unity of the country. Even before the royal visit had provided me with such overwhelming private evidence, I had been impressed and surprised by the depth of King's personal attachment to the British connection. On 20 March 1939 an incident occurred which revealed his thinking on the issue.

In the usual cumbersome, infuriatingly detailed, and exhausting way and in the atmosphere of tension and short temper in which all of King's major speeches were produced, the final text of an intended statement in Parliament was being hammered out in his East Block office as the House of Commons was about to assemble. The last typing and checking was still in progress as the carillon struck three o'clock and the Speaker's procession began to move towards the chamber. The Prime Minister got to his feet, was helped into his overcoat, and the papers were thrust into his hand as he descended to his car and was whisked over to the Centre Block. Hurriedly he took his place in a chamber which was crowded and expectant. He was recognized immediately and began to speak. Well into his text he seemed suddenly to have lost his place. He stopped and fumbled amongst the papers in his hand and on the desk before him; then, with a perfunctory bob in the direction of the Speaker, he bustled out of the astonished chamber. Out to the Speaker's entrance and back to the East Block he hurried to locate a page he had discovered to be missing from his typescript. In the scurry of final preparation it had somehow been detached. King recognized at once that its omission would distort the careful balance of his statement and give an opening to those who suspected him of disloyalty towards Britain and the Commonwealth. After some minutes of embarrassed pause, the Prime Minister returned to his place and started again. This time the critical paragraph was there:

If there were a prospect of an aggressor launching an attack on Britain with bombers raining death on London, I have no doubt what the decision of the Canadian people and Parliament would be. We would regard it as an act of aggression, menacing freedom in all parts of the British Commonwealth.[1]

1 House of Commons, *Debates,* 20 March 1939, vol II, p 2042.

In the light of the record since revealed it is ironic that the impression persisted over the war years that Mackenzie King preferred Washington over London, the continental association to that with Britain and the Commonwealth. We who worked with him closely had reason almost daily to know the fact was quite otherwise. King was ever wary of those he suspected of wanting to make of the British connection the fabric for a centralized political authority, but his attachment to Britain and things British was pervasive and no sudden consequence of his exposure to the King and Queen the previous summer.

In the two months following the departure of the royal couple the attention of the East Block was concentrated on the rapidly deteriorating situation in Europe and such secret preparations as could be made interdepartmentally against the prospect of Canadian involvement. The Prime Minister, increasingly pessimistic as he poured over his External Affairs reports, divided his time between Ottawa and Kingsmere. In July I was able to get away for a short break and drove my family down to the Maine coast. While we were at the seaside there occurred an incident which, unimportant in itself, cast a first shadow on my relationship with Mackenzie King.

I had gone to Ottawa on the explicit understanding that I would undertake the organization of a secretariat to the cabinet on the British model. One feature of the arrangement, essential in my judgment, was that I should not be involved in the Prime Minister's party politics. It was not that I had any distaste for such activities, but I was convinced that involvement on my part would jeopardize the possibility of establishing a permanent institution of the kind that was needed. It soon emerged that King saw things differently. With him, as with other prime ministers, it was instinctive to assume a coincidence between the interests of the party and the state. In any event, when I received an invitation to the dinner in Toronto on 8 August to celebrate the twentieth anniversary of King's Liberal leadership (whether or not at his instance I do not know) I declined on the ground that attendance at such a party gathering would be inconsistent with my intended functions. It was not long after my return from Maine that I learned that the Prime Minister had been disappointed and hurt by my action. He attached great importance to personal anniversaries. I was, however, becoming anxious at my failure to make any significant start towards organizing the cabinet business, and I was increasingly sceptical of King's willingness to enable me to do so. For one reason or another, he refused to sanction the simplest, most obvious procedural proposals designed to bring some order into the increasingly chaotic way of dealing with government business. The prospect which had brought me to Ottawa, namely appointment to the Privy Council Office with the mandate to perform the functions of secretary to the cabinet, seemed as remote as ever.

It was in this frame of mind that I drafted and sent a private memorandum to the Prime Minister later that summer. Doubtless it revealed my impatience and frustration; quite possibly it was importunate and unduly legalistic in its reference back to our exchange of correspondence a year before. When, at his request, I went out to Kingsmere to discuss it with him it was obvious that King resented its tone and its substance. His attitude was an infuriating blend of disappointment and tried patience as he explained the need for taking things slowly, awaiting the right moment, and so on. Tense myself, I interrupted to say that if he had changed his mind and no longer wished to go ahead with what had been agreed I would happily return to my profession; my old firm would always make me welcome. 'Arnold,' the reply came, 'that was unworthy of you!'

What followed in the development of the Privy Council Office under the pressures of war is set down in a later chapter. In the clearer vision of hindsight, however, I have since come to realize that in one important respect our minds had never met. To Mackenzie King it would have been in the natural order of things for me to share in all his activities, and to progress from his office – whatever my style and title – into direct participation in political life under his auspices. My idea, on the other hand, was to create and set to work a new and permanent mechanism which would rationalize and accelerate the business of government at the cabinet level. Because of this difference, I proved a disappointment to King after the first year of our connection. Under the pressure of events, however, a good relationship was soon re-established, on a less exalted, but for me more satisfactory, basis.

In the morning of 1 September 1939 Canadians learned that Hitler had struck at Poland just after midnight. Word had come to me early. After a hurried breakfast in the kitchen with the radio blaring out the bulletins of the first shattering blitzkreig and a telephone call to Norman Robertson, I was off to the East Block. The Prime Minister had sent word that he would expect the cabinet to be assembled by nine o'clock. By eight the ministers and their chief advisers had been summoned.

What followed is well known. After the cabinet meeting the Prime Minister made the announcement that he had prepared for this situation. Parliament would meet in six days and 'in the event of the United Kingdom becoming engaged in war in the effort to resist aggression, the Government of Canada [had] unanimously decided ... [to] seek its authority for effective cooperation by Canada at the side of Britain.' Meantime, necessary actions were being taken for the defence of Canada. The War Measures Act was proclaimed, the armed forces were put on active service, and the other steps set out in the recently revised 'War Book' were taken under the authority of the act. On 3 September Britain declared war. Exactly one week later, after a brief but remarkable debate in the House of Commons, Mackenzie King cabled the High Commissioner in London to make a formal submission to the King for a declaration of war. For the first time Canada was at war by its own act.

During the following five years my duties at the centre of the government mechanism brought me in daily working contact with those who shaped and directed the Canadian war effort. This meant, first of all, the Prime Minister himself and those colleagues upon whom, because of their personal qualities, ministerial functions, or both, King relied most in the conduct of affairs. It also meant the chief officials of government, military and civil: the chiefs of staff, the deputy ministers, and senior members of the key wartime departments, some drawn from outside for the duration but most of them from within the permanent service. On the whole they were a remarkable group who served the country well under circumstances of almost continuous pressure and frequent anxiety as events unfolded overseas and at home. All were moved by the interests of Canada as they saw them and, until late in the war, they remained united in their major convictions. A few are among the great figures of our country's history.

Of the Prime Minister as the head of a wartime administration much has already been written, not least in the notable and monumental *Record*[2] drawn from the immense mass of diaries in which he recorded his daily comments on people and events. Much still remains to be written and it seems likely that for many years political historians will continue to argue the virtues and frailties of that strange man. My own estimate will emerge from these pages as I recall the dozen years of our close personal and official relationship. For the moment it is enough for me to observe that at no time during the war years was there the slightest doubt that Mackenzie King was in fact and in law the head of the government and the master of his cabinet.

When the war began, King had about him an inner team of experienced colleagues with a variety of talents. Soon after my arrival in the East Block, I came to realize that, in terms of personal relations with the Prime Minister as well as authority and prestige in the cabinet, in Parliament, and in the country, Ernest Lapointe towered over the others. He was the only minister, other than Rogers who had been his secretary, whom I ever heard King address by his first name. On the most delicate and confidential affairs, Lapointe was uniquely the Prime Minister's confidante whose loyalty and judgment he trusted; more than that, he was a friend for whom the Prime Minister had deep affection. After Lapointe's death in November of 1941 no other colleague took his place. St Laurent had King's respect from the time he joined the ministry and, increasingly as the war went on, his admiration and confidence. Yet there remained a certain formality in their relationship, a feature absent in King's communion with Lapointe.

2 J.W. Pickersgill and D.F. Forster (eds), *The Mackenzie King Record,* 4 vols (Toronto: University of Toronto Press, 1960-70).

King asked me to accompany him to Lapointe's funeral in Quebec City. I was glad to do so, for like everyone who had had personal dealings with him I had developed affection as well as respect for that warm and devoted Canadian. After the procession and funeral mass at the Church of St Roch we boarded the train going on to Rivière-du-Loup for the burial. Weary and depressed after the heavy emotional experience of the afternoon, the Prime Minister's mind was nevertheless obsessed by the succession to his Quebec lieutenant. It was one of the rare occasions during the war that King asked me to have a drink with him – he had foresworn 'stimulants' as a contribution to the war effort. As the funeral train rolled on down the south shore of the St Lawrence, he began by telling me, as I already knew, that the problem of finding someone to take Lapointe's place was worrying him greatly. It was clearly essential that, if the unity of the country in the war effort was to be maintained, a Quebecker of the highest standing be brought into the inner councils of government. He was having great difficulty in finding anyone who could come close to filling the great gap. He admired and trusted Adelard Godbout, but Godbout felt that his place was in the province. He mentioned Louis St Laurent, and another leading advocate at the Quebec Bar. As it happened I had known them both; St Laurent rather more than casually because of my earlier experience[3] with him, the other man as a successful and skilful practitioner. I told King of the impression St Laurent had made on me on that occasion years before. He was, I said, a person of cultivation and charm and, most important of all, of character; of that I was certain. As for his intelligence, his position at the Bar was the best evidence of that; there was no one whose opinion was more valued. The alternative possibility he had mentioned was an able lawyer and intelligent citizen but not a patch on his first choice. If he could bring St Laurent into the ministry, King would acquire a colleague who would be a comfort and strength to him as head of a wartime government and who would perform a great service for Canada. I do not presume to think that my opinion weighed much in the balance. King received the same advice from his Quebec colleagues and others whom he consulted. Nevertheless, I happened to have expressed myself at the critical time and, of course, like to think that my view helped to tip the balance. However that may be, St Laurent was invited and persuaded that it was his duty to accept. He entered the government on 10 December 1941, less than two weeks after Lapointe's death. Immediately he assumed a role of major importance in the conduct of affairs.

The career of Norman Rogers as minister of national defence was cut tragically short by his death in an airplane crash on 10 June 1940. As with Lapointe the relationship of King and Rogers had an unusual personal element.

3 Chapter 3, p 28.

After Rogers' death King wrote: 'Rogers was the best man I had in the administration, bar none, for this period of war. No loss could possibly be greater to the ministry.'[4]

Of Mackenzie King's other colleagues in the early days of the cabinet War Committee, the strongest – those who carried the heaviest guns in discussion and had the most influence on decisions – were C.D. Howe, J.L. Ralston, J.G. Gardiner, J.L. Ilsley, and C.G. Power. T.A. Crerar, as minister of mines and resources, had a special position. King's personal relations with them were not in any sense intimate, though I think he had affection for Chubby Power even when distressed by his conduct. Yet to each he accorded the respect due to capacity and political power. He recognized 'C.D.' as uniquely equipped to develop the industry of war and gave him free rein. Ralston had returned to the ministry at King's urging but they had little in common. As Finance Minister Ilsley was devoted and conscientious but King found him infuriatingly rigid, while Gardiner felt that he had to be watched. As the war went on, others were added to the cabinet War Committee: J.T. Thorson came in as minister of national war services; Angus L. Macdonald as minister of national defence for the Navy. Altogether the calibre of King's wartime administration was, if not an executive of all the talents, surely as strong a group as we have had for any extended period in our history.

In 1939 two remarkable men, O.D. Skelton, undersecretary of state for external affairs, and W.C. Clark, deputy minister of finance, were the government's most influential non-political advisers, and directed the execution of high policy. Both from Queen's University, they had deserved and been accorded the confidence of Conservative as well as Liberal administrations. The war multiplied their responsibilities and the Prime Minister and his colleagues relied still more heavily on their counsel. Skelton was not only King's deputy in international affairs but his closest adviser over the whole spectrum of government. Even when it could not be accepted for political or other reasons, the judgment of that able, quiet, and devoted Canadian could be relied upon as loyal and disinterested. Clifford Clark, though less involved personally, stood high in King's confidence and no major economic measures were adopted without his advice. More than anyone else it was Clark, indefatigable and imaginative, who provided the leadership in the formulation and direction of critical wartime financial policies. I became closely associated with these two during the first years of war as we prepared material for ministerial consideration and am proud to recall that both became close friends of my wife and me. For each I came to have affection and respect; to the memory of each I acknowledge a deep debt of gratitude.

4 Pickersgill, *The Mackenzie King Record*, I, p 90.

Of the dozen or two others who were in frequent attendance on the Prime Minister and his colleagues in 1939 and 1940, I recall especially Norman Robertson, who was to succeed Skelton as undersecretary in March 1941, and Donald Gordon as he took firm grasp of the economy. I also remember the Prime Minister conferring with L.B. Pearson and Hume Wrong, both of whom I then knew only slightly, having met them during their visits to Ottawa from London and Washington respectively.

In the Prime Minister's own office Jack Pickersgill became the mainspring. Concerned primarily with the exacting task of assisting King with his speeches in and out of Parliament, he rapidly extended his usefulness to virtually every area of prime ministerial activity. We saw much of each other and our friendship has endured. Although King continued to complain to his diary and others of the inadequacy of his personal staff, the fact was that he was well and truly served in his own office throughout the war. Henry, Turnbull, Pickersgill, C.W.G. Gibson, and most of all J.E. Handy, the Prime Minister's personal stenographer and secretary, made up a team which set a standard of loyalty and competence for all of us.

One of the first important questions for the wartime government was that of the training in Canada of aircrew from the Commonwealth. The story of the negotiations leading up to the agreement in December 1939 has already been told in detail. Nevertheless, since it was the first such business in which I was involved I might refer to one or two episodes which cast some additional sidelights on the affair.

My initial impression of the United Kingdom's delegation, and the behaviour and bearing of some of them as the negotiations proceeded, hardly fitted with my conception of what should be expected of Whitehall. Clifford Clark and I were sent down to the Chateau Laurier to meet them when they arrived on Sunday evening, 15 October 1939. We were received in their suite by Lord Riverdale, the Sheffield industrialist who was their head, and introduced ourselves to his sizable party of senior civil officials and staff officers from the Air Ministry. After assuring ourselves that all was in order for their comfort and convenience, and before we had had a chance to mention arrangements for the following day, Lord Riverdale drew Clark and I aside and asked us to go with him into the next room. There he proceeded to fish in the drawer of his bureau and select two small tissue-wrapped packages which he solemnly presented to us. They turned out to be pen knives clearly marked with his firm's name. Poised as we were for immediate exchanges on urgent issues, Clark and I found it incongruous that the first move by the noble Lord, however kindly intended, should have the colour of sales promotion rather than serious negotiation between governments.

Initially the discussions went forward in business-like fashion, and solid progress was made towards agreement with Britain and the other Common-wealth nations. At an early stage the cabinet War Committee had decided that training of aircrews would be an important contribution to the joint war ef-fort and one peculiarly suited to Canadian capabilities and physical conditions. Before the negotiations were well underway the preliminary work had begun for the rapid provision of aircraft, airfields, and men. The training program became one of the most imaginative and successful achievements of the war.

Agreement with the British on several critical features of the plan, among them the issues of financing and Canadianization, was not, however, achieved without difficulty, misunderstanding, and delay. In the process a good deal of heat was generated on both sides. The Prime Minister kept in close touch throughout and did not hesitate to deploy the full power of his office on is-sues he regarded as important to Canada. In doing so he could be devastatingly preemptory as the British discovered to their surprise. The manner in which he finally brought Riverdale and Air Chief Marshal Sir Robert Brooke-Popham to the point of signing in the early minutes of his birthday on 17 December has already been told.[5] Skelton and I, and later Turnbull, were with him as he took personal charge of the final act. The British representatives were out-manouevred and they knew it.

Earlier in the autumn I had had an experience in this same matter of the sure touch and decisive power King could bring into play to achieve his pur-poses. There had been long argument with the British over the provision of groundcrew, required in large numbers for the training establishments spread across Canada. Not unnaturally the RCAF could take little satisfaction in the prospect of having the great majority of its own men prevented from going overseas and limited to training duties, however important. The situation of Canadian aircrew in combat areas was difficult because they had to operate within the RAF, but an agreement had been reached whereby RCAF squadrons would be set up. That of the groundcrew was at an impasse, the Canadian air staff being unwilling to contemplate all Canadian groundcrews remaining at home while Canadian squadrons overseas were serviced by the RAF. The inevi-table result of such a policy would be to jeopardize the immense groundcrew recruiting requirement of the RCAF. Few Canadians would choose the Air Force if their prospect for the duration was Penhold, Alberta, or Summerside, Prince Edward Island, whatever their charms. Persuaded that the Canadian delegation would not budge, the Air Ministry put forward a proposal to have Canadian groundcrews proceed overseas in the course of the concentration of Canadian aircrew in RCAF squadrons, the so-called 'Canadianization' process.

5 See Pickersgill, *The Mackenzie King Record,* I, pp 52-9; see also, James Eayrs, *In Defence of Canada* (Toronto 1965), II, p 114.

The RCAF were favourable. Their difficulty would be met and, ultimately, there would be completely Canadian overseas formations in the air and on the ground.

I was with the Prime Minister on 14 December when Norman Rogers gave him Riverdale's letter describing the British proposal. Taking off his glasses, he said at once that this would not do at all. The British must be told so without delay. Already irritated by the stubborn opposition of the British on the Canadianization issue, King saw the groundcrew proposition as a scheme for sending Canadians overseas to the fighting zone and replacing them on safe home bases by Englishmen (which of course was exactly what it was and what the RCAF wanted). 'You are to see Riverdale at once,' he instructed me, 'and tell him from me as Prime Minister of Canada that, unless this proposal is withdrawn immediately, there will be *no* agreement for an air training plan and that I shall cable Chamberlain to that effect immediately. Tell him that I want the proposal withdrawn at once and without qualification.' In vain I tried to explain that the proposal was in response to the RCAF's determined pressure to give Canadian groundcrew an opportunity to serve overseas and that the British had finally agreed to put it forward despite the formidable arguments against it on grounds of economy and shipping. 'Do as I say, Arnold,' he concluded. 'The consequences of accepting such a proposition as this would be disastrous.' Off I bustled to deliver my message to Riverdale at his office in the Senate. The old man was dumbfounded. 'But,' he spluttered, 'we thought that this [the UK proposal] was exactly what you wanted.' Finally, despite Rogers' intervention with the Prime Minister, the proposal was withdrawn.

King, for reasons of public policy, did not hesitate to reverse his subordinates. If, in this instance, there was reason to sympathize with the British negotiators, it must be said that generally we found them strangely insensitive to Canadian considerations. Riverdale and Brooke-Popham, the two top members of the delegation, quite clearly started with the assumption that the Canadian government would accept the position that mother knew best. Before they were through they had learned better. The result was a much better agreement and a much better plan, for what finally emerged provided for partnership and co-operation in mutual respect.

My appointment to the Privy Council Office was made literally on the eve of the general election of March 1940. Mackenzie King had delayed earlier action ostensibly on the improbable ground that his colleagues might resent having an official present as secretary in ministerial meetings. My reminders of his undertaking to have me named before elections took place did nothing to lubricate our personal relations nor did the fact that, faute de mieux, I was already being pressed into service of war ministers by the force of events. It was in King's nature to withhold decisions on such matters to the last possible moment. In the end, however, all went well. My presence at meetings of the cabinet War Committee were legitimized by my being given the dual title of 'clerk' and 'secretary'; the government, spearheaded in Quebec by Lapointe and Power, won a smashing victory; and in the East Block we were able to get on less spasmodically with the administrative business of the war. As the crowded weeks and months went by and we moved into a second year of hostilities, the Prime Minister came to accept me and to display confidence in my new office. If I had failed to come up to his notion of what Hankey had been to Baldwin and to take full advantage of the opportunity he had given me, at least I was performing (if, for him, with somewhat excessive efficiency) a useful and necessary wartime job. Our personal relations returned to normal, the temperature fluctuating with external events and the private moods of that anxious, lonely man.

Late in March I made the short but significant move into the office of the clerk of the Privy Council. Before moving in I had known my new quarters as the dim sanctuary of my predecessor in the clerkship, E.J. Lemaire, a courtly survivor of an earlier day whose civilized working hours seemed to be occupied chiefly in affixing his signature to copies of orders-in-council. Situated at the centre of the north end of the East Block, the office remains to this day one of the nobler rooms in official Ottawa. Well proportioned and high-ceilinged, its large window looks north over Parliament Hill towards the distant Gatineau. It is connected on one side with the council chamber through a small anteroom which in those days was a cluttered but not inelegant Victorian cubbyhole to which ministers repaired during cabinet meetings to receive officials or merely for a breather or a cigarette. On the other side of the clerk's suite are the corridors which provide the entrance way to the Privy Council Office, still happily insulated from the remainder of the East Block by the swinging neogothic doors with their coloured glass. It is fitting that now Mackenzie King in imperious bronze should be situated just outside, his eyes directed towards the windows behind which later privy councillors and their officials continue to wrestle with the nation's familiar problems. For the next nine years that ancient office was to be the principal scene of my labours. The proceedings of the cabinet War Committee, its deliberations, and the carrying out of its decisions became the centre of my existence. It was a full-time occupation and more, and from where I laboured the course of current history could be perceived.

One of King's major wartime objectives was to draw Great Britain and the United States together. To this end, as well as for narrower Canadian purposes, he cultivated assiduously and successfully the personal relationship he had already established with Roosevelt. He was acutely sensitive to the kinds of difficulties likely to characterize direct encounters between the United States and Britain, and from the early days of the war did much by personal intervention to avoid and reduce friction. The important part that he played as mediator in the 'destroyers-for-bases' arrangement is a case in point.

After his meeting with the President at Ogdensburg in August 1940, when the situation in Europe seemed almost hopeless and Roosevelt himself was almost openly sceptical of Britain's survival, King wrote to father in a rare wartime letter:

I know of course how wholeheartedly you would endorse and rejoice in all that was accomplished at Ogdensburg, and much besides which has been the fruit of the combined efforts of those of our country and other parts of the English-speaking world who have sought to bring the United Kingdom and the United States into closer relations with each other.

How thankful we all ought to be that the voice of men and women of good-will has become, of late, if anything stronger than that of the men and women of ill-will, who are responsible for the terrible state of affairs in the world at this time.

I really believe that history will record the period of the Ogdensburg Agreement and that of the exchange of United States destroyers for British bases as that of the tide of British affairs which was taken at the flood, and which will lead, in the end, to victory. Had that moment and its opportunities been lost, I do not know what, in the end, would have saved us all.[6]

For King it was evident that the Ogdensburg Agreement, and the Canada-United States Permanent Joint Board on Defence it created, would serve not only, in the President's words, 'to help secure the continent for the future' but also the wider and more critical objective of Canadian policy, namely the welding of Washington and London in solid alliance against the aggressors. King's visits to Washington and to Hyde Park in April 1941, which resulted in the Hyde Park Declaration, provided further almost dramatic testimony of his success in encouraging United States involvement and assistance. A noteworthy feature of King's visit to Britain in August was the time given to discussion of relations between London and Washington. King's conversations with Churchill were largely devoted to reporting and advising upon American developments. King earnestly hoped that the United States would move to support the British cause, but felt it must not be a reluctant entry into the war to save others. Events must be allowed to convince the Americans that they must get in for their own salvation. Pearl Harbour was only four months in the future.

One curious manifestation of King's anxiety to exploit every opportunity to bring Britain and the United States together in fighting the war was the

6 WLMK to WBH, 21 September 1940.

despatch with which Canada declared war on Japan. By coincidence, at the Prime Minister's direction I had spent part of the morning of 7 December 1941 with Norman Robertson discussing reports of Japanese naval units threatening the Malay peninsula, and the rest of the morning in arranging completion of the formalities for declarations of war against a number of the minor Axis allies. For some reason we had not until then dealt with Finland, Hungary, Rumania, or Bulgaria; I cannot recall why it was that Sunday morning was chosen to fill in the gaps. I do, however, remember well that the drafting of the orders and proclamations and attendance at Government House to obtain the Governor General's signature occupied my time until noon. Despite our care, we forgot Bulgaria, though when that omission was drawn later to King's attention he refused to sanction the necessary action. He had 'had enough of declaring war for one day!'

When word of the Japanese attack reached him that afternoon, however, he felt relief that the Japanese had chosen to attack the Americans first. He acted at once. Awakened from a sound sleep after late lunch with my neglected family, I was directed to call a meeting of the cabinet War Committee for early that evening. I was to prepare the necessary papers to put before them. Since I was already well-practised in declaring war that day I was able to produce the documents in sort order. When the War Committee met they agreed to the Prime Minister's proposal that action be taken at once; the order-in-council recommending the necessary submission to the King was signed at 9:15 that night. Since by then further telegrams had arrived, the Canadian advice was based upon Japanese hostilities against Britain as well as against United States territories and forces. It was the exact situation which King had hoped would provide the spur to final United States action. To him there was a dramatic justice in the fact that Canada's declaration of a state of war, from 11 o'clock that same evening, preceded rather than followed the action of the United States Congress.

The climax of Mackenzie King's hopes to help in establishing the Anglo-American relationship on a solid basis came two years later when he was able to play host to both Churchill and Roosevelt at the first Quebec Conference held in August 1943. During the war, notably at the two Quebec meetings, I had several opportunities of observing Mackenzie King in the company of Churchill and Roosevelt and, on one occasion at least, of watching the trio perform. It is not easy to describe confidently these personal relations other than to state the obvious, that the three were on terms of familiarity and friendship. In appearance, manner, and behaviour the differences among them were striking, yet it was evident to the beholder that each had respect for the other, the mutual respect of allies united in a common purpose. It was also the special kind of respect accorded successful politicians by their fellow practitioners. Both Churchill and Roosevelt demonstrated this attitude towards King whose longevity in leadership had far exceeded their own.

King's demeanour in the presence of them was a curious blend of diffidence with a persistent sometimes embarrassed assertiveness. Churchill and Roosevelt were to meet in Quebec, each with his great and glittering staff and all the manifestations of authority in imposing array. King was delighted to have them do so and pleased that they should meet together on Canadian soil. Nothing was to be spared for their comfort and convenience. On the other hand, he was not willing to have Canada, or himself, left out of the party. While not strictly a part of the conference, the Canadian Prime Minister was in Quebec, staying at the Citadel, during its entire course. The Canadian chiefs of staff were on hand, as were the ministers of the cabinet War Committee. The Canadian Ensign flew at the Queen's Bastion alongside the Union Jack and Old Glory, and King was in the final group picture with Churchill and Roosevelt and the combined chiefs of staff. King's determination to achieve a place for Canada at these high councils of the alliance may have caused some irritation in certain quarters and some embarrassment in others. Nevertheless, it was because of King's stubbornness that a measure of Canadian influence was brought to bear upon the deliberations of the two major allies at points and upon issues of vital interest to Canada.

It had been agreed that, before the President arrived, the British Prime Minister and his chiefs of staff would meet with the cabinet War Committee and our own chiefs. The meeting took place in the Chateau Frontenac and the two prime ministers presided jointly. Churchill was in top form; at King's invitation he opened with a masterly tour d'horizon analysing the course of the war thus far and forecasting the developments to be anticipated in the months ahead. The meeting then proceeded to discuss questions affecting the employment of the Canadian forces and Anglo-Canadian co-operation in a number of areas. It proved an exercise useful to both sides. When the time came to adjourn, Churchill, turning to me where I was sitting behind and between him and King, asked whether I had a piece of paper. 'This is a great occasion. We must have a communiqué.' When I produced paper and pencil and gave them to him, he then uttered as he wrote:

On this ('what date is it?') – 1943, there met at the ('what is the name of this place?') – Chateau Frontenac in the historic City of Quebec, the ('what do you call these Ministers of yours?') War Committee of the Canadian Cabinet and the (here a pause and looking up 'Ah I see the Lord President is here') the War Cabinet of Great Britain. Matters of mutual interest were discussed.

In this way the world was informed that the British War Cabinet had been meeting in Canada with its Canadian counterpart. When Clement Attlee, who was acting prime minister in London, and his colleagues read their papers next morning they were, no doubt, more than somewhat surprised.

Among my duties as secretary to the cabinet was to keep the Governor General informed of what was transpiring in the ministry. The Prime Minister had customarily called at Government House for the purpose; but not long after my appointment to the Privy Council he agreed that some regularity should be introduced into such communications with the crown's representative. Accordingly, I was instructed to see the Governor General once a week and to give the high points of what had gone on in the council chamber; in fact, this came to mean in the cabinet War Committee. King's own calls were reserved for special occasions.

My weekly visits to the Earl of Athlone at Rideau Hall turned out to be among the more agreeable of my wartime duties. I became very attached to him and I believe he was fond of me. He possessed, in notable degree, the traditional royal qualities of style and presence without the merest trace of pomp or condescension. He felt much involved personally in the progress of the war. While he genuinely enjoyed his life in Canada, he had been a solider and his thoughts and his warm heart were with old comrades and friends in embattled Britain and across the globe. When I would be shown in, he would greet me and at once offer me a drink, once with the admonition that 'you should always wet your throat, Arnold, before you light a cigarette.' More often than not he would begin with a few observations of his own. Not infrequently, these were exceedingly difficult to identify or place in any given context. This proved awkward when the old gentleman was under some emotional stress. On one occasion I remember his greeting me with tears in his eyes, at the same time repeating several times as he moved about the room: 'Very tiresome. Very tiresome. Very tiresome!' It transpired that he had just had word of the destruction by bombing of a country house in which one of his oldest servants had perished. He was bowed down in grief. Yet he could allow himself no stronger expression. Later in the war when the British in Burma were retreating upon India and for some days the news had been consistently bad, Athlone greeted me in passionate emphasis and without any preliminaries: 'They should never have given up their horses!' It slowly emerged that he had just been reading an account of the passage of the Blues, his old regiment (long equipped with armoured cars), across the Irrawaddy river in the face of devastating Japanese fire. The casualties had been heavy. So was the old man's heart.

When the time came for the Athlones to leave, he and the Princess Alice were sad. They had a touching farewell at Rockcliffe Airport. As they came down the line to where I stood Athlone was obviously moved. If I ever came to London, he said, I must look them up. Then turning to the Princess he asked: 'But where will Arnold be able to get in touch with us?' 'Kensington Palace will find us,' his wife replied.

From the time he had concluded that war was inevitable Mackenzie King was haunted by the memory of the conscription crisis of 1917 and the fear that, with the continuation of hostilities, the country would be rent asunder once again over the issue of compulsory overseas service. To most others, the electoral victory of 1940 seemed to lay the ghost; not so for him. His suspicions and anxieties on this score were never far from the surface of his consciousness. Yet when the crisis came in the autumn of 1944 he was taken by surprise. In mid-September when he went for the second time to meet Churchill and Roosevelt in Quebec he was in a sanguine frame of mind feeling that the danger was past. The fighting in which the Canadian Army had been engaged since D-day was proving to be more severe than had been anticipated by the experts, nevertheless King remained confident in the assurance of the government's military advisers, confirmed in conversation by Montgomery himself, that available reinforcements would be adequate.

The principal members of the cabinet War Committee with their handful of senior advisers, civil and military, accompanied the Prime Minister to Quebec. As before it had been arranged that the Canadian party would confer with the British delegation before the arrival of the President. We were to meet after lunch in the long gallery of the Citadel which opens out to the broad platform overlooking the St Lawrence. As the hour approached we assembled in the sunshine outside the conference room, and Churchill strolled happily up and down flanked by two of his senior officers. A few minutes before the time fixed all was in readiness. Except for one thing. King had not arrived. In some anxiety, since I was responsible for the meeting's arrangements, I was watching Churchill. I saw him stop, take his watch deliberately from his waistcoat pocket and look at it. Then, raising his head, he beckoned to me. 'Young man,' he pronounced solemnly, 'where is your Prime Minister? We cannot,' indicating the chiefs of staff, 'keep these great men waiting.' I explained that the Prime Minister had a speaking engagement at lunch time, that it was an obligation of importance, and that I felt sure he would be with us soon. Churchill grunted but seemed satisfied. A few minutes later King turned up, having just delivered to the Quebec Reform Club the speech reaffirming his opposition to overseas conscription which was so greatly to upset Ralston, then minister of national defence.

While I have little to add to the several other accounts of the reinforcement crisis already made public, I can hardly omit reference to it. In the nine years of my attendance at meetings of ministers there were many occasions of tension, but none to compare in dramatic quality with the sessions between 18 October and 1 November 1944. Most of the action took place in the cabinet

War Committee, but as events moved to their dénouement the scene shifted to the full cabinet. Even now, twenty-six years later I do not feel at liberty to reveal what passed between ministers in the Privy Council chamber other than what was subsequently made public in the House of Commons. Yet because I was the only disinterested witness of much that transpired, I should give some personal evidence from my recollections of that critical fortnight.

After Ralston's return in October from his visit to the army in Italy and northwest Europe, the cabinet War Committee was in almost constant session, or so it seemed to me. With the close and admirable collaboration of Major General Maurice Pope, the military secretary, I was responsible for recording the interminable discussions and for following up the decisions taken in that body and in the numerous ministerial and interdepartmental committees set up to go further into the critical arithmetic of reinforcements. Pope's own restrained account of what transpired conveys much of the flavour of those exhausting and depressing days and nights in the Privy Council Office.[7]

All the effort and ingenuity which could be brought to bear, however, were to no avail. The central problem, whether or not compulsion for overseas service should be employed, continued to defy solution. The division between the protagonists had by this time become known outside the chamber. The Prime Minister then directed that the subject go to full cabinet, and in the cabinet meetings that followed the differences of opinion and judgment went deep. Emotion, heightened by fatigue, confused the issues while they were debated and redebated, just as they subsequently confused the recollections of some of the participants. At the time it seemed to me that ministers about the table, with few exceptions, were conscious that they were dealing with a subject of supreme national as well as political significance. Certainly the future of the Liberal government was in jeopardy; most of them believed its fall would mean national disaster.

The final scene in the drama was played out on 1 November. I was in the chamber when King made his fateful pronouncement which the newspapers summarized the next morning as 'Ralston out; McNaughton in.' I remember the time as in the evening, after dinner, though others present have fixed it in the afternoon. I recall the chill of frozen silence which transfixed all present as King stopped speaking. Ralston rose immediately, made his way about the table shaking hands with each of his colleagues and the Prime Minister and exchanging a few quiet words. His manner was calm, courteous as always, and without sign of bitterness or resentment. His farewells made, he opened the red baize door into the Privy Council corridor for the last time. Shaken myself, I left my little table in the corner and popped out through the anteroom

7 *Soldiers and Politicians* (Toronto 1962), pp 247-51.

to intercept him as he was putting on his coat. I told him how sorry I was to see him leave. Gentle and genuine, calm, and in complete control of himself, he thanked me, said a few words of appreciation of my work and asked whether he could give a short letter to my secretary. We went into Mae Roe's room together and he dictated the letter of resignation upon which the Prime Minister subsequently acted.

Japan's rapid advances in the Pacific after Pearl Harbour had greatly increased United States interest in defence activities in northwest Canada. The construction of the Alaska Highway by the US Corps of Engineers and the development of the North West Staging (Air) Route by the Canadian Department of Transport were already well advanced when the United States entered the war. Thereafter, requests from Washington for leave to undertake further substantial operations such as the Canol road and pipeline over the Mackenzie mountains appeared with increasing frequency on the agenda of the cabinet War Committee. By the summer of 1942 the United States Army had a large headquarters in Edmonton and there were considerable US Army and Air Force units engaged in various undertakings from Fort McMurray down the Mackenzie valley to the Arctic Circle and northwest to the Alaskan boundary. Preoccupied with the war effort in Europe, no one in authority in Ottawa was aware of the extent and nature of what westerners had begun to call the 'American occupation.' Nor was anyone anxious to take on the additional job of finding out. One day in the cabinet War Committee someone had the idea of assigning to the retiring commander, Major General W.W. Foster, the task of looking into our agreements to co-operate with the United States on northwest defence. The War Committee readily concurred. When the question arose as to the department which would be responsible for Foster's operations, C.D. Howe, who had been insistent that something be done promptly and was himself concerned about most phases of the United States efforts in the area, looked round the room. I was the only civil official present. 'Why not attach him to Heeney?' he asked. So began my personal and official contact with continental defence to be continued many years later through my chairmanship of the Permanent Joint Board.

In the autumn of 1942, armed with the splendid title of Special Commissioner for Defence Projects in North West Canada, Foster established his own modest advance headquarters in Edmonton with an over-age colonel from Kelowna and a first war group captain from Winnipeg. Then he and I set off together to assert the Canadian presence in our own country. It was an unforgetable autumn journey. Flown in an old Lysander by an uncanny bush pilot masquerading as an RCAF squadron leader, we descended the Mackenzie, stopping along the way to show the flag at every landing strip from Waterways to Norman Wells, then across the mountains to Whitehorse and back down the

Staging Route. We found Americans everywhere, all engaged in massive operations with elaborate and exotic machinery. We found a work battalion of blacks at Fort Smith unhappily anticipating the onset of another winter, military engineers struggling to build roads that would not stay put west of Fort Norman, and everywhere steak, marmalade, peanut butter, ice cream, and a warm welcome. I think our visitation achieved its purpose. From it I developed a regular system of surveillance and reports. Certainly for me it was a happy and stimulating diversion from the East Block in the company of a man who knew and loved the Canadian north.

Among the other extramural activities attached to government through the Privy Council Office during the war was 'information.' This had the official result of requiring me, as the responsible deputy minister, to try to keep some semblance of administrative and financial restraint in costly operations. I did what I could. This responsibility had the personal result of bringing me into close association with a very gifted public servant, John Grierson, head of the National Film Board and later director of our Wartime Information Board. Our forays together to Washington and New York in the interests of projecting Canada's wartime image in favourable terms, and my time on the WIB, taught me much about the possibilities and limitations of disseminating information abroad.

Such, as I remember them thirty years later, were some of the highlights of my war. Now, as then I think, I recognize how fortunate I was. All this time our children were developing at that pace to which parents, despite the clear evidence of experience, seem never to become accustomed. The war had little direct affect upon our family life in Rockcliffe. There were of course the minor irritations of rationing and limitation on movement. For us, however, the abnormal features of our life were but the welcome pressures of wartime tasks and the shared anxieties and sorrows of friends. In the summers we were able to get up the Gatineau where we constructed a cottage high at the north end of Danford Lake. From our broad verandah we could look down to the narrows at which Luke's house still stood, as it does to this day. There in conditions to which wartime restrictions contributed some flavour of the pioneer conditions of my Heeney forebears, my wife laboured and our children prospered. I joined them when, conscientiously, I could escape from the East Block.

6

Secretary to the cabinet

Mackenzie King had brought me to Ottawa for the specific purpose of developing a secretariat for the cabinet along the lines of that set up in Britain during the first world war. Yet it is at least doubtful that the venture would have succeeded under his administration had it not been for the pressures created by the second world war. As it turned out, the circumstances that permitted the radical reorganization of the central executive machinery in Ottawa beginning in 1940 were essentially similar to those that in 1916 enabled Lloyd George and Maurice Hankey to effect the changes at Whitehall which provided us with our model. By the time King approached me on the subject, the idea of 'a Canadian Hankey' was well established in his mind. He had discussed it earlier with at least one other candidate, Burgon Bickersteth, at that time warden of Hart House, and probably with others. Obsessed by the feeling that he was inadequately served by those about him, he sought relief in what seemed a new remedy for an old complaint. The fact was that few prime ministers had had better or more loyal personal staffs. King's problem was only in part institutional.

Mackenzie King's notion of the responsibilities which Hankey discharged in Britain was far from precise and, in a number of important respects, far from the facts of British practice. He had written to me that the Canadian cabinet secretary should be 'a kind of Deputy Head of a Government Department ... in immediate touch with the Prime Minister,' and that he should 'exercise a general superintendence over the work of the Prime Minister's office'; he was also to provide 'liaison with other Ministers of the Crown.'[1] In fact, many of my early duties as secretary of the cabinet took the form of personal service to the Prime Minister. At no time did King give the impression that he had any real interest in the secretariat as an institution; never did he appreciate its significance in the administrative scheme of things. He re-

1 WLMK to ADPH, 13 July 1938.

sented my refusal to serve him in his capacity as leader of the Liberal party, and he failed to see that such meddling in politics would jeopardize the development of a new and valuable institution of government. In the establishment of the cabinet secretariat, as in other organizational changes effected during his administration, Mackenzie King's primary, if unacknowledged, purpose was to enhance his authority as prime minister by strengthening the means of its exercise.

On 25 March 1940, literally on the eve of the wartime election, the order-in-council of my appointment was passed. For the first time the designation secretary to the cabinet was added to that of clerk of the Privy Council. For the first time the instrument of the clerk's appointment set out the duties of the incumbent and included a summary statement of new functions:

The great increase in the work of the Cabinet, of recent years, and particularly since the outbreak of war, has rendered it necessary to make provision for the performance of additional duties of a secretarial nature relating principally to the collecting and putting into shape of agenda of Cabinet meetings, the providing of information and material necessary for the deliberations of the Cabinet and the drawing up of records of the results, for communication to the departments concerned; and that provision for the performance of the said additional duties, referred to in the preceding paragraph, can most conveniently be made by providing that they be undertaken by the Clerk of the Privy Council, and that for such purposes it is desirable that he be appointed to the Cabinet.[2]

It was inevitable that the new arrangement which King himself had initiated, albeit somewhat hesitantly, should affect the easy informality of pre-war ministerial meetings. King had accepted the necessity of the change to a more orderly process as a consequence of the wartime situation. Yet, as the business of bringing order out of chaos moved inexorably forward under the pressure of events, he must have often regretted the loss of greater freedom of earlier times. He could not be expected to feel affection for the monster he himself had created. For the rules and procedures which, bit by bit, he felt compelled to approve in order to get things done could not but restrict in some degree his personal management of affairs.

Before 1940 the decision-making process of the Canadian cabinet seemed incredibly haphazard to someone such as myself, coming to Ottawa from a St James Street law office and accustomed to the procedural niceties of legal practice. I found it shattering to discover that the highest committee in the land conducted its business in such a disorderly fashion that it employed no

2 Order-in-council PC 1121, 25 March 1940.

agenda and no minutes were taken. The more I learned about cabinet practice, the more difficult it was for me to understand how such a regime could function at all. In fact the Canadian situation before 1940 was the same as that which existed in Britain before 1916.

Before the war there was no real distinction between 'council' and 'cabinet' in the minds of the ministers who composed both. The only senior official then serving the Prime Minister and his colleagues as a group was the clerk of the Privy Council who had an assistant clerk and a very small junior staff. The principal duties of these officials were the drafting of the formal proceedings of council (orders and minutes) by direct transposition from the submissions made by ministers, the swearing in of ministers and civil servants, and the maintenance of the formal records. When ministers met they normally did so in the council chamber, seating themselves at the table (which in those days was still round), the Prime Minister in the highbacked chair originally designed for occasions upon which the Governor General attended. In front of each minister was a red leather folder upon which his office was stamped in gold letters. In front of the Prime Minister, in addition to his portfolio, stood a large, deep open box divided in the centre by a partition. Before the ministers assembled, the clerk of the council would place at the Prime Minister's place the draft orders and minutes which had been prepared for disposition. The clerk then withdrew. When the ministers had dispersed, he returned to the chamber to find his orders and minutes in the two compartments of the great box at the Prime Minister's place. Those in the right hand compartment had been signed as an indication of approval for transmission to Rideau Hall for the Governor General's signature; those in the left remained unsigned as an indication that they had been deferred or rejected. The clerk had no more than this remote contact with the Prime Minister concerning the proceedings in the chamber; under no circumstances was he present while a meeting was going on, unless sent for to receive directions or to provide information. Furthermore, the clerk was concerned solely with the council aspect of the ministerial meetings, that is to say, with those items of business which involved documentary advice to the crown's representative in the form of orders-in-council and formal minutes of council.

Having disposed of the council business, the ministerial meeting would usually resolve itself into cabinet, without one may suspect many of the participants being aware of the significance of the change. At this point it was Mackenzie King's practice, and doubtless that of his predecessors, to turn to the colleague on his right (when I first attended this was Ernest Lapointe) and inquire: 'Have you anything to bring up?' So on round the table he would go, or rather as far round as time permitted. Time, I soon discovered, was an important, often a crucial, factor at all cabinet meetings. In King's day, when the cabinet met at noon in the Centre Block during the parliamentary session, it was not infrequent that ministers to the left of the Prime Minister found themselves and their business cut short by the bell summoning them to the House of Commons. For the Prime Minister, on the other hand, there was wide scope in the presentation of business. He could always alter the normal order to give place to matters he considered of special urgency or importance. Indeed, it was quite clearly understood by all that the Prime Minister could bring up whatever he wished, whenever he wished. King took full advantage of this prerogative.

Under such a regime, apart from any special arrangement the Prime Minister might have made with individual colleagues, there was no way for a minister to tell in advance what subjects would be brought up at any given meeting or in what order. King himself would sometimes have little notes from one of his private secretaries, or from O.D. Skelton or perhaps W.C. Clark, on matters he wished to be reminded to raise. Occasionally, very occasionally as I remember, some minister would send to the Prime Minister, and even more rarely to one or two of his other colleagues, a written proposal upon which he wished to have a cabinet decision. But advance notice, let alone advance briefing, was rare. In consequence, ministers were frequently taken by surprise by proposals introduced by their colleagues and important questions would have to be suspended and decisions deferred so as to enable interested ministers to take advice and to reflect upon a proposed course of action.

In those days there was no record whatever of the decisions taken by the cabinet. As a result ministers frequently had different, sometimes quite contradictory, ideas of what had been decided. In Britain prior to 1916 there was at least the record contained in the letter which the prime minister customarily wrote to the sovereign after each cabinet meeting. Yet British political memoirs are full of references to the difficulties arising from doubt as to the precise nature of cabinet decisions. In Canada the situation was much the same, although in the early days of the war, before proper minutes were authorized for the cabinet War Committee, the Prime Minister would occasionally ask one of his secretaries who had been present to make a memorandum of some particularly important decision. From time to time, King would dictate his own notes of what had transpired for his diary and so that he might have a source of reference in case of any disagreement as to what had been decided.

Because of the rapid march of events in Europe and the increased attention which ministers were giving to defence problems at the time of my arrival in Ottawa, my first duties related not to the cabinet as a whole but rather to the War Committee of the cabinet (which later became the Emergency Council, a cabinet committee with senior officials in attendance). From the time of its formation after the outbreak of war the cabinet War Committee progressively assumed the direction of the Canadian war effort. From then until after the end of hostilities in Europe its proceedings and business occupied virtually all my time and energy.

The idea of locating the cabinet secretariat in the Privy Council Office originated with O.D. Skelton whose ingenious proposal to graft on to the ancient office of clerk of the council the new set of functions and the new title was adopted. Before I went to Ottawa, it was known that the opportunity to put this scheme into effect would occur early in 1940 when the then clerk of the council, E.J. Lemaire, was due for retirement. After consideration of the legal implications, it was determined that Lemaire's successor, without the necessity of new legislation, could be assigned the additional duties contemplated and the additional descriptive title of secretary to the cabinet. The new institution would then be created by the simple expedient of defining its functions in the act of appointment. This solution was not only appropriate but eminently practical and it appealed to King because it involved no legislation and was unlikely to attract much notice. The fact that the headship of the Privy Council Office carried with it the highest status in the Civil Service hierarchy, traditionally and perhaps apocryphally because of the insistence of D'Arcy McGee's brother Francis at the time of his own appointment, was an added advantage. For it was important that the new secretary should have the standing among ministers and senior officials which his new duties would require.

Accordingly, it was by this simple executive means that the cabinet secretariat, an institution hitherto unknown in Canada, was established in the spring of 1940. The only description of the secretary's duties and responsibilities remains that set out in the order-in-council of my appointment. Students of cabinet government will recognize in its terms the echoes of British practice modified by Canadian experience to meet Canadian requirements. In fact, in setting up the secretariat and developing procedures for the conduct of cabinet business, especially in the first years, we leaned heavily on British models as described in all the texts and studies we could lay our hands on. We also profited greatly from the personal interest and assistance of the two secretaries of the British cabinet, Sir Edward (later Lord) Bridges and Sir Norman Brooke (later Lord Normanbrooke). These able and generous men made freely available to us in Ottawa a mass of private and highly relevant material which, despite the immense wartime pressures upon them, they supplemented by copious personal and practical advice from their own long experience. We even received the benediction of Lord Hankey himself. In the development of our affairs, I owe a special debt to the late Lord Ismay, whose knowledge of combined civil and military affairs before, during, and after the second world war was unique. He too was most generous in sharing with us his experience, wisdom, and good sense. The post of military secretary to the cabinet (and staff officer to the prime minister), to which Major General Maurice Pope was appointed later in the war, was a Canadian parallel to that held by Ismay under Winston Churchill. Altogether, the close collaboration and the friendships which developed between the two cabinet offices in London and Ottawa was one of the happiest and most constructive features of the early years of the Canadian cabinet secretariat.

The procedures adopted for the conduct of the cabinet War Committee's affairs from 1940 to 1945 were developed under the pressure of events and in response to actual need. In essence, they consisted of simple clearcut rules for the systematic disposition of business. They dealt with the form and manner of introducing items for the agenda, adequate notice of proposals calling for decisions, preparation and circulation of papers, maintenance of suitable transcripts of discussions, and the recording of agreed conclusions and arrangements for follow-up to ensure that decisions were promptly effected by the responsible ministers and their departments. The development of these rules was essentially a pragmatic process, involving much trial and error. The objective was to establish an uncomplicated practical regime of procedure, combining flexibility and precision, which would enable ministers to deal quickly and efficiently with a heavy volume of important business.

I cannot say that Mackenzie King was ever enthusiastic about these developments. When, in 1940, he accepted the principle of having an agenda for the cabinet War Committee, he refused at first to allow it to be circulated to ministers in advance of the meeting; indeed for some time he insisted on keeping the agenda to himself. Similarly, it was well on into the war before he permitted copies of the 'conclusions' to be circulated to his colleagues, even to those directly responsible for the implementation of the War Committee's decisions. It was only some time later that the circle was extended to all ministerial members. Even then King insisted that the copies sent them be returned promptly for destruction so that the only record remaining was the original in the Privy Council Office and the copy retained for the Prime Minister's own use. I well remember, too, in the very early days of the cabinet War Committee, how difficult it was to keep the Prime Minister to the agenda. Also, to obtain his permission for the introduction of other Privy Council officers into ministerial meetings was a long, slow process. Early on, in my capacity as secretary, I was admitted to the cabinet War Committee to take limited notes. But when the volume of business and long hours of meetings made it impossible for one person to handle such matters adequately, it required a great deal of persuasion before King would agree that John Baldwin might attend as the first assistant secretary.

It was the same with virtually every procedural reform adopted over the war years. Instinctively Mackenzie King recoiled from efforts to formalize the business of the cabinet, an institution whose genius, historically and in his own experience, had been its flexibility and informality. Nevertheless, it is to his enduring credit that, step by step, he did recognize the necessities of the new situation. Albeit reluctantly, he came to accept, and for a long time only for the cabinet War Committee, the need to put in order the process of ministerial decision-making.

The role of the secretary to the cabinet did not work out the way King had hoped and expected, but the war had made revolutionary changes in the affairs of government. It had so increased the volume and importance of ministerial business that the old methods collapsed. It became essential that the Prime Minister and his principal colleagues have assistance in their deliberative sessions to put their work in order, to co-ordinate the various departments involved, to record agreed decisions, and to follow up with the officials who had to carry them out.

The clerk of the Privy Council, in his new guise of secretary to the cabinet, became responsible for the discharge of these duties. As a result I had little or no time to act as the personal staff officer to the Prime Minister, which I believe was the role which King had principally had in mind. Nevertheless, my job did come to involve a good deal beyond the strictly secretarial role, though still within the ambit of cabinet business. From the outset, I was in very close touch with the Undersecretary of State for External Affairs, Skelton and later Norman Robertson, and with the chiefs of staff, all of whom sat in the War Committee. It was also natural that I should be employed by the Prime Minister to consult with colleagues on matters of government policy not yet ready for cabinet consideration. Frequently, too, I and members of my staff would prepare memoranda on subjects of major interest for the Prime Minister's own guidance, either on direction or on my own initiative. Finally, it was in the capacity of staff officer that I was included in the Canadian delegation to the Peace Conference in 1946. For hadn't Hankey himself been at Paris in 1919? These and other functions gradually accumulated in the Privy Council Office as the idea of the cabinet secretariat became accepted by King, his colleagues, and his senior officials as a normal and necessary part of the machinery of government.

The procedure which the cabinet has followed since 1945 has been essentially that developed during the second world war for the cabinet War Committee, improvements and changes being made as time has passed. The composition of the secretariat has been altered and increased in recent years as new responsibilities have been assigned to special task forces and located in the Privy Council Office. It was natural that during the war the concentration should have been on matters of defence and foreign policy and that the mixed civil and military composition of the secretariat should reflect that fact. It seems to me to be a matter of regret, nevertheless, that the military element was subsequently removed from the Privy Council Office and located in the Department of National Defence. Something has been lost in the surgery, for in my view the process of determining defence policy should be as closely and continuously associated as can be with the formulation of decisions upon other great national questions. Detachment of the defence secretariat from that of the cabinet was thus an administrative error; the fact that the same mistake was made in London brings no comfort.

An important event in the short history of the cabinet secretariat in Canada occurred after the general election of 1957 when the defeated Prime Minister, Louis St Laurent, met his victorious opponent John Diefenbaker to arrange the transfer of the administration. One of the questions which they had then to decide was that of the disposition of cabinet records for which there was no Canadian precedent. We may count ourselves fortunate that these two men agreed that the British tradition should be followed and that the secretary to the cabinet should be accepted as the custodian of cabinet papers, responsible for determining what communication should be made thereof to succeeding administrations. With that agreement, the cabinet secretariat became a permanent institution of Canadian government.

In his foreword to the Public Record Office handbook which accompanied the opening of the records of the British cabinet office to 1922, Harold Wilson referred to the essential purpose of the cabinet office as being 'to assist Ministers in the task of discharging their collective responsibility for the government of the country and the conduct of its affairs both at home and abroad.'[3] This remains the chief purpose of the cabinet secretariat in the Privy Council Office of Canada. The manner in which it discharges its task will doubtless alter from time to time as the requirements of government change, but the essence of the operation will not. The secretary to the cabinet is one whose chief interest and concern remains the formulation, recording, and communication of the decisions of those who compose the cabinet of the day. It is and will remain the chief function of the secretary and his colleagues to do everything possible to facilitate and assist the deliberative process onward to informed decision. This involves doing everything that can be done to see that the issues are put clearly before ministers in due form and in due time and to see that all relevant considerations are brought to their attention before

3 Public Record Office, *The Records of the Cabinet Office to 1922,* Handbook 11 (London: HMSO, 1966).

decisions are taken. At that stage it is the responsibility of the secretary to see that decisions are recorded clearly and precisely and communicated to those responsible for implementation. It is also his duty to see that items of business are put before the cabinet in an order of priority which takes account not only of urgency but of importance. In so doing, as in all his duties, the secretary is first of all the servant of the prime minister, as the prime minister is the 'master,' to use the old expression, of cabinet business.

After more than a quarter of a century I can assert with some confidence that the cabinet secretariat, based firmly in the ancient Privy Council Office, has achieved a permanent and accepted place in the machinery of Canadian government. That this is so is due in part to each of the prime ministers who, since 1940, has presided in the Privy Council chamber. But most of all, it is due to William Lyon Mackenzie King who, while he may have had little interest in the administrative process, had a sure and subtle instinct for the business of government.

7

Last years with Mackenzie King

The dramatic resolution of the political crisis of 1944 and the steady progress of the allied forces in Europe in the months which followed eased the emotional tension in the East Block. At the same time the volume and pace of cabinet business continued unabated as the prospect of early victory added urgency to the need for preparing solutions to postwar domestic and international problems. The agenda of ministerial meetings included increasing numbers of important questions of peacetime policy in addition to those relating to the war effort. By early 1944 the Prime Minister, sensitive as he was even then to the serious political implications of the problems of demobilization and reconstruction, had turned his attention and that of his colleagues in these directions. He was determined that Canada should avoid the misery which followed the 1914-18 war.

During the period after the reinforcement crisis, as attention to postwar questions increased, the full cabinet began to resume the primary role it had virtually surrendered to the cabinet War Committee in 1940. King was actively planning extensions of social legislation, notably family allowances and unemployment measures which he was determined to launch once the war was over. In these matters he was aided by Brooke Claxton, his parliamentary assistant, upon whom he increasingly relied. Primary responsibility for planning the conversion of the nation's vast war industry which he had done so much to create was assigned to C.D. Howe.

On 13 October 1944 the cabinet was reorganized, and Howe became minister of reconstruction the same day and officials under the leadership of Clifford Clark and W.A. Mackintosh were directed to prepare measures and programs for the ministers' consideration. Before the end of 1944 the cabinet agenda included many of their proposals which were to provide the outlines for the White Paper on postwar economic policy which the government published in April 1945. To the remaining ministers and officials other areas were allotted. Proposals were debated interdepartmentally and brought forward for consideration and approval. As a result, when hostilities ended in Europe, the main directions of domestic policy had been determined, and King was ready to go to the people.

At the international level postwar planning proceeded apace during 1944 and 1945, and Canada participated fully with the Prime Minister's blessing. However, I do not recall much discussion in cabinet or in cabinet committees about the United Nations as its charter emerged from the Dumbarton Oaks deliberations. Nor do I remember consideration being given by ministers to the major issues which emerged at the San Francisco conference on the United Nations. Such matters were dealt with principally by King and his senior advisers in the Department of External Affairs. King himself headed the delegation to San Francisco and remained for the first part of the conference. He was, however, discouraged by the course of events there and, particularly after V-E day, was preoccupied by the coming general election. He knew it would be his last.

His mind kept turning from the problems of peace and security to those of party organization and strategy at home. In the East Block we were not allowed to forget that our master expected to be kept up to date week by week, day by day, virtually hour by hour, on what was taking place at the seat of government. Nor were we permitted to forget, when he was away, that he took the burden of office with him. In a letter to me on the eve of his leaving San Francisco for the extraordinary coast-to-coast tour of Canada which was to be the old man's final campaign, he indicated what was at the top of his mind:

This is just a line before leaving San Francisco to thank you for the splendid way in which you have kept me posted on the happenings at Ottawa, and in seeing that the many exacting duties of each day of this exceptional time have been speedily and effectively met.

I have found the time here very difficult. With the war ending when it did, there came the burden of messages to be prepared and acknowledged, the broadcast and much else. I cannot say that this was wholly unexpected. It certainly was not unwelcome but it imposed heavy additional burdens.

What has been most distracting of all has been the inability to make any preparation for the speeches which will have to be made in the campaign. Today, for the first day, I have been able to get something underway for the broadcast to be delivered from Vancouver on Wednesday afternoon. From then on, everything will have to be prepared, so to speak, en route. This is not an easy task where one has really nothing prepared in advance. However, the time since we have left Ottawa has gone by quickly.

A right beginning has been made with the work of the Conference. I think my presence here will, in the campaign itself, prove to have been helpful to the party and, in some respects, the change has, I believe, been beneficial. I am, however, still very fatigued and have to watch myself closely not to get too overtired.

I am much looking forward to being back in Ottawa in a fortnight's time and reviewing with yourself the problems of the Ministry and covering the many important matters which will have to be attended to before the day of election itself.

I am immensely pleased about the flag.

Then, in his own hand: 'It is best I think to await a resolution to the House of Commons or of the two Houses before discontinuing the flying of the Union Jack.'[1] The final reference was to the cabinet decision after the victory in Europe (in which King had participated from San Francisco) to employ as 'the Canadian flag' the flag which the Canadian Army had used overseas: the Red Ensign with the shield of the Canadian coat of arms in the fly. In Ottawa we felt that there had been wide acceptance of the decision and that the flag question had been settled in the most propitious circumstances. But King changed his mind, and the resolution necessary for formal adoption of the new flag was never submitted to Parliament. Perhaps it was just as well in the light of what took place years later when the flag question assumed larger symbolic importance.

Voting took place on 11 June 1945 and the result was an unexpectedly overwhelming victory for Mackenzie King. He was elated. Wanting to share the joy of his triumph, he telephoned me at home during the course of the evening and inquired diffidently whether he might come out and join my wife and me in listening to the returns as they came over the radio. As it happened my friend and a colleague in the Privy Council Office, Evan Gill, and his wife were with us. I said that of course we would be happy to have him. Within a few minutes he arrived, like a schoolboy in his delight as the proportions of the victory became evident and the casualties among his opponents mounted. No other therapy could have had such dramatic results. The fatigue of the years disappeared as if by magic. For a few hours the old politician was young again.

On 22 June the Prime Minister returned to San Francisco to take part in the next day's ceremonial signing of the United Nations Charter. St Laurent, to whom King was by then turning to an increasing extent on external matters, accompanied him along with a small group of advisers in which I was included. This allowed me to get some personal flavour of what had been going on from Robertson and my other friends on the delegation, and of seeing President Truman and hearing him perform for the first time at the closing ceremonies of the conference.

1 WLMK to ADPH, 14 May 1945.

In September 1945 Mackenzie King was confronted suddenly with the kind of problem he most resented and which he would have done almost anything to avoid. The defection of Igor Gouzenko, the cypher clerk at the Soviet Embassy on Charlotte Street, cast him and Canada in a role he considered unsuitable and uncalled-for. What had we to do with espionage, cyphers, secret agents, and all the sordid paraphenalia of intrigue associated with older more sophisticated and less fastidious states? He struggled to escape, but there was no avoiding the necessity for action. Consultations in Washington and London confirmed beyond doubt the advice which Norman Robertson and the few other officials privy to the circumstances had unanimously tendered to him; so the notorious 'secret' order-in-council which provided for detention without trial was drafted and passed on 6 October 1945.

Once the decision had been taken, St Laurent as minister of justice did not hesitate. On his instructions I drafted the appropriate order under the emergency powers still in effect. I then took it round for immediate signature by four ministers, a quorum of council for such purposes. St Laurent, the initiating minister, with the Prime Minister's authority signed first. I went next to Ilsley, minister of finance, one of the senior privy councillors. By that time the strain and burdens of his wartime service over the previous five years had begun to tell, and he was tired and nervous. The order he was being asked to sign seemed to him to be inconsistent with principles he had regarded as fundamental. Yet he had great respect for St Laurent; if St Laurent saw no other course to ensure the country's safety he would go along. Sorrowfully, still expressing his distaste, he added his name. Two more signatures, the approval of the Governor General, and the deed was done; a train of events was set in motion which was to reach into many countries and affect many individuals. It is ironic that the principal adviser to government in this affair, was Norman Robertson whose deep attachment to the traditional liberties was known to all of us and doubted by none, even those most critical of the course the government pursued. In fact, no tolerable alternative was available. In February 1946 under the authority of the order a royal commission was set up to investigate the affair and the loyalties of some Canadian citizens who had been arrested and held incommunicado.

In 1946 King began to relinquish his supreme personal authority in the government. This happened partly because of his age and the increased physical and nervous fatigue which followed sustained effort, especially when his emotions became involved, and partly as the result of his deliberate calculations. It was not that he was no longer capable of demonstrating the reality of his command over his colleagues and intervening with finality when the occasion seemed to require it. But as the year went on King was prepared to leave more and more to his colleagues, notably St Laurent whose prestige rose steadily and who in September 1946 became the first secretary of state for external affairs who was not simultaneously prime minister.

At this time the first of the 'musical chairs' shifts of senior foreign service officers took place. Robertson became high commissioner to London, Pearson took his place as undersecretary, and Hume Wrong, the associate undersecretary, went back to Washington, this time as ambassador. It was an admirable deployment of the best talents in the right places at the right time. The fact that I had myself been considered for the Washington embassy, while flattering, did not alter my opinion of the wisdom of the decisions.

The Prime Minister, as good as his word, had included me in the delegation which accompanied him to the Paris Peace Conference that summer, my first serious involvement in such multilateral diplomacy. Brooke Claxton was deputy leader of the group, and he mingled well with the 'official' members of the delegation: Robertson, Vanier, Wilgress, Pope, and myself, most of whom he had worked with closely in the East Block when he had been the Prime Minister's parliamentary assistant. Others joined us from the department in Ottawa and from our European offices, including Charles Ritchie from Canada House in London and Jean Chapdelaine, later the knowledgeable and cooperative representative in France of the province of Quebec. We were a small but closely knit group.

I had not been in Paris since my undergraduate days. To be back again after so long induced something of the symptoms of a remembered love affair. It was curious, too, and nostalgic that once more Norman Robertson and I should be there together. Sitting next to one another behind the Prime Minister in the great salon of the Palais de Luxembourg during one of the first of the long sessions of the steering committee, we found our minds reverting to that first visit. Did I remember, he whispered, that more than twenty years before we had had rooms within a stone's throw of where we were sitting? Now we were in Paris again, listening to Soviet Foreign Minister Vishinsky's long tirades and taking our part as Canadians in the interminable charade of a conference which from the outset seemed unlikely to bring peace.

Of the many prominent actors on the scene I shall mention only two, both representative of smaller powers: Jan Masaryk, who headed the Czechoslovak delegation, and Herbert Evatt, the Australian minister of external affairs. Masaryk was a sad and haunted figure reflecting in his demeanour the outlines of the prison house in which he was soon to be enclosed. From time to time his normal civilized self was able to escape and on some social occasions he comported himself with his natural humour and humanity. In the chair in plenary or in committee, however, he had begun to behave as the tame captive of the communists which indeed he was. His bearing, like his speech was lifeless, that of a great marionette whose strings were manipulated by others.

Lunching one day in his honour at the Czechoslovak embassy I remarked that both the Minister and the Ambassador behaved as men who knew that their days were numbered. Both host and guest of honour were very obviously surrounded by the communist elements which dominated the Czech delegation. It was a sad occasion.

The Australian delegation was led by Herbert Evatt whose determination to become president of the conference exaggerated unpleasant features of a personality which required no additional emphasis. His behaviour in Paris in pursuit of his ambition jarred the sensibilities of many, not excluding the members of his own delegation. Few can be more successfully abrasive than a determined Australian, and Evatt was a past master in giving offence. We were not, it is true, without means of retaliation when the aims of this ungentle politician led him into courses with which we disagreed. I recall one evening while the steering committee was in session that Charles Ritchie, by what means I never discovered, was seen to persuade Evatt to rise from his place at the table, circumnavigate the room, work his way through the periphery of advisers to the head of our delegation, and apologize abjectly for a slighting reference to the Canadian attitude attributed to him in a local newspaper. I remember too that Maurice Pope, our representative on the committee dealing with the Bratislava bridgehead, when questioned on the reasons for the attitude he had taken replied quite simply: 'I wait till that bastard [Evatt] takes his position then take the opposite.'

The presence of the Vaniers in the charming little 'hotel' in the rue Dosne which was the provisional embassy residence was a source of comfort and delight to all of us on the delegation. Their generosity was untiring and their helpfulness to us temporary Parisians never failed. More than that, the repute and standing of both of them in the official French community, especially among those who had been in the de Gaulle entourage in Algiers and those officials who had come up from the resistance, was unique among foreign representatives and from that we drew further advantage for Canada. In everything but name Georges Vanier was dean of the diplomatic corps (a position held ex officio by the papal nuncio) and had a personal welcome everywhere, from the Palais de l'Elysée to the lower levels of the government apparatus. As Canadians, we had many occasions to be proud of them both.

Before leaving Canada the Prime Minister had determined to visit the battlefields where Canadian troops had been engaged. For this purpose Vanier and his staff had provided an extensive program and invoked the appropriate local auspices. The first sortie in which I participated was to the Normandy beaches and on to Caen and Falaise. Vanier, along with a mixed civil and military group, went with us and I shall not soon forget the spectacle of his 'translating' to the little groups of local inhabitants who greeted our party the few words Mackenzie King pronounced at various crumbling crossroads. The brief and pedestrian sentences in English were transmuted at some length into deliberate and moving French which never failed to evoke a warm response. In such ways did Georges Vanier serve his country and enhance the effect of his Prime Minister's pilgrimage.

One other disengagement from the conference is worthy of mention. In Berlin the Prime Minister's party was received and put up by Maurice Pope who had become the head of our military mission. At that time Pope and his wife lived in a family house in Charlottenberg which somehow had escaped the almost total reduction of the area by allied bombers. For me it was a strange and uncomfortable sensation, in the midst of destruction, to be put up in comfort in such an intimate domestic establishment. The owner lived in the cellar as a kind of caretaker; yet everywhere above stairs there were the signs of earlier days: the name plates of the various children beside the towel racks on the bathroom wall, the garden still bearing the evidence of loving care.

One of King's desires on this visit was to see again the house in which he had stayed as a student before the 1914 war. For an hour and more our party moved in convoy in search of the site, among the massive ruins and piles of rubble surrounding the Tiergarten. In vain the Prime Minister sought some recognizable landmark. Time passed and the hour approached for Pope's official lunch to which the whole allied command had been invited. At last, with suspicious unanimity, our guides announced that the elusive objectives had been identified. Dismounted before yet another mound of destruction, King stood bare headed for some minutes, reflecting no doubt on his vanished youth and the catastrophes which had since befallen. Then, sirens screaming, we were off to lunch.

We returned to Paris via Nuremberg, for King was determined to witness the trial of the Nazi leaders. From the front rows of the visitor's gallery we watched that wretched, sick, and disconsolate group as they filed into the dock. The sight was repulsive; and yet despite our revulsion to it, it was also pathetic. The prison palour and with a few exceptions the abject bearing of most of the prisoners at the bar was nauseating. Goering, in particular, his vast tunic draped over his wasted belly, his face like sagging putty, was a miserable spectacle. King, however, was fascinated, noting every detail as the trial proceeded at its deliberate pace. He observed the absence of Hess and was told that he had pleaded illness that day. Later when we visited the nightmarish prison block in which the principal defendants were housed, King leaned down and peered through the spy-hole into Hess's cell and reported to us in detail the appearance and surroundings of the wretched inmate. Despite the eminence of the judges and the fastidious dignity of the proceedings the whole experience left me depressed. The memory of evil and decay stayed with me days after we had returned to Paris.

Apart from ceremonial occasions, and these were few, the Prime Minister attended few of the conference sessions. He occupied himself in Paris, visiting friends, paying homage at the shrine of one of his heroes, Pasteur, and alternately basking in the historic quality of the occasion and worrying about what was happening in Ottawa. Our delegation was staying in the dated splendour of the Hôtel Crillon on the Place de la Concorde where King had managed to obtain the suite Woodrow Wilson had occupied in 1919. From time to time he would meet the members of the delegation and, when he was not taken up by grand occasions, Norman Robertson and I would often take meals with him in the hotel restaurant. At such times King would usually manage to have one of us sign the bill, not so much to take advantage of us but in order that his own expense account should be kept to the minimum against the possibility of criticism in Parliament. As a result of such harmless stratagems the Prime Minister's expenditures invariably appeared to be among the lowest of the Canadian delegates, on one occasion actually below those of his valet, the loyal and invaluable Nichol. In the same way he was consistently suspicious of what the rest of us were doing with the public purse. On one occasion when Brooke Claxton had organized a modest delegation vin d'honneur in his honour to celebrate one of the many anniversaries in the Prime Minister's year, King said to me as we left: 'I hope Claxton hasn't put the cost of that champagne on his expense account.'

By the end of August the Prime Minister had had enough of Paris and the conference. He was taking virtually no part in the negotiations and he found the round of social and ceremonial occasions increasingly tiring as well as boring. Leaving the leadership of the delegation in Claxton's competent hands, and accompanied by Robertson, myself, and his personal staff, he left Paris on 25 August, at once relieved and anxious at the prospect of returning to the familiar tensions of life in Ottawa. As the special train provided by the French authorities pulled out of the Gare du Nord, Robertson and I settled down gratefully to a cup of tea. 'Do you realize,' he inquired, 'that we are at the end of a month constantly in the immediate presence and without a single untoward incident?' I agreed that we had been most unusually lucky. But the spell was about to be shattered. In the few days we spent in London, it became painfully obvious that our master had fallen into one of his despondent moods when nothing could be right and no one about him could or would provide him the comfort and support he felt were his due. What his strange visits to the friends who put him in touch with the other world, of which I first heard on this occasion, may have contributed to his darkened mood I do not know. The voyage home on the *Queen Mary* did nothing to lift King's spirits.

Because his diary contains an extended and highly subjective account of the events of those days, I feel bound to give my own account of what took place.[2] Pearson had joined us in London for the crossing. Appreciating the delicacy of the situation, he, Robertson, and I consulted as to what we could do to dispel King's black mood. To begin with we decided that it would be best not to offer to sit at the Prime Minister's table, for to do so might be taken as putting ourselves forward; better leave it to him to invite us should he wish our company. This turned out to be a mistake. Long before the journey ended King made it abundantly clear to me that he had felt 'let down,' 'deserted,' by those he had a right to count on. Furthermore, we had all 'neglected' him in London, Pearson and I running off to Canada House and leaving him to toil over correspondence and other matters where we could have helped. In fact, I had proferred our services at the Dorchester and been turned down on grounds of 'personal' business. So when we arrived at Halifax all three of us made certain to be at King's side when he met the press. He immediately indicated his disappointment that, having ignored him when we were alone at sea, we should turn up so promptly when the reporters and photographers were on hand. When the mood was on him no one could win; the line between devotion and aggressiveness was narrow and often impossible to identify.

I would date from that autumn the beginnings of King's growing fatigue. From my own point of view this showed itself in a decreasing interest in cabinet business and an increasing tendency to work at Laurier House rather than at his East Block office. There were more frequent instances of impatience and unreasoned testiness with members of his personal staff and even with some of his colleagues, notably Ian Mackenzie and James Gardiner. It is well known that he was always inclined to ignore the existence of any private life on the part of those nearest to him. This was true especially with stenographers and typists. For them, and above all for Handy, King's unorthodox timetable imposed a heavy and relentless burden. Those of us who worked closely with him as prime minister found his continuous complaints about the inadequacy of his staff, voiced to any who would listen and recorded repeatedly in the diary, intensely irritating. One would imagine that he had always been badly served and at no time less adequately than in these last years. The fact was quite the reverse. In my judgment, during the years of my own servitude, the level of assistance was very high indeed. I have never known anyone in high office who had a better team to support him at every level, and that in terms not only of intelligence and character, but also in the constancy of their devotion.

2 Pickersgill and Forster, *The Mackenzie King Record*, III, pp 329-32.

If King's attitude towards his officials, and his colleagues for that matter, was often tainted by pettiness, suspicion, and disregard for their personal feelings, he still was capable on occasion of graceful and sincere gestures of appreciation and warmth. For example, when he learned that Norman Robertson's father and mother had come to Ottawa after Professor Robertson's retirement, King decided that it would be fitting to have them and my own mother and father, who had similarly settled in the capital, dine at Laurier House along with Norman and me and our wives. There was to be no one else at the party, only the Robertsons and the Heeneys and the host himself; yet the details of menu and seating were planned as for a state occasion. It was charming as, to do him justice, were most of King's parties. He was at his best, the considerate and entertaining host who quickly put our excited parents at ease. When we had finished our meal, and before we left the table, King rose to his feet and embarked upon an extravagant and lengthy paean of praise for Norman and me, who found ourselves unexpectedly in the role of guests of honour. 'Never,' he finally concluded, 'would I have been able to endure the heavy burdens of office at a time of war had it not been for Norman and Arnold.' Our parents, of course, were delighted, satisfied that we were being paid a tribute no more than our due. Our wives, I fear, took a less lofty view; indeed they had obvious difficulty in concealing their amusement during the purpler passages, remembering, as they did, the numerous occasions upon which King had shown little consideration for our private lives. Yet his entertainment and his praise that evening were perfectly genuine, as were the many occasions on which he would set aside urgent government business to write letters of sympathy on bereavement and congratulation on success.

During the war and in the immediate postwar years the British were represented officially in Ottawa by a succession of able and effective men. It was a particularly fortunate circumstance for both countries when Winston Churchill decided that Malcolm MacDonald should be appointed high commissioner to Canada in April 1941. His term in Ottawa was notably successful in the development and maintenance of a relationship which was not without serious difficulties at that time. Mackenzie King had known Malcolm's father, Ramsay MacDonald, as one of the group of rising socialist politicians before the first world war and was predisposed to think well of his son. In fact Malcolm played his cards very skilfully with the Prime Minister and quickly developed a personal relationship with him which served his country well. On a number of occasions MacDonald's personal intervention with King was able to pave the way to the resolution of difficulties between the two governments.

At that period and since, I have had the impression that in choosing their representatives in Ottawa, Britain has taken more than normal care in their selection. Certainly no country, in my experience, has had such consistently effective spokesmen. Representation of the United States has been uneven, as has that of France. There have been occasional outstanding professionals, but the record remains mixed and neither government has always resisted the temptation to treat Ottawa with scant respect when ambassadorial appointments were being made.

When Malcolm, who had been a friend of mine since Oxford days, was to be married to a beautiful Canadian widow late in 1946 and I undertook to organize his bachelor dinner, it was natural that Mackenzie King should be included. He was delighted to accept and on the occasion was at his most relaxed and engaging. In the speech he was inevitably called upon to make he was graceful, witty, and warm. The following day he wrote me by hand to say how much he had appreciated taking part. After thanking me for being invited to such 'an exceedingly happy affair,' he went on:

I must thank you as well for the many kind attentions paid myself. As I talked with so many of those present of remembering their fathers and grandfathers before them, and of recalling the occasion of their own coming into the world, I began to realize how much closer I was drawing to the exit than I had hitherto felt. Time seems to be passing very rapidly.[3]

The year 1947 witnessed a noticeable decline in the Prime Minister's vigour. He complained more frequently of fatigue and of lack of adequate assistance and support in bearing the burdens of office. Nevertheless, he managed several visits abroad during his last two years in power and, as the *Record* shows, greatly enjoyed his contacts with Attlee and Churchill as well as with lesser public figures. He also took pleasure in his friendship with the King and Queen. Yet the effort involved proved increasingly tiring. His reactions to events in the ministry and in Parliament seemed to me to be more emotional than formerly and he tended to be sharper with officials and colleagues. In the manner of older people he became more vulnerable to his own feelings, and his attitudes tended increasingly to vary with his physical well-being. He was immensely pleased when he received the Order of Merit and effusive in his expressions of gratitude for congratulations. He was equally irritated by the pressure for honours on the part of others, including long-time colleagues. He was even less patient than hitherto about interruptions in his personal routine and more abrupt with those who failed to fall in with his own ideas of what should be done.

On the other hand he remained to the end in fact as in law the first minister. I am satisfied for example that his rejection of the United States government's offer of a free trade, a 'new reciprocity,' in the spring of 1948 was not,

3 WLMK to ADPH, 7 December 1946.

as has been suggested, the result of any increase in his sentimental attachment to the monarchy developed during the last years. It was, rather, the instinctive reaction of the old politician. I was with him when he made his decision on the report of John Deutsch and Hector McKinnon on their private talks in Washington. As is now known they had an attractive package to present, one which accorded well with traditional Liberal economic doctrine. Yet the old man did not hesitate in reaching his conclusion. To the surprise and chagrin of the group who had reason to think they were producing precisely what Mackenzie King would want, his response was categorical and negative. The terms were tempting and, if embodied in an agreement, would no doubt have been beneficial. But he would have none of it. He was not going to be responsible for a second 1911 and disaster for a Liberal government.

Mackenzie King's dominance of his cabinet persisted well into 1948. In May of that year, however, an incident occurred which to those of us close to the centre of power had major significance. The occasion was whether or not Canada should be represented on the United Nations commission to be set up to oversee elections and troop withdrawals in Korea. Ilsley, as head of the Canadian delegation, had agreed to Canadian membership on the commission and his decision had been backed unreservedly by St Laurent as secretary of state for external affairs. Increasingly concerned that, under Pearson and St Laurent, Canada was becoming much too deeply involved in dubious UN adventures, increasingly suspicious of the United Nations itself, King brought the matter to cabinet and bitterly opposed Canadian involvement. Ilsley, with St Laurent's backing, stood firm to the point of threatened resignation; King, in the end, gave way gracefully. Power was beginning to shift.

One of the endemic hazards of the professional civil servant is that his political masters will change their minds and repudiate for one reason or another the positions taken by their career subordinate. Sometimes ministers leave it to officials to convey an unwelcome government decision, implicitly reserving the option of modifying it themselves later on. This makes for distrust all round and undermines the official's authority and usefulness. Curiously, this often happened in our postwar dealings with the British, to whom no one wanted to be beastly.

One such incident occurred in 1946 when Anthony Eden was visiting Ottawa to discuss financial matters, including a long-term wheat agreement, with Canadian authorities. Norman Robertson and I, under specific instructions, called on Eden at Government House to explain to him the reasons why our government was unwilling to follow a course proposed by the United Kingdom. We made our case late at night and with some difficulty, for Eden was openly sceptical that we were accurately representing the Prime Minister's attitude. Sure enough, the following day when King and a group of ministers met with Eden they proved much more bland and more accommodating than they had instructed us to be. I felt certain that ever after that incident Eden and other British ministers were convinced that if only they could circumvent the senior officials in Ottawa and deal at once and directly with ministers they would have less difficulty in having their way with the government of Canada. And I am not at all sure that they were wholly wrong.

During Eden's visit, King had invited the Governor General, Lord Alexander, his secretary, Major General Harry Letson, Robertson, Pearson, and myself, as well as one or two others, to an informal dinner with the British minister. Eden was in one of his elated moods and talked a great deal. His main preoccupation was the British financial situation which at the time was very grave. Letson, in answer to Eden's question as to how best to explain the British position, suggested partly, but not wholly, in jest that one way of improving the UK dollar reserves would be to sell Bermuda to the United States. The island was already in the US sphere of influence and of no strategic importance to Britain. At that point, as Letson observed later on, 'the balloon went up.' Eden, who had been talking with Letson and one or two others of us at one end of the room, bounded to his feet, stamped up and down saying that he had been insulted, never expected to have been spoken to in such a way in Canada, and more of the same. He then demanded his hat, took leave of a surprised host, and stalked out. King, who had been at the other end of the room, was totally mystified. When Robertson and I explained what had happened he seemed not wholly surprised.

By April 1948 King had outdone Walpole's record and had stated publicly that he would not lead the party in another general election. One morning I had sought and obtained his somewhat reluctant leave to take up with him at Laurier House a number of urgent matters awaiting cabinet action. It had become increasingly difficult to have him concentrate on government business, but on this occasion he seemed relaxed and good humoured and spontaneously inquired how things were going in the Privy Council Office. Before I had had a chance to reply, he picked up a letter that lay on his blotter and read me a passage from it. It went somewhat like this: 'They tell me that you are thinking of retiring. Take my advice – never retire.' Looking up, King then asked me if I could guess who it was from. When I made the obvious reply, he said: 'It's from Churchill. But he's wrong. I am going to retire and very soon.' That was the first that I heard him talk in a definite way of his intentions. By the end of 1948, intention had become reality. King had retired and St Laurent had succeeded him to the leadership of the Liberal party and the prime ministership of Canada.

For Mackenzie King, 1949 was a year of solitude and illness. He passed virtually from public view as is the fate of former prime ministers once they have

left office. After he died, on 22 July 1950, I took part with the other hon-
ourary pallbearers in the final ceremonial and his final journey, and I could
not help wondering what he could have found wrong in 'the arrangements.'
One thing I know he would have approved of was the long memorial address
at St Andrew's Church. It seemed to me ironic and sad that in expressing his
admiration for the deceased, the pastor, in addition to acceptable expressions
of respect, felt called upon to predict 'that as the years pass the figure of Mackenzie King will grow in stature and increase in greatness until he enters into
his true and rightful place in the affection and gratitude of the Canadian public.' As I reflected upon my own experience with King I certainly felt respect
and gratitude, but I doubted that many felt affection for that great but strange
man.

8

Other end of the East Block

Before Lester Pearson accepted St Laurent's invitation to enter the government as secretary of state for external affairs and severed his long connection with the Civil Service, he discussed the problem with me and with a few personal friends. I had no doubt that he should and would accept, as indeed he did after some anguish of spirit in the autumn of 1948. I was satisfied that Pearson's governing motive in taking this critical step was his feeling that by becoming a member of the St Laurent government he could most effectively advance the objectives of the Canadian foreign policies he had done so much to develop. Of course the invitation was flattering and acceptance would crown his already distinguished diplomatic reputation. No doubt too there was a healthy element of personal ambition involved. Nevertheless, I am certain that the main impulse which moved him to leave the relatively sheltered environment of the service and surrender his associations and friendships at the professional level – an increasing personal sacrifice as time went on – lay in his strong sense of public duty, just as nine years later when duty led him to seek the leadership of the Liberal party. Failure to appreciate this moral aspect in his character has, over the years since 1948, led to some sad and sorry estimates of his essential nature.

As he considered his own translation to politics, Pearson asked me if I would be willing to become his deputy and to succeed him as undersecretary of state for external affairs. I was flattered and attracted at the prospect of working under one I liked and admired. Under the leadership of St Laurent and largely at the instance of Pearson and his principal colleagues in the department, a remarkable revolution had already been accomplished in Canadian foreign policy. The long years of fear and reluctance to become more involved in external affairs and the tendency in King's thinking to shy away from peacetime commitments had been dispelled by developments in the preceding three years. The North Atlantic Treaty Organization was already on the way to being set up, and Canada was on the verge of a new era in its external relations. The prospect of being directly involved as head of the department in charge of these matters was exciting. Hitherto as secretary to the cabinet and through close association with two prime ministers, with Pearson, and with other senior officials during and after the war, I had already been closely involved in the development and execution of decisions in external matters. And although the new post held many mysteries, I did not think of myself as wholly unqualified. Furthermore the senior officers of the department – Robertson, Wrong, Pearson, and many others – were among my closest personal friends.

Such were the undoubted attractions to me of Pearson's offer. On the other hand, after eleven years in the East Block, the idea of a complete change, perhaps into one of the large 'outside' departments of government or perhaps back to the practice of law, was not without appeal. I had even been tempted by the opulent prospect of a job in industry to which in those years a number of wartime civil servants were turning. However, the attractions of external affairs outweighed such considerations and I agreed to take over the undersecretaryship for a period of about three years. After that it was understood that I would be appointed to some senior post abroad.

The order-in-council appointing me undersecretary of state for external affairs was passed on 19 January 1949, to take effect during March. At the same time Norman Robertson was appointed to succeed me in the Privy Council Office and Dana Wilgress, then deputy minister of trade and commerce, was to succeed Norman in London. On 15 March I moved into the large, high-ceilinged office at the southeast corner overlooking the statue of Sir Wilfrid Laurier and across Wellington Street to the 1914-18 War Memorial. There I was to spend most of my waking hours over the following three years.

It was not long before I came to realize that, despite my previous close association with the department, I was very much an innocent in diplomacy and had a great deal to learn. I don't suppose that many have had a more concentrated or more sympathetic crash course in diplomacy than I received those first few months at the hands of Escott Reid, who had been acting undersecretary since Pearson's ministerial appointment, and the half dozen other senior officials upon whom I had been parachuted.

Events, however, did not wait for the completion of my education. Within a couple of weeks of my taking over the department, the North Atlantic Treaty was signed in Washington and we were immediately engaged in all the problems of developing the administrative apparatus required to put flesh on the bones of the agreement. Relations between the West and the Soviet Union were critical. The Berlin blockade continued. We were in the process of establishing a mission in Bonn. Our missions in London and Washington were deeply engaged in other issues of great importance. Everywhere economic as well as political problems beset the foreign offices of the world including the East Block. Pearson himself was heavily engaged in his new ministerial duties in cabinet and in Parliament, and he was frequently absent from Ottawa. Apart from policy matters upon which the undersecretary was expected to advise and inform, the administrative problems of the department, in the throes of a program of expansion and reform, demanded attention in a hundred different areas. Always there were meetings that required the undersecretary's presence, meetings of interdepartmental committees and meetings of cabinet committees among others. There was also the obligatory diplomatic social round of which I had had until then only some selective experience.

Pearson had little time, indeed little taste, for administrative problems. His flair was for developing and negotiating avenues of solution, for action at the policy level. It has often been said and written of him that he disliked the business of running a department and that, in consequence, he was no good at it, and that he left to his officials, ultimately his deputy minister, the unpleasant decisions of personnel management and housekeeping. There was much truth in this. For example, in March 1950 while I was staying as a guest at our legation residence in Copenhagen, and in receipt of the attentions and hospitality of Laureys, the minister, and his wife, I had to tell him that he must retire and make arrangements to leave Copenhagen within the next few months. He was the victim of a new rule, approved by Pearson, that all heads of missions, whether regular professionals or from outside the service, must retire when sixty-five or over on completing ten years' service. It was the duty of the undersecretary to administer the coup de grâce.

If I became the bearer of unwelcome news – of retirement, transfer, refusal of pleas for improved treatment – to official colleagues, I had no real grounds for complaint. There is much to be said for leaving such matters to the undersecretary. Such a policy, however, must be accompanied by a willingness on the minister's part to back up his subordinate, and on this score I had no difficulty. Pearson was always ready to defend the actions of his officials, in and out of Parliament, even in the most distressing circumstances. The best example of this last was his total and unreserved expression of confidence in the reliability of Herbert Norman, who was named during the McCarthy hearings in the United States, following the private recommendation which I had made to him on the evidence which had been so exhaustively and painfully assembled. I recall no instance in which Pearson failed to back me up in the decisions I had to take as undersecretary.

I have no doubt that one of the reasons why Pearson invited me to become his deputy was so that I might undertake the extensive reorganization which the department quite obviously required, leaving him free to concentrate on the important policy developments taking place at that period. Not that I was relieved of the normal function of the undersecretary as the final stage in the channel of advice on all policy questions. Indeed during my three years the flow of advice originating and brought together in the departmental and interdepartmental apparatus increased in volume and accelerated in pace as a result of events in Europe and in Asia. Of these the most notable and influential were policies on the consolidation of the NATO response to the Soviet Union, and the United Nations reaction to the outbreak of war in Korea in 1950. Nevertheless, it was to urgent administrative and especially personnel problems that I bent my first efforts. I soon came to realize that, although there was a tendency in the East Block, as in all foreign offices, to subordinate such matters to the more stimulating and prestigious business of formulating policy for ministerial decision, the need for firm, decisive, and prompt action in such affairs as departmental organization at home, recruiting, training, and perhaps most of all, suitable manning of our posts abroad, was of immediate, and in some cases of first, importance.

Among my beginning administrative tasks was the lowly and infuriating business of mission housekeeping: the acquisition of premises for chanceries and residences, the provision of furniture and supplies, the manning of embassies and consulates, and dealing with the people involved, men and women at home and abroad. It is hard for anyone who has not had actual experience to appreciate how much is involved in this aspect of a foreign service. In the one matter of 'supplies and properties,' for example, the postwar expansion had led to a great accumulation of problems – purchases, rentals, decoration in a variety of places, and a wide variety of circumstances. It seemed that everyone and his wife had, and expressed, strong opinions. Robertson, and Pearson after him, had been concerned primarily with policy. It was up to me to bring some order into the prevailing chaos. After a concentrated five-week fact-finding tour of our European missions in the spring of 1950 and with our ambassadors' and ministers' woes still ringing in my ears, I adopted the standard bureaucratic device of setting up an advisory committee on properties abroad with special reference to furnishing, decoration, and related problems.

One of the features of Canadian representation abroad that worried me, was the relationship between the officers of External Affairs and those of Trade and Commerce. The two departments at home were all too clearly totally autonomous. External Affairs had the formal statutory responsibility for the conduct of Canadian foreign policy, yet the department had no direct control over our trade commissioners in the field whose functions obviously formed part of our external position. It seemed to me that there should be the closest co-operation abroad, that the heads of our missions should feel a personal responsibility for our commercial representatives, and that they should, as a minimum, do everything possible to support the commercial service in its efforts to encourage Canadian exports and provide commercial intelligence. Ideally, too, heads of missions should be in a position to deploy the commercial officers in economic and business reporting.

Not everyone in my new department shared these views. Incredible as it may seem, there were some in External Affairs who conceived of the department as something apart from the rest of the Civil Service, concerned with 'diplomatic' and 'political' affairs outside of Canada, rather than with trade or even economic policies. This attitude was, in fact, common to the staff of many foreign offices. To their own serious detriment, diplomats of many nationalities had become isolated from the general community of the public service of their countries and remote from the realities of popular requirements. In Canada, the tendency to separation was also due to some obstinacy and rigidity on the part of officials in other departments. In our own Department of External Affairs some, including several senior officers, would have had us administered, not by the general law governing the Public Service of Canada but by a special foreign service act which would have established a separate and distinct diplomatic service free of the Civil Service Commission's authority. I had no patience with such a course which I felt sure would be disastrous. Canada was still a small country in terms of the human and material resources it could afford to employ in the conduct of its business abroad. Anything which detracted from the efficiency and unity of the total effort should not be tolerated. And any ambassador who did not put the advancement of Canada's commercial interest near the top of his priorities was not fit to head a mission.

After the signing of the North Atlantic Treaty 1949, the affairs of NATO were among the most important with which I had to deal. In November 1951 I attended the NATO Ministerial Council in Rome with Pearson who was flanked by Brooke Claxton, minister of national defence, and D.C. Abbott, the minister of finance. Over the next few years these able men were to become the familiar trio who represented Canada whenever the council met at the ministerial level. By any standard it was a formidable team. This meeting of NATO foreign ministers gave me the opportunity to see Anthony Eden in action at the head of the table and at the various social functions which were so glitteringly organized for the occasion by the Italian government. I had, of course, seen him in Ottawa for bilateral discussions during and immediately after the war, but Rome gave me my first impression of Eden on a larger stage. For one who had been a hero to so many of us after his resignation at the time of the prewar crisis over sanctions against Italy, he proved a disappointment. As chairman of the council he performed well enough, but in and out of meetings I thought him singularly lacking in gravity, frequently impatient, and even ill-tempered. Nevertheless the meeting proved memorable, though more for the grandeur of its setting than for its accomplishments.

As the United Nations was meeting in Paris that autumn, Pearson and I took the train from Rome and in the course of the journey managed to accomplish a good deal of departmental business without interruption. In Paris we had decided to call together all of our heads of mission in Europe, a practice which was useful politically and administratively as subsequent meetings amply proved. During the morning Pearson had each of our ambassadors and ministers describe to us the situation of the government and country in which he was discharging his functions and give an appreciation of the general situation from his vantage point. When this was over Pearson himself in an easy and entirely extemporaneous fashion commented upon what had been reported on the state of NATO as revealed in Rome, then went on to express his own views as to the nature of the problems confronting us all and the solutions which seemed to him to offer the best chance of success in terms of collective security. To the obvious disappointment of the assembled ambassadors, and to a degree to my own dismay, when the time came to break for lunch he declared that he would be occupied with important conversations at the Quai d'Orsay and elsewhere during the afternoon. He understood that some wished to bring up administrative questions. In fact such items were at the top of most of their minds: personnel, accommodation and allowances, and the hundred and one practical problems of the ambassador's lot. Pearson with an engaging smile shattered their hopes of ministerial redress: 'The Under-Secretary would deal with such questions in the afternoon sessions!' And so I did.

From my new position in the East Block, the Ottawa scene continued to be absorbing and fascinating. I found that each day I looked forward eagerly to my work in the department. There were, as well, other aspects of the undersecretaryship which distinguished it from the position which I had had in the cabinet office. My relations with ministers were less frequent and more specialized. Because of developments at that time in western Europe and the United States, my most frequent contacts, in addition to Pearson and the Prime Minister on occasion, were with the Minister of National Defence and the Minister of Finance. Here I was fortunate because both Brooke Claxton and Doug Abbott were old friends of mine from Montreal days where all three of us were members of the Quebec Bar. With them and with other senior officials I now spent many hours hammering out the various aspects of Canadian external policy, especially on NATO which was in the forefront of our concern.

I found it interesting and helpful during my undersecretaryship to appear before the House of Commons Committee on External Affairs where I was subject to the usually but not always friendly cross-examination of members on both government and opposition sides. Of these Howard Green, subsequently himself secretary of state for external affairs, was one of the most persistent and hardest to satisfy on departmental details. He was especially fascinated by the large telephone and telegram accounts of the department, finding it difficult to understand why we had to have so many communications between our various offices. Later on he was to learn the reasons and himself contribute a good deal to these very expenses. On the whole on questions of policy there was virtually no disposition amongst the members of the committee, whatever their party, to criticize government action. It was in many ways the golden age of Canadian diplomacy and Pearson enjoyed enormous prestige amongst all members of Parliament.

Then there were the social obligations connected with the job, the diplomatic dinners and luncheons, to say nothing of receptions and cocktail parties. Such events became a regular feature of the life of my wife and me. Great fun at first, they tended to become tiresome and too frequent with the increase of diplomatic missions in Ottawa; at least we found it difficult to maintain a high level of enthusiasm for all our comings and goings. There were also state visits. President Auriol of France came in 1951, Churchill again in 1952, and many others during those years. The pattern for these occasions was always the same: the government dinner at the Country Club, a luncheon or dinner at Government House, a reception at the Chateau Laurier, and a similar routine at the appropriate embassy. It was all very exciting for a while, but exhausting when one was working six and seven days a week.

During my last years in the East Block father and mother were in Ottawa. They had an apartment in the Roxborough – a venerable Ottawa institution now sadly and prematurely demolished in the cause of progress in the capital – whose proximity allowed me then to slip down Elgin Street for lunch two or three times a week. These short visits during the last years of father's life remain among my happiest memories of my parents. In the Roxborough father had formed a number of new friendships among fellow residents, notably Colonel 'Pat' Edwards and his wife whose kindness and generosity to the day of father's death and after, I shall never forget. Then there was 'Bill' Herridge, the former minister to Washington, by that time quite crippled, in whose company and conversation father took much pleasure.

In February 1952 I attended the North Atlantic Ministerial Council meeting in Lisbon. Whether the NATO headquarters would be in London or Paris had already been virtually settled in favour of the latter, much to the irritation of the British who continued to feel that Canada had somehow let them down in supporting the French capital. There remained however the critical question of naming a secretary-general. Here, in part as a compensation for London having lost the headquarters, it was agreed that a British nominee would be desirable. By common consent, Oliver Franks was regarded as the one who would fill the position admirably. I remember the phone call from Lisbon to Franks, then British ambassador in Washington. It had not apparently occurred to Dean Acheson who was making the call that it would be very early in the American capital. Franks was just up and shaving when Acheson came on his line. However, despite his urgings and those of Pearson who had been asked to lend his support to the proposition, Franks's considered answer a little later was negative. However, the subsequent selection of Lord Ismay proved to be admirable and universally popular.

The main question of substance before the council was that of the elaborate 'infrastructure' required for the common defence across the territory of France and the Low Countries. This called for the expenditure by the alliance of large sums for airfields, pipelines, depots, and the rest of the solid necessities for a modern defence system. Brooke Claxton was the principal Canadian representative on the infrastructure committee and he laboured hard and long, supported by his civil and military officials, to produce the complex formula which ultimately determined the shares the various allies should bear in this vast undertaking.

It was not all hard work in Lisbon, however, and we in the Canadian delegation managed as well to have fun and see a good deal of the environs of the capital. The Portuguese authorities had put a car and driver at my disposal so that my wife, unencumbered by official engagements during the day, was able to wander farther afield in the glorious sunshine along the rocky coast and even some distance into the interior. A number of us went one Sunday to Cintra, in part I suppose to pay homage to the great figures of nineteenth-century British literature whose aura still remained. I recall one Sunday encountering Dirk Stikker, the Netherlands foreign minister, strolling on the esplanade in front of the cathedral. He told us that a minute or two before he had run successively into ex-King Carol of Rumania, ex-King Humber of Italy, and ex-King Peter of Yugoslavia. 'Where else,' he wondered, 'could one encounter three former monarchs in such a short space of time?'

When at the conclusion of the meetings we left for home, we carried with us the Governor General designate, Vincent Massey, who was to be installed on 28 February. He was anxious to obtain opinions on the conduct of his new office, although his own disposition was to make few changes. I remember his inquiring of my wife whether he should retain the curtsey. When she suggested it might be a good occasion to drop the traditional obeisance Massey seemed doubtful; in fact, the curtsey remained throughout his term.

My days in the East Block were numbered. At the end of 1951 Pearson had approved a pattern of senior postings and cross-postings which would send Norman Robertson to London once more, Wilgress to the undersecretaryship in Ottawa, and me to establish the new Canadian mission at NATO. Immediately upon my return to Ottawa from Lisbon I was plunged into the personal and official preparations which such an uprooting required and in the plans which the setting up of new offices and assembly of a new staff for NATO made necessary. My years abroad were about to begin.

9

NATO interlude

When the time came to leave the East Block it proved a sorry wrench. However strenuous the work, however long the hours, the years I had spent there imbued me with the sense of being at the centre of affairs, of being part of the strange decision-making process. Yet from every point of view I was due for a change of environment. The prospect of having a mission of my own and being able to build it from the ground up, and in Paris at that, was an attractive one. So there were few regrets when my wife and I said goodbye to friends and colleagues at the Ottawa station on 16 April 1952.

I arrived in Paris on 25 April in advance of my family. As there was no permanent residence, I had to find temporary quarters in a hotel. I appealed for advice on that account to Charles Ritchie who had had extensive Paris experience. For reasons never fully explained he recommended the George V. There, amid the glittering distractions of that celebrated hostelry, I set myself up as Canada's first ambassador and permanent representative to the North Atlantic Council. It was to be six months before I could find a house and resume more suitable domesticity.

As Saul Rae, who had been lent to me by Canada House in London, had already established our delegation's headquarters, there was nothing to prevent my taking over at once. I made my first call on Lord Ismay, the secretary-general. Ismay had only recently arrived, having been abruptly snatched by Churchill from his brief tenure as secretary of state for Commonwealth relations. I had known him from wartime days in the Cabinet Office. Despite the frustrations of insufficient staff and temporary offices in the Palais de Chaillot – where he remained for almost two years – he was cheerful. He welcomed me warmly and rapidly filled me in on the current state of affairs in the council. Even at that early stage it had become evident that there would be difficulty in putting together an efficient secretariat and that Ismay would find himself under great pressures from national governments for the preferment of their own nominees. Indeed, over the months that followed he was to encounter every sort of practical administrative problem. French officialdom, to which he had to look for the solution of many such matters, proved far from helpful and he had constantly to appeal to higher authority in many of the smallest details.

Soon after I arrived the first morning at our office in the annex to the Château de la Muette, my secretary came in to say that one of my Nordic colleagues, whose offices were at the other end of the hall, wished to call on me at once. Busy with setting my own affairs in order and settling in with my own little staff, I sent word back rather peevishly that, if he could give me half a chance, I would be making my call on him very shortly. The reply returned within minutes. It was not a courtesy call that was proposed but a matter of business. Curious that so soon there should be some business with a NATO colleague, I responded that I would of course be glad to see the ambassador at once. Thereupon there entered Steensen-Leth of Denmark, tall, ruddy, and cheerful. He came straight to the point. 'It so happens,' he said, 'that when I was sixteen I developed a taste for Canadian whiskey. Until recently I had no trouble in satisfying my requirements. But now, as you no doubt know, my country along with many others is in some difficulty in meeting its dollar requirements.' I intervened to say I did not think he needed to go any farther; I appreciated his problem. He nodded his head. 'I was wondering whether it would be possible for you and I to make some arrangement.' He supposed that I was not particularly fond of a certain liqueur for which his country was celebrated. When I replied that I liked his product well enough but hardly in large quantities he shook his head sadly. On the other hand, I observed, his country's breweries were famous. His face brightened, we shook hands warmly, and he took his leave. Next day began the process of supplying my modest requirements for beer in return for which I was able to prevent any serious interruption in my colleague's customary tipple. It was the beginning of a beautiful friendship.

The first business with which the council had to deal was the appointment of a successor to Eisenhower as supreme allied commander in Europe (SACEUR). As yet, the council had no established procedures for such a purpose. Nevertheless we all felt it important that such a major decision be taken by the council with some formality. Not that there was any disposition to refuse the nomination of Matthew Ridgeway, whom Washington was putting forward, but merely that the proprieties should be observed. It was in the course of consultations on this point that I made my first acquaintance with members of the British and US delegations.

The British were headed by Derek Hoyer-Millar whom I had already met and liked. He had displayed in other assignments the common sense, determination, and sense of proportion that were to make him one of the best permanent undersecretaries the Foreign Office had in my time. The relations between our two delegations were splendid from the beginning and I never had the slightest hesitation in consulting Hoyer-Millar on delicate and confidential matters. He was supported by a professional staff of typical British competence, his number one (on the economic side) and principal agent at Organization for European Economic Co-operation (OEEC) was the able and accomplished Eric Roll.

The United States delegation was by far the largest. When I arrived at NATO the United States had no less than five full ambassadors in Paris of whom three were in their NATO delegation. It was reported at the time that when William Draper, the president's personal representative in Europe as well as the head of the US delegation to NATO, asked that a meeting of his staff be convened, the Marigny Theatre had to be provided for the 1100 people who answered the summons. Numerous as they were, however, and with their usual tendency to trip over one another's feet, they were friendly, immensely hard working, and full of good will. It was in their company that I first met Livingston Merchant, Draper's second in command. From that time on, Merchant's path and mine were often to cross and run parallel.

The quality of that first North Atlantic Council was high. Governments had made an effort to select able representatives. I was particularly fortunate in my Canadian colleagues in the Permanent Delegation of whom Wynne Plumptre and Marcel Cadieux headed respectively the economic and political sections. Among the ablest of those from other countries I came to know well were Hervé Alphand (later French ambassador to the United States) and André de Staerck, the Belgian. De Staerck was outstanding and could, I understood, have had any appointment within his government. A bachelor, an intellectual, sensitive, humourous, extraordinarily effective in negotiation, he was also a dear person.

A month after I reached Paris I was present at the ceremony for the hand-over of command of the Supreme Headquarters Allied Powers Europe (SHAPE) from Eisenhower to Ridgeway. It was an impressive, well-arranged occasion at which Eisenhower made an eloquent and moving reaffirmation of his faith in the Atlantic community. In contrast to the familiar departing commander, Ridgeway seemed cold and severe. Nevertheless, he was given a good start and, with the popular General Grunther as his chief of staff, I was able to report home that he should do well. In fact it turned out that way and we soon became accustomed to the different style.

Generally speaking the atmosphere in the council and within the delegations in those early days was one of optimism, mutual respect, and mutual confidence. The permanent representatives felt they had been given an important task by their governments and the manner in which the organization had been launched in Paris gave ground for the belief that the alliance would be bucked up materially from the various capitals. Our behaviour those first few months reflected this conviction and the assumption round the table that each country would discharge in good faith its commitments to the alliance to the best of its ability. There was thus a spirit of unity in the council and a freshness which encouraged all of us to do our best to make the organization function and to overcome cheerfully the confusion and difficulties of the initial period.

Notwithstanding this initial atmosphere of optimism and the momentum engendered by the early spirit of unity, there were problems of importance from the outset. The first of these arose from the preoccupation of a majority of the permanent representatives with strictly European issues, notably that of the European army. Until the signing of the European Defence Community (EDC) Treaty on 27 May 1952, many of my colleagues were continuously engaged in the complex and delicate negotiations of this agreement. And when the permanent representatives were all invited to attend the signing of the European treaties at the Quai d'Orsay, there was little or no Atlantic flavour to the occasion. France, under Foreign Minister Schumann's guidance, was concentrating public attention upon Europe; my council colleague, Alphand, and his team had little time for NATO in its wider context. Indeed, in his opening statement, Schumann used the word Atlantic only twice, once merely to indicate what documents were to be signed. Not that NATO was being deliberately sidetracked; rather France and most of the continental powers were convinced that settlement of major European problems was a precondition for the sound development of the Atlantic alliance.

The second element in our affairs, which loomed larger as the months went by, was the process by which national contributions to the alliance were related to the goals agreed upon at the ministerial meeting at Lisbon. Here the secretariat sought to take the initiative and develop an independent role to effect the goals. Because of the attitude of most national governments this effort proved quite unrealistic and unacceptable; indeed, it came near to creating a serious crisis within the council. It was natural that the secretariat should begin to develop an independence of the permanent representatives, and to a degree this was sound and in accord with early NATO doctrine. But there was also a real risk that the process would go too far and that the council would become a mere advisory committee. Ismay himself never intended that things should go that way, but there were others who did. The United States delegation in particular took quite readily to the concept of unfettered 'management' by an independent secretariat, despite the obvious danger of failure to obtain congressional support for this position. The Canadian delegation, on the other hand, felt that such a development would be destructive of the hopes we had for an effective operating alliance resting on the consent of the council after due deliberation and debate. It was unfortunate that Ismay, harassed as he was by the frustrations of administrative incompetence and indecision, only just fell short of making a personal issue of the secretariat's authority. As it was, he deliberately let his patience run out and employed all the elements of his personal prestige in asserting the secretariat's right to control the budget. In the end the situation was defused and the issue side-stepped. But it had been a near thing, and only the respect and affection which all of us had for Ismay enabled us to avoid a minor disaster.

By the middle of that first summer the process of the annual review of national contributions to the alliance, measured against the Lisbon goals, was underway and had already run into difficulties. There were some who felt that the shortfall between Lisbon profession and Paris performance was the fault of the Permanent Council. Field Marshal Montgomery, lecturing to the NATO Staff College that summer, did not hesitate to attribute such failures to the weakness of the permanent representatives in Paris. The facts, of course, were quite otherwise. Each government in the alliance insisted on determining by its own domestic processes the nature and extent of the forces it would commit and the funds it would obligate. Their representatives in NATO had no authority to make decisions on their own. The council, in fact, was a continuing conference of delegates subject to instruction and little more. By July it had become evident that the Lisbon goals were unrealistic and would have to be sharply revised. Even Pearson felt that 'much of our optimism and most of our brave talk about the value of the new and permanent Council and its importance in the building up of the Atlantic Community seem to have disappeared.'[1]

In this connection the situation of the United States delegation was a curious one. Pressing the other countries to live up to the Lisbon goals, as they felt it their special duty to do, they included in their own response to the secretariat that autumn a figure for military aid which no realistic observer could expect the Congress to approve. My assessment of the situation as I wrote home was that 'American constitutional schizophrenia impedes our joint endeavours and we have in our planning to deal with theoretical assumptions which are likely to bear little relation to the final outcome of the congressional processes.'

The military too were operating in a watertight compartment, insulated from the council and making plans which, by any realistic assessment, they were quite incapable of fulfilling. Well before the end of the year it was evident to all of us that everyone would fall short in some particular, including

1 L.B. Pearson to ADPH, 18 July 1952.

the United States. The only comfort for me was the fact that Canada ran no risk of embarrassed isolation.

As the time for the first ministerial meeting of the council in the new headquarters drew near, tension over the annual review and national contributions increased. The French were insisting, to the point of virtual ultimatum, on the strict application of a rigid burden-sharing formula, and Alphand's statements in the council became increasingly provocative and irritating. At one point when I had taken him up sharply on a proposal to include Bizerte, Tunisia, in the allocation of allied forces, he had the effrontery to say that his ministers would take a very serious view of the Canadian attitude on the subject when he reported to them. Meantime, the French government itself was introducing a defence budget openly conditional upon a level of US aid which the United States did not, and certainly would not, accept. The soldiers still pressed for their military goals with no apparent appreciation of the political and economic difficulties, and SACEUR's report continued to include what I characterized as 'cardboard targets' for the next year. The United Kingdom delayed replying to the secretariat's questionnaire, the EDC Treaty remained unratified by France, and finally, the United States elections had taken place and the US delegation had concluded that the reconciliation between what NATO should have and what it could have would have to wait until the following spring.

In these sorry circumstances in a personal letter to Pearson I assessed the prospects for the ministers' December meeting in this way:

At any rate, we now have reason to hope that the Ministers' discussions in December of the Annual Review and the future NATO defence programme will be confined to general issues and not focussed upon impossible statistical gaps between what we have and what the soldiers think we should have ... Politically, of course, Germany's relationship to NATO will be the all-pervading issue. And this for two reasons; first, because it will be evident that, without Germany's contribution, the levels to be achieved in 1953 will be unacceptably low; and second, because of the backing and filling which has been done by the French on the EDC and the pall of doubt which now overhangs the prospects of ratification. I confess that latterly I have come to wonder whether we ought not now to plan for a spring meeting of the Ministers with the twin object of approving a sound and realistic defence programme for the years ahead and for bringing Germany directly into NATO at the same time. Certainly a lot of people will begin to think this way if the prospects of ratification and of Franco-German rapprochement within the EDC framework do not improve radically by the beginning of the new year.[2]

2 ADPH to L.B. Pearson, 24 November 1952.

In fact the ministerial meeting in December went off much better than we had anticipated. Perhaps because our expectations in Paris had not been high, we felt in the Permanent Delegation that the level of discussion had been reasonably good; for one brief period, when American Secretary of State Dean Acheson made his farewell speech, the level had never been higher. Our ministers were Abbott and Claxton. Pearson, kept in New York by his duties as president of the UN General Assembly, left the diplomatic representation to Wilgress and myself. Kraft of Denmark turned out to be a better chairman than we expected, and the discussions on political questions were frank and sensible. I had a long talk with Acheson at what we called the 'Kraft dinner.' He was in splendid form, but I knew he would miss the great events in which he had participated so gracefully in the preceding few years. Lord Alexander was on hand in his guise of British minister of defence and, at a dinner that I held for our two ministers attended by Hoyer-Millar, Ismay, Draper, and Grunther, we gave him a rather hard time over British reluctance to play any real role in the European army which was struggling to be born.

There was no visible alteration in the attitude of the United States after the inauguration of President Eisenhower in January 1953. In fact one of the first directions given to Draper was to impress upon the French and the council the importance which the United States attached to European integration and in particular to early ratification of the EDC Treaty. Eisenhower and Dulles were following the same course as their predecessors and, as Alphand pointed out, were running the risk of having the 'new Europe' considered as a solely American objective. I found it hard to see how the EDC could be ratified by the spring, either in France or Germany. And if it were not, what would the Congress think and do?

In February of the new year we had a visit from John Foster Dulles accompanied by Harold Stassen. Before they came, Draper warned us that we were to expect nothing much from the 'new boys.' They were coming to Europe 'to look and to listen and then to go home and think.' While the abbreviated timetable for their visit to NATO was the occasion of some private sarcasm among my colleagues, it was I think of some value, as I wrote at the time, that the Secretary of State of the United States should actually sit down at the council table with us: 'It is something for the members of the Council to have looked upon the countenance of the new US Secretary of State, even though it is a good deal more forbidding than that of his predecessor.'[3] Dulles took the occasion to emphasize the place held by NATO in United States foreign policy and underlined the importance of EDC ratification. When he left Paris I was worried nonetheless that he had gone home with a greater optimism for ratification by France than the facts justified.

3 ADPH to L.B. Pearson, 5 February 1953.

The ministerial meeting held in April 1953 was my last in the Paris post. The ministers came together at that time in circumstances quite different to those of the previous December. There was uncertainty concerning Soviet intentions after the astonishing and rapid series of developments which had taken place since Malenkov had assumed Stalin's mantle. There seemed every reason to reaffirm the intention of the member countries to proceed with the planned build-up of forces. Nevertheless, there was bound to be a temptation to relax and NATO was already having enough difficulty in maintaining an acceptable level of preparedness. As has so often been the case, the West found itself in the dilemma of having to persist in a policy of strength and at the same time avoid giving an impression that it was not genuinely prepared to discuss an overall settlement with the Russians.

From time to time, sometimes with my colleagues on the council, I engaged in official visitations of Canadian and other NATO forces in various parts of Europe. I remember being particularly impressed by our airmen attached to General Lauris Norstad's command at Fontainbleau, and Norstad himself described his RCAF element as among the best, if not the best, under his command. I was gratified too by the smart appearance and creditable performance of our naval forces in the NATO exercise code named MAINBRACE, held in Norway. Although it rained almost steadily during the exercise, the sight of the fleet at the head of the fjord impressed all the members of the council with the military reality of the alliance. In November 1952 we went to sea for naval manoeuvers in the Mediterranean; another time we observed an armoured exercise in Germany. Such sorties among the allied forces proved refreshing to all of us after the often tedious and unreal debates round the council table in the Palais de Chaillot.

I doubt that many of the Parisians who daily passed the brave cluster of flags before NATO headquarters gave a thought to what was going on inside the Palais de Chaillot. NATO had been installed in Paris, but somehow it never became part of the life of the city. Perhaps it would have been different had the French government succeeded in its efforts to have us take over the monumental stables of Louis XIV at Versailles, or even had their offer to make the Gare Montparnasse available to the organization been accepted. Years later a permanent headquarters was finally established in a shining new building on the edge of the Bois, ironically not very long before the French decided that they could do without us and the weary move to Brussels had to be undertaken. All of which, I suppose, is merely an indication of the transitory nature of human organization in the life of a great city which has grown over the centuries by a process quite other than deliberate diplomacy.

My wife and children had joined me in the early summer of 1952, and we moved into a suite which I had acquired at the Trianon Palace Hotel in Versailles. By the autumn, we had leased a small but really quite elegant 'hôtel particulier' in the 16th arrondissement, just off the avenue Victor Hugo. It was barely large enough to accommodate us and our daughter (our son returned to Canada in the autumn), with the usual box-like quarters for the personnel. It was, however, decorated and furnished to the last detail with exquisite taste. The boiserie in salon and dining room was superb, and all the small objects had the mark of delicate personal choice. One impressive luxury was the silver gilt hardware in the richly carpeted bathroom off the master bedroom. I was told that the house had been built originally to accommodate the mistress of some wealthy unknown. Certainly it admitted of such a history. When we were able, through Pauline Vanier's intervention, to secure a competent maître d'hôtel and, even more important, an excellent cook and an accomplished upstairs maid, we were comfortable indeed.

To many, the 16th arrondissement may not be the real Paris, although my own experience led me to conclude that all quarters of that fascinating human creation are not real in their own way. No doubt the 16th was rather plutocratic and bourgeois and lacked the chic to be found in the rehabilitated hotels of the older quarters. Yet for us, at least, our own particular quarter had great charm, and it was not long before the local bakery, butcher, chemist, café, and the rest became part of our lives.

What happens to people who have the good fortune to be translated to the most sympathetic of all cities has been told a thousand times. If Parisians have a certain arrogance of their own, they have surely some reason for it. This may make it no less irritating, however, to the rest of us. It is a sort of natural quality crossing the boundaries of class and education. For example, our chauffeur Louis had travelled a bit about Europe. Yet he seemed to regard everything outside the great boulevards that encircled his capital as terra incognita, wasteland inhabited by ignorant foreign folk. One evening we were to dine with a friend who lived near St Cloud. My secretary had warned Louis to be on hand to drive us there for the given hour. Word came back to me that he would be unable to find the house as the country beyond the Bois de Boulogne was quite unknown to him, whereupon I sent him a map with the location quite clearly indicated. Under some pressure he consented to do his best and ultimately, with no difficulty at all, delivered us to our destination. However, he refused to return to Paris while we were dining, on the grounds that he would never be able to find his way back again. When we emerged some hours later and entered the car for the homeward journey we could feel Louis' sense of relief as we neared the great boulevards. Once through the Bois he turned over his shoulder and said, with manifest relief: 'Ah Monsieur, encore une fois, rentrés dans la civilization!'

And because of Louis my wife and I are unlikely to forget the first occasion upon which we were received at the Elysée Palace. Elegantly attired, we came downstairs in good time for Louis and the official car. Ten minutes before the hour set for dinner he had not shown up. It was raining; yet we must be off if we were not to be unacceptably late. There was no option but for me to go into the street and hail a taxi. At length I secured on the Rue Longchamps one of the oldest and most disreputable cabs. When I announced our destination rather grandly to the driver as 'le Palais de l'Elysée,' he at first totally failed to comprehend. Then, as we became desperate, the truth dawned on him. 'Oh,' said he, 'you mean chez Monsieur Vincent Auriol!' Whereupon he set off at a rattling pace and in due course turned into the palace courtyard on the rue du Faubourg St Honoré. Our driver performed with great style and thoroughly enjoyed the red carpet, the floodlights, and the flashing sabres of the Guarde Républicaine as we descended from his ancient vehicle which had taken its place in the line of diplomatic and ministerial limousines. At the end of the evening Louis was waiting full of apologies. His wife, he said, had suffered an accident, and we had no cause to doubt his story.

On two or three occasions during that crowded year of 1952-3 we managed to get over to England. One time I had been invited to speak at a dinner being held in the hall of Christ Church, Oxford, the final event in a conference devoted to NATO problems. Grandly turning down the offer of hospitality at another college, I wrote St John's that a room be reserved for me for the night. After considerable delay I received a note from the bursar's office acceding to my request and citing the price. When I arrived at the college my reception was somewhat less cordial than seemed to me suitable to an alumnus who had travelled from Paris on an ambassadorial occasion. Shown my room by an unknown porter's assistant, my attention was drawn to a note on the table beside my bed. Ah, thought I, a message of greeting. Not at all. It was another note from the bursar drawing attention to the fact that the cost of the room would be thirty-five shillings, and adding that for a payment of so many guineas I could maintain my membership in the college. That was all.

The coronation of Queen Elizabeth occurred while we were at NATO. In default of a more exalted personage, I was called upon to visit the Canadian brigade in Germany to play the role required for appropriate celebration of the event. As my wife was unable to come, I took Tish, our by now teenage daughter. The troops were splendid; the hospitality, both military and civilian, was excellent, and my daughter enjoyed herself, especially when the ADC assigned to me reported that one of the party had observed: 'The Ambassador seems a nice enough fellow but what a cute little wife!'

On 14 May 1953 Pearson wrote that the cabinet had approved my transfer to Washington as ambassador, the posting at which I was most anxious to try my hand. The announcement of my appointment to the United States was made on 10 June. Again, the change involved departmental 'musical chairs' as familiar names and faces shifted within the same orbit: Dana Wilgress was to replace me at NATO and the OEEC; Hume Wrong was to leave Washington to take over from Wilgress as undersecretary. Leaving my wife and daughter to spend July in Austria, I said goodbye to my friends and colleagues at NATO and returned to Ottawa for a two-week refresher on US affairs in the department, and a couple of weekends with father and mother up in the Gatineau.

Mr and Mrs William Heeney, ADPH's greatgrandparents

Mr and Mrs Henry Heeney, grandparents of ADPH

ADPH with his parents, Mr and Mrs William Bertal Heeney
(*from a photograph loaned to the Public Archives of Canada*)

Homestead at Danford Corners with Mrs W.B. Heeney on the right

Canon and Mrs W.B. Heeney, 1942

ADPH at Oxford

ADPH called to the Montreal Bar

W.B. Heeney, Mackenzie King, and ADPH at Kingsmere, 1938, with Pat
(*Public Archives of Canada*)

Principal secretary to Mackenzie King,
1939

On the royal tour, 1939

The Canadian delegation at the Paris Peace Conference, 1946: Norman Robertson, Mackenzie King, Brooke Claxton, ADPH

With President John F. Kennedy in the White House, 1962
(*Associated Press*)

The International Joint Commission, 1970. Standing are commissioners
B. Beaupré, E.W. Weber, A.D. Scott, and C.R. Ross. Christian B. Herter, Jr,
American chairman, and ADPH, Canadian chairman, are seated.

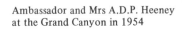
Ambassador and Mrs A.D.P. Heeney
at the Grand Canyon in 1954

Son Brian at graduation
from Trinity College, 1954

Daughter Patricia, 1970

10

Washington

My first four years in Washington began against an international background which was relatively relaxed. In Europe the forces of the North Atlantic Treaty Organization were regarded as sufficient at least to delay a conventional Soviet attack by several weeks. Stalin had died and the Soviet leaders were obviously having difficulty among themselves and with their satellites. Eisenhower had been able to fulfil his promise of bringing an end to the fighting in Korea and only a couple of days before I reached the United States capital at the end of July 1953, the armistice agreement had finally been initialled. Altogether international tension had perceptibly lessened.

Over the three years which followed, however, a number of issues arose which raised the temperature of relations between Canada and the United States. Early in 1954 Dulles made his 'massive retaliation' speech indicating that the United States would retaliate with considerable force and even use atomic bombs anywhere in the world. From that time on Ottawa was almost continuously anxious about the course of United States foreign policy; indeed, similar anxieties characterized US relations with the other allied capitals. And although the Indo-Chinese armistice came about in 1954, the intransigent attitude of the United States on the offshore islands and relations with Peking led to recurrent periods of difficulty which affected Canada. Furthermore, not long after my arrival in Washington the activities of Senator William Jenner and Senator Joseph McCarthy began to capture the headlines, evoking increasing Canadian criticism of United States behaviour. In fact security problems remained high on the embassy's agenda during the whole of my first tour in Washington. There were also recurring problems of economic policy: United States sales of agricultural surpluses were cutting into traditional Canadian markets, and a general rise in protectionism which found expression in a stumbling retreat from the liberal trade policies of the previous administration served to frustrate the development of a dependable US market for Canadian goods. Finally, the Suez crisis in 1956 led to the most severe breach in British-

United States relations since before the war. Inevitably this was of direct concern to Canada for it clouded and impaired our own dealings with both London and Washington.

My official arrival in Washington took place on 30 July 1953 and was rather grand. I travelled in a special RCAF aircraft because it was thought more appropriate that the Canadian ambassador arrive by such identifiably national means rather than by commercial flight. Assembled to greet me on arrival was a considerable company headed by Sidney Pierce, who had been chargé d'affaires since Wrong's departure (his own appointment as ambassador to Brazil was imminent), and by the head of our joint staff, another old friend Admiral Harry de Wolfe. At that time, too, it was the custom that the heads of all Commonwealth missions should turn out to welcome a new colleague. So it was that an acquaintance of some years, Roger Makins, the British ambassador, was in the line. He was to become a highly valued colleague and one of our closest friends in the next three years. The other diplomats were new to me as were most of the Canadian newspaper, radio, and television people except for James M. Minnifie, at that time senior CBC representative in Washington.

This was my first experience of how desperately hot and humid it could be on the tarmac of the National Airport. I was relieved to hear later that it was the hottest day of the summer and the hottest 30 July on record. But it was not only my heavy British flannel suit and the excitement of the moment that induced the soon-to-be-familiar light-headedness that always took me by surprise. After uttering a few bromides into the microphone for the benefit of the considerable number of newsmen assembled for the occasion, I was whisked off to the embassy where I was greeted for the first time by the butler, Henry, and where I lunched and talked with a number of my senior officers who explained to me the nature of my program over the next few days.

It had been arranged that I should call on the Secretary of State that afternoon after meeting John Farr Simmons, the chief of protocol. At this first official encounter I found John Foster Dulles pleasant, even jovial. He was, as usual, pressed for time yet he was relaxed and easy and talked of his island in Lake Ontario while our photographs were being taken. As I took my leave he said he was looking forward to our association.

The next few days were occupied in meeting my staff at the chancery, making my first contacts with de Wolfe's considerable Navy, Army, and Air Force group, and attending my first meetings at the State Department. At one of the latter Dulles, without a note, made a competent and comprehensive presentation to a group of ambassadors representing the 'fighting' countries in Korea. He seemed then to be very conciliatory, very sensitive to the views of the allied countries, and altogether more 'pleasant' than I had expected.

My call upon the President to present my credentials took place rather earlier in the day than was normal because the President was leaving Washington immediately after the funeral that day of Senator Robert Taft. At 9:15, on the morning of 2 August 1953 I arrived at the White House with the Chief of Protocol. We were promptly ushered into Eisenhower's study, and despite the formal wording of the document which, as an ambassador of the Queen of Canada, I conveyed to the President, there was little ceremony. I had known Eisenhower briefly in Paris when he was supreme commander of NATO forces, and this morning, entirely relaxed and at ease, he talked vigorously and enthusiastically about NATO. The council, he thought, should have more authority. We should be able to toss problems to the council and have it come up with the solutions. At present, he complained, the permanent members were only a group of national representatives, each of whom had to refer back to his government for instructions: 'They will not make decisions.' I did not think it the time to suggest that the national representatives would find themselves in deep trouble, the Americans most of all, if they started to take decisions without authority from their government; they could exercise the authority their governments conferred on them and no more.

Eisenhower went on to ask about wartime Canadian friends. How were Foulkes and Simonds and Claxton, and that man who 'hated everybody' in the Mediterranean, Andy McNaughton? He obviously liked McNaughton, and his recollections of the Canadian general were marked by real affection. He recalled with some amusement the occasion upon which McNaughton had called upon him in North Africa, furious with Montgomery for trying to prevent him from visiting the Canadian troops in Sicily. McNaughton, as commander of the Canadian Army, did not propose to stand for conduct of that sort. If necessary he would withdraw the Canadians from their combination with the British. 'Remember General,' Eisenhower said he had to remind him, 'we are fighting the Germans, not the British!'

Eisenhower impressed me on that occasion and throughout my time in Washington by the same qualities of informality, sincerity, and humour which had earned him his reputation as an allied commander. It was not difficult to discern the reasons for the immense personal popularity which had carried him into the White House on a wave of public enthusiasm. In my dealings with him he was uniformly friendly and I was never in doubt that his sentiments of friendship for Canada and Canadians were as sincere as their expression was unaffected.

Later in the morning, still finding it a little hard to believe that I was the Canadian ambassador, I went to my first official function with my new colleagues of the diplomatic corps, the state funeral for Senator Taft in the rotunda of the Capitol. It was to me a strange and soulless occasion climaxed by the verbose funeral oration delivered by Senator John Bricker standing in the centre of the sombre inner group: the sorrowing widow, the rockbound sons, the Vice-President, General MacArthur, and the legendary Joe Martin, long-time Republican minority leader in the House of Representatives.

As a diplomatic post, Washington is unique. Not only is it the capital of the country with which Canada has by far the most numerous contacts, private as well as governmental, it is also the 'super power,' the policies and actions of which affect in a major degree the course of events in our whole world. For these reasons Canadian representation in the United States is larger than in any other country. The embassy and the joint staff during my years comprised, in all ranks, something over four hundred people. In addition we had consuls general and consulates in a number of the principal cities in the United States, and our military element included a considerable number of officers integrated into various US formations and performing liaison duties throughout the country. For these outside offices as well as for the administration of the embassy itself and the conduct of the joint staff the ambassador had general responsibility.

The life of a diplomat in Washington, that beautiful, exciting, and troubled capital, is strenuous and demanding. Very soon I became obsessed by the feeling that whatever happened, in the White House, in the vast government departments and agencies, in Congress, in the press, on television, even at the endless dinners and receptions, might somehow affect my country's interests and influence the course of world events. Washington is an especially exacting post for Canadian representatives, not only because of the massive and intricate mutual involvement of the two countries but also because of traditional sensitivities so easily aroused in our dealings with 'Uncle Sam.' Nevertheless, if the official and personal demands were heavy and anxiety never far from the surface, I was quick to recognize that the rewards were equally great. From the professional point of view, Washington must surely be the most stimulating post on the globe. As one crowded day followed another I became increasingly aware that I was in the midst of history in the making. And one of my wise and experienced senior colleagues remarked when I paid my first call on him: 'Washington is good theatre. There is only one catch. The curtain never goes down!' Nor did it take me long to appreciate the other large compensation of service in the United States, namely the traditional hospitality and friendliness of Americans. Finally, there was satisfaction in the physical beauty of much of the city and its surroundings and in the agreeable nature of our own situation at the embassy. All of these things were genuine benefits to set against the costs of the busy and worrying life which we had to lead.

As the months went by my acquaintance with United States officials was gradually extended. By good fortune my colleague of Paris days, Livingston

Merchant, had become assistant secretary for Europe, a position which at that time included responsibility for all the Commonwealth countries as well; I quickly renewed my friendship with him. I made it my business to meet Bedell Smith, the undersecretary of state, clearly one of the key officials of the administration not only because of his position but also because of the special confidence the President had in him as his trusted wartime chief of staff. I already knew Freeman ('Doc') Matthews, deputy undersecretary for political affairs, and liked him; we were colleagues many years later on the Canada-United States Permanent Joint Board on Defence.

Of the senior officials at the State Department, one of the most engaging and at the same time most exasperating was the Assistant Secretary for the Far East, Walter Robertson. A political supporter of Eisenhower from Richmond, Virginia, Robertson was by choice and background an enthusiastic anglophile, constitutionally prejudiced in favour of everything British. Fortunately for us he seemed to include Canadians in this category and was most friendly with me from the outset. Nevertheless, his deep emotions combined with his inflexibility to the point of irrationality on Korea in particular and the Far East in general made him an exceedingly difficult person with whom to deal. During my first call on him my mention of Korea let loose a flood of argument and emotion. Without bitterness or sarcasm but with determination and obvious sincerity, Robertson made the extreme United States case against any political conversations with 'the other side' – and at such length that it was difficult for me to get away at the end of forty minutes. Finally he ended by assuring me that, despite our differences of viewpoint, he knew that we would get along well. And we did.

Before autumn set in, I was able to have a good chat about my mission with Pearson in New York where he was heading our delegation to the United Nations. Since he had been a most successful ambassador in Washington I was glad of the chance to hear his ideas on how the embassy could best be conducted. As it turned out, his views corresponded very closely to the tentative conclusions I had reached in the months since my arrival. He told me first that I should 'get and keep close to the new crowd' – the Eisenhower administration – because Canadian contacts hitherto had been almost wholly with the Democrats, and a new ambassador had a good opportunity of cultivating a new administration. The leads which I had already made should be followed up. Second, he said that my colleagues of the diplomatic corps should have low priority in the allotment of my time and energy as compared with US officials and members of Congress. Certain ambassadors, however, of whom he mentioned two or three, could be helpful. Third, Congress should be given more attention than had customarily been the Canadian practice. This was a delicate and slow process; better to get to know a few individual congressmen and senators well than to cast the net wider in large functions. Fourth, the press was important and should be unostentatiously cultivated; I should have a good press officer. Fifth, I should travel and speak as much as possible; visits to our offices outside Washington could be the occasions for addressing appropriate groups. Finally, on the social side, his experience had been that small and well chosen lunches and dinners were more effective than big affairs.

That autumn I met Sherman Adams, 'the Governor' as he was universally known although his formal title was 'Assistant to the President.' His personal qualities as well as his official position gave him much influence with the President in those first years, and his assistance and friendship were to prove of great help to me in the resolution of a number of issues which arose during Eisenhower's first term. Until the wretched business of the vicuna coat, Adams was the central focus of authority in the White House.[1] He was a New Hampshire Yankee of wide political experience, blunt, shrewd, and devoted to the interests of his country and his party. Fortunately for us he knew Canada well and had close Canadian friends. At our first meeting he chuckled with me about his friendship with Jack Pickersgill and some of the incidents of the Newfoundland campaign. Adams introduced me that day to a number of his colleagues, including Vice President Nixon.

Another friend we had at the cabinet level was the Secretary of the Treasury, George Humphrey. He had a close knowledge of Canadian business, in part through his personal friendship with C.D. Howe of whom he spoke as 'the best man in any government anywhere,' but I never thought that he had much understanding of Canadian political attitudes. Humphrey told me on one occasion that he'd rather do business with the Canadian government than with any United States government and with any Canadian official rather than with Tom Dewey, sometime governor of New York state. When I tried to draw him out on external commercial policy, he agreed that this topic would be high on the agenda in the months ahead. So far as Canada and the United States were concerned 'our interests were the same'; he saw no reason for any

1 The vicuna coat incident was an affair, the nature of which has become all too familiar to the Canadian public over the past decade. While he was a junior member of the New Hampshire legislature, Sherman Adams had become friends with Bernard Goldfine, a local textile manufacturer. In 1958 the Goldfine enterprises came under the scrutiny of the House Committee on Interstate and Foreign Commerce. It was discovered that Goldfine, whose relations with the Federal Trade Commission and the Securities and Exchange Commission the Committee was investigating, had over a period of three years paid certain of Adams' hotel bills to the sum of $2,000. As well, Goldfine had given him a vicuna coat which was manufactured in his mill. The committee alleged that because of his friendship with Adams, the two regulatory commissions had given Goldfine preferred treatment. Although he was not legally obliged to, Adams appeared before the committee to clear his name. Rumour persisted, however, and two months later he was forced to resign.

barriers. When I observed that, politically, reciprocity or continental free trade would be at best a dubious element in any Canadian party's platform since it would inevitably be related in the public mind to the maintenance of our political independence, I got the impression that Humphrey did not know what I was talking about. In this he was not by any means unique, for among the highest of US officials I was to encounter all too frequently reference to 'the sameness of our two peoples and the perfect relations which existed between us.'

About the same time I had a long conversation with Vice President Nixon at a dinner for Sean Lemass at the Irish embassy. He also made a pleasant impression on me. As we talked about Asia which he was then about to visit, his manner was serious and unaffected. There was no evidence of the qualities of priggishness and self-absorption I had been led to expect. Before we parted he urged me to visit California soon, and when there to speak in San Francisco at the Commonwealth Club, 'the best platform on the Pacific Coast.' To my surprise a few days later I received a call from the secretary of that organization to the effect that Nixon had telephoned them and, at his suggestion, they were inviting me to make my first appearance on the west coast at a luncheon which they would be happy to arrange. I accepted and in the spring of 1954 spoke to the Commonwealth Club in San Francisco.

Another cabinet member who became a close friend was the Attorney General, Herbert Brownell. When I sought to call on him for the first time he responded by inviting me to lunch at the Justice Department with all of the senior officials including his deputy, William Rogers. I spent an interesting noon hour and came away with the impression of an attractive, keen team, full of a sense of mission to clean up the Justice Department. As I remember, all except one were new men. This departmental introduction was to prove valuable in the succeeding years. Further, Brownell's friendship was not only personally enjoyable; he also assisted in my attempts to interpret the inner workings of the United States administration, its policies, and attitudes.

While I was making my official calls and getting to know the members of the cast with which I would have to perform, my wife was organizing the residence and its personnel, surely the most delicate of all our embassy's departments, for failure in this area can seriously diminish the effectiveness of one's mission. We began to have people in to lunch and dinner and to provide the numerous 'receptions' called for by the presence of miscellaneous Canadian delegations, official and otherwise, whose frequent descents upon Washington became a regular feature of our existence. My wife also began to develop her interest in the arts and those concerned in their promotion in the capital.

My first considerable encounter with Bedell Smith in November of my first year was occasioned by the preparations for the President's forthcoming visit to Ottawa and diplomatically was close to a disaster. Without assigning any reason he had asked me to call on him alone in advance of a scheduled meeting in the State Department with a small group of senior Canadian and United States officials on current defence questions of concern to both countries. When I presented myself in his office Smith, without any preliminaries, put to me a problem which had raised temperatures in both Ottawa and Washington concerning the personal security arrangements when the President was in Canada. He reminded me that United States law made the Treasury responsible for the person of the President. This put the US authorities in the difficult position of having to insist on having Treasury agents around Eisenhower at all times wherever he was. 'Even in Canada,' he added, where admittedly the RCMP were at least as efficient and reliable as their own people. He hoped I would appreciate his position and that I would persuade Ottawa to make the necessary minimum adjustments in the arrangements. 'Just because we have to be childish about this business, that's no reason why you should be,' he concluded. The US law, however stupid, would have to be complied with.

To this last proposition, I took immediate exception. After all we were talking about a situation in Canada, not in the United States. In the circumstances he described I could give him no assurance whatsoever that we would modify our attitude. It would be hard to explain to the Canadian people, or to anybody else for that matter, why overweight and middle-aged US agents should replace the RCMP in the personal protection of our guest. Other heads of state, including our own sovereign, had found the RCMP altogether satisfactory. Smith was furious. Picking up the papers on his desk he rose to his feet exclaiming that, if he'd thought that I'd have responded 'as a diplomat' he would never have raised the matter with me. He stalked in silence from his office and into the next room where our colleagues were already assembled for the meeting. Taking the head of the table, he called the meeting to order. Then he pulled a pad towards him and immediately started to write. As I began to cool down myself in the chair next to him, I speculated as to what was coming from this odd and violent man. Some sort of ultimatum perhaps? Would the President's whole Canadian visit be cancelled? He had, indeed, threatened to do just that if we were unable to comply with US security requirements. The Undersecretary completed his writing, folded the paper, and passed it to me. Opening it I found a short, simple, unaffected apology. From that moment we were friends and I know of no one with whom my dealings in Washington were more satisfactory or fruitful officially and personally. His departure from the inner councils of the State Department and the White House constituted a grave loss to the administration.

Before the year 1953 was out I had the first of a number of unpleasant experiences on the subject of 'security' in relation to congressional proceedings.

A subcommittee of the Judiciary Committee of the Senate, under the chairmanship of the ineffable Senator Jenner, had decided that they wanted to import Igor Gouzenko to appear before them. Their request to the Canadian authorities for his appearance was in typically abrupt and provocative language. This stimulated considerable public resentment in Canada and strong criticism of the US Senate and administration for making such a demand. My interventions with the State Department were vigorous and categorical. Bedell Smith was frank and sympathetic, referring to the Senator in terms I myself would not have employed outside the Canadian embassy. But he was virtually powerless and the State Department had little influence. Ultimately, however, this incident passed off without too much difficulty; Gouzenko was interviewed in Canada by Jenner and a colleague under the presiding presence of the Canadian Chief Justice. But not before the *New York Times* had referred to the 'rift' between Canada and the United States and the 'deterioration' in Canada-US relations.

The President and Mrs Eisenhower made an official visit to Ottawa in the middle of November 1953. In accordance with custom my wife and I accompanied the presidential party. During the trip we had the opportunity to chat privately with both the President and his wife. Eisenhower again talked about NATO developments in which he continued to have great interest, and he emphasized the necessity for early European integration 'in the interests of all of us.' He spoke of the importance of having an objective, uninstructed North Atlantic Council, though without any indication that he yet appreciated the constitutional and practical difficulties involved. Once more he was friendly, frank, and articulate. He gave the impression of being a good man who was anxious to do what was right but who felt he had few bearings to lead him through a largely unmarked jungle.

The Eisenhower visit to Canada was a popular success. As usual, the arrangements made in the Canadian capital were admirable, and the President responded to his welcome with warmth and grace on all occasions. For his address to Parliament he had a good text and delivered it firmly and with conviction. In the cabinet afterwards he was informal and forthright on every subject and left a most favourable impression upon the Canadian ministers. On that occasion, however, I was struck once again by the reluctance of Canadian ministers to take issue with a celebrated guest or to raise embarrassing questions. I had no doubt that Eisenhower and his advisers left with the impression that Canada had no problems of any consequence with the United States; it was left to the officials on other occasions to say the unpleasant things.

That December we attended our first formal diplomatic dinner at the White House. My wife was seated at the extreme end of one section of the forked table, with no one on her left, no one within normal conversational distance opposite, and of all people the Soviet Ambassador, G.N. Zaroubin, on her right. The situation had a certain piquancy as Zaroubin had been in charge of the Soviet embassy in Ottawa throughout the Gouzenko affair. During the course of the long and rather spiritless meal, I noticed that my wife and the ambassador were in animated conversation and that Zaroubin was smiling and even laughing from time to time. This aroused my curiosity as to the subject of the conversation. As it turned out, my wife had got Zaroubin going on the ballet, of which he was very fond. I was caught between the wife of the Rumanian Minister, who spoke no English and little French, and the wife of the Minister of Lithuania with whom I found little in common. I concentrated, therefore, on the standard and uninspired food and the passable drink. After dinner we were quickly whisked into a drawing room and exposed to a reasonably good musical program. When it was over the President got quickly to his feet and we all filed out. It was hardly a lively evening, and I wondered afterwards what purpose was served by such purely diplomatic occasions.

An interesting feature of Washington's social pattern was the survival, in lingering elegance, of a number of prominent residents. Known irreverently as the 'cave dwellers,' they continued the capital's tradition of measured hospitality. One of the more celebrated was Mrs Truxton Beale whose Decatur House on Lafayette Square has now become a national monument. My wife and I were included in some of her occasions such as her gaslit parties after the annual White House reception for the diplomats. I must say they lived up to the reputation Mrs Beale had acquired over the years. Other social notables of an agreeable and out-of-the-ordinary sort were the remarkable Mr and Mrs Robert Woods Bliss of Dumbarton Oaks fame, Mrs Virginia Bacon whose parties for visiting celebrities were conducted with great style, and Mrs Nicholas Longworth, the daughter of Teddy Roosevelt and the widow of a speaker of the House, who could be counted upon to provide some of the best conversation in the capital.

The social whirl continued. In a long gossipy letter that I wrote to my predecessor Hume Wrong, who was mortally ill and who died just a month later, I tried to put together for his Christmas entertainment a series of unconnected and unimportant items:

This morning December 17th, is apparently regarded by the local residents as *very* cold, which means that it froze last night and that today's temperature is hovering around the freezing point. For my money, it is a lovely day, bright and crisp, so that I allowed myself an extra five minutes' walk from the house and circled round by the Shoreham Hotel and down Connecticut (this involves thirty minutes as opposed to the twenty minutes which it takes me to walk down Massachusetts). There is hardly a leaf left on the trees in Rock Creek

Park. We can see the windows of the Shoreham from our bedroom (which as you may have heard, is the room that you unselfishly used to give to your distinguished – and sometimes undistinguished – guests). And I could see the top of the Embassy from the far side of the Connecticut Bridge when I crossed ...

Outside of the office, the social and diplomatic whirl has me pretty dizzy at the moment. Many of the occasions are, of course, great fun and very stimulating. Others are pretty much of a bore, as you so well remember. But it is the constant absence from one's own board (I might also equally accurately add 'bed') that seems to develop a special kind of fatigue, at least in me.

Then after referring to a large and elaborate dinner dance which my wife and I had attended a night or two before in Anderson House I went on:

Never I think in my life have I been to such a lush (not to say vulgar) affair. The Davies (our hosts) had transported a considerable proportion of their gold plate and other finery, and the tables set for dinner on the second floor were positively creaking under the weight of immense gold candelabra and bon bon dishes and other evidences of (no doubt perfectly legitimate) looting in various parts of the world. The display of flowers and their exotic variety – orchids, camelias, white roses, and God knows what else – gave the curious impression of an overloaded greenhouse. Peggy and I, as the third ambassadonial couple ... were seated at the 'white' table (meaning white orchids of course!). There were so much flora and other junk piled on top of the lace table cloth that I only got occasional glimpses of any of my fellow diners except for those with whom I was immediately seated.[2]

Later in the same letter, continued the next day, I described other more agreeable and profitable social events, including our first dinner at the French embassy which had obviously been great fun. At that time Henri Bonnet was the ambassador, and a very good one he was, while his wife had become one of the best known women in the United States. There was a great deal of talk on that occasion about McCarthy and Jenner in the context of Canada-US relations, on which I commented to Hume Wrong:

How often have you been told that we should stand up to people like Jenner and McCarthy? I was able to boast that although I had only been in the United States for something over three months as Ambassador, no less a journal than the *New York Times* had commented recently that US relations with Canada had not been in as bad a way since 1812![3]

---

2 ADPH to Hume Wrong, 17 December 1953.
3 *Ibid.,* 18 December 1953.

The death of Hume Wrong at the beginning of 1954 was a personal loss to many of us who had been his friends as well as his colleagues. This was especially true for Pearson whose friendship with Wrong extended back to their days at the University of Toronto. And it was Pearson who had to find a successor in the undersecretaryship, where Wrong's tenure had been so tragically brief. After a careful canvass of the ablest remaining officers within the department, Pearson's choice for the succession fell on Jules Léger.

From New Year's day 1954 the weeks succeeded one another more and more quickly. In and out of the office my ambassadorial life pursued its course. My contacts with the East Block, with the Ottawa hierarchy, were all that I could have asked. Pearson seemed to trust me. In addition to communication by teletype, he used to telephone me frequently, and from time to time we met in one of the two capitals or in New York during UN sessions. I felt that we were on a frank and confident basis in our dealings. Whenever I went back to Ottawa I saw the Prime Minister and brought him up to date on our affairs with the United States.

One of the areas which Pearson had suggested that I cultivate somewhat more than had been customary was the congressional one. The relations of an ambassador in Washington to Congress are inevitably tricky. In law they do not exist, for the ambassador is accredited to one element in a severely divided government, namely the executive, and the legislature is jealous of its independence. Yet senators and congressmen are essential parts of the nervous, spinning life of the capital where political talk is continuous and uninhibited. Consequently, in his encounters with legislators it is sometimes difficult for the ambassador to maintain the measure of reserve which the Constitution imposes and which is supposed to be one of the essential qualities of the diplomatic profession.

Indeed, relatively early in my time in Washington, I could not forbear from exchanging words with a certain member of the Senate. The occasion was a dinner at the South African embassy and the person whom I encountered and with whom I permitted myself to exchange words was Senator Bourke Blakemore Hickenlooper. As my wife and I were on the threshold of the embassy we observed a car stuck in the snow in the driveway, its wheels churning. I was able to assist its harried driver on his forward course, only to find on entering the embassy that, unknown to me, I had come to the rescue of the Senator from Iowa. I am not sure, however, that he recognized me as his good Samaritan. In the course of dinner conversation, across the bosom of the hostess, Hickenlooper launched into an attack on the United Nations as 'futile'; the organization had 'let the United States down' over Korea. Furthermore, he went on, the allies of the United States who were doing only five per cent of the job, had stopped the United States from going beyond the Yalu. Nor could the UN do anything in Europe. Finally, and this was what really set me off, 'the Canadians, like the British perhaps, were prepared to fight to the last American.' To me, Hickenlooper's outburst seemed an incredible and depressing burlesque of an isolationist US senator at the time of the first world war. I frankly enjoyed allowing my temperature to rise and made a reply in kind. I was still new on the job.

For an ambassador to intervene directly with a member of either House of the Congress is a delicate, risky undertaking which may easily backfire; the legislative branch is traditionally resentful of anything approaching foreign interference or attempted pressure. Near the beginning of my mission, I remember one of my more experienced diplomatic colleagues advising me on the subject. He told me that he deliberately included in his social occasions senators and congressmen who, because of their committee assignments, seniority, or for other reasons, were influential in matters of concern to his country. Over the course of his considerable time in Washington, he boasted, this technique had been successful in preventing congressional action which could have seriously affected the commerce of his country. A few months later I was still reflecting on this advice when a tariff change which this gentleman had sought to frustrate by his hospitable attentions was enacted.

My own experience led me to conclude that direct recourse to congressional friends should be reserved for the most critical situations in which no practical alternative was available. Indeed, I recall only one occasion upon which I felt justified in going directly, and literally, to 'the Hill.' I had learned one morning of the imminent threat that one of the recurrent bills to authorize further diversion of Great Lakes water at Chicago would be adopted by the Senate within a matter of hours. This was something that Canada, with the support of the State Department, had resisted successfully over the years. What to do? The State Department had done its best but was impotent. I drove post-haste to the Hill. Once there, a couple of discreet telephone calls from a friendly senator brought me quickly into the presence of the majority leader. I explained the basis of Canadian opposition to further diversions at Chicago, and within minutes the crisis was avoided. The bill, he assured me, would not pass. The majority leader was Lyndon B. Johnson.

Another of Pearson's admonitions had been that I should travel and 'make speeches.' Over my first term I certainly complied with this direction. One of my first efforts was at the Oxford-Cambridge boat race dinner, an annual affair in Washington which brings together a surprising number of Oxford and Cambridge graduates of different generations. To my horror, on arrival I found that I was to speak between Dean Acheson and Felix Frankfurter, two of the most formidable after-dinner speakers in the country. The consequence was to reduce me to a relatively brief and banal effort. The performances of Ache-

son, an honorary graduate of Oxford, and Frankfurter, a former George East-
man visiting professor at Oxford and an honorary member of the Balliol Common Room, were characteristically brilliant, the former including, however, a
number of caustic essays into current politics that I found strange for such an
occasion. Seven years later I was in a similar situation when I was invited to
address the annual Harvard dinner at a time when Harvard men were conspicuous in the seats of power. On that occasion, at the last moment, I was brack-
eted with Kenneth Galbraith and spoke immediately after a sparkling performance by that self-confident celebrity. The fact that President Kennedy, who
was expected, did not turn up was only partial solace. I had been upstaged again.

As time went on I went further afield and spoke to a variety of audiences
on many different occasions, not so much in Washington where there was little chance of conversion and too much competition, but in other cities across
the country. Often I would base our travels (most times my wife accompanied
me) upon our consuls general and consulates. This served the double purpose
of making Canada known and, at the same time, gaining knowledge myself of
the conditions in which our representatives operated. My notes indicate that
between the time of our arrival and May 1956, I travelled to twenty states
and spoke in no less than sixteen of them. It was a relief to get away from
Washington and a pleasure to travel and to meet people in other parts of the
country who were uniformly hospitable and obviously less bored with ambassadors than the inhabitants of the capital.

It was the custom for every British ambassador, and many others from the
Commonwealth, to address the prestigious Pilgrims Society of New York. This
I did early in my first term at a luncheon organized in my honour at the Waldorf. I had worked very hard on my text thinking of the distinguished persons
and notable speeches that had preceded me and conscious my words would
appear later in elegant print and receive a wide distribution. When the time
came for me to rise to my feet I found myself rather nervous, but under the
sympathetic chairmanship of John W. Davis I got under way. About half way
through my speech, just as I was reaching a climax, there was a disturbance at
the back of the hall and by stages, the whole audience stood, faced about, and
began to applaud. Edmund Hillary, the New Zealand conqueror of Everest,
had just arrived. My speech ground to a halt. Hurriedly I tabled my notes and
joined in the welcome as Hillary was escorted to the high table. When he had
been settled in his place next to the chairman I was invited to resume my address. But the spirit had gone out of me and I could do no better than to read
lamely the remainder of my text and get the thing over.

I used to make it a practice each year to visit Wall Street where I was entertained rather grandly by principal United States bankers having Canadian interests. To them I would speak of Ottawa's current economic policies and

problems. With few exceptions they were well informed on Canadian financial matters, though much less knowledgeable when it came to understanding our political environment. During these years our consul general in New York played an important role in representing Canada to the US financial community. I was increasingly impressed by the importance of our New York office, especially in the matter of finance, which is of such critical interest to our provincial as well as our national governments, to say nothing of private citizens.

In the spring of 1954 my wife and I made our first extensive sortie from the capital. Beginning with a stop at Denver, Colorado, we then went on to the Pacific coast to visit our consuls general at Seattle, San Francisco, and Los Angeles, winding up in Chicago. At each of these stops we had a carefully planned routine which included calls upon the 'local dignitaries' – mostly governors, mayors, and bishops – receptions, dinners, and of course speeches. In Colorado I made my first contact with the Air Defence Command at Colorado Springs and found that even at that early stage the United States Air Force regarded a unified command essential to continental defence. I also made it a point to visit local universities and colleges wherever possible and to have some contact with the students. Our consuls arranged for me to meet, as well, local publishers and editors.

Our first visit to Los Angeles was great fun. Apart from the routine events admirably arranged by Leslie Chance, our consul general there, we had a day in Hollywood. In the morning we visited Walt Disney and his studios, in the afternoon the Warner Brothers. The contrast was striking. The Disney outfit was enthusiastic, creative, excited, and exciting, wholly involved in the creation and carrying out of their complicated, patient process of animation. The lunch at Warner Brothers, 'hosted' by Jack Warner, was a production in itself. Guided by an elegant and self-possessed chef de protocol, a large company, including half a dozen of Warner's leading stars, among them Doris Day and John Wayne, proceeded in to a lunch of regal proportions and quality. Our subsequent visit to the back lot seemed a crude and massive letdown after Disney.

One of the built-in features of the life of Canadian ambassadors in Washington is the frequent visits by 'official' guests from Ottawa. The extent and variety of Canadian involvement in the United States combine with proximity to make movement between the two capitals both possible and convenient for ministers and officials. This is helpful in every way and contributes materially to the conduct of relations on a business-like basis. For my wife and me such visits were among the happier features of our diplomatic role in Washington. Prime ministers, ministers, and senior officials came and went; in the process, in our role as hosts, we were able to arrange many occasions of pleasure and profit.

The Governor General made a formal state visit in 1954, the arrangements for which took a good deal of planning with the White House and the State Department not only because of the formal character of the program, but also because of the meticulousness of Vincent Massey himself. We had managed to secure for him an invitation to address Congress and he sent me a copy of the draft of his proposed speech, asking for my comments. I was not very happy about it, especially as there was a good deal in it calculated to confuse Americans as to the relationship between the Commonwealth, the United Kingdom, and Canada. There were also, I thought, many too many references to Britain, for example a mention of Brooks' Club, which which would mean nothing to his audience. I managed to obtain minimal changes but it was a delicate operation, and the reference to Brooks' stayed in. On the whole, however, the visit was a great success. Massey conducted himself with dignity and his infallible sense of theatre stood him in good stead. The Americans went all out to greet him with treatment accorded a chief of state, and his own deportment, even when the heavens opened at the District ceremony, was impeccably royal. His speech to Congress was delivered to perfection, the manner almost, if not altogether, making up for what I regarded as the weakness of the substance.

The dinner we gave at the embassy in the name of the Governor General provided us with our only opportunity to receive President and Mrs Eisenhower. The evening turned out to be a huge success, despite the scores of secret service men and District police who seemed everywhere, and despite what my wife thought was the worst meal we had served at the embassy up to that time. We had, in fact, returned home only shortly before Massey's arrival to find the cook gone. The President, however, didn't seem to notice any culinary lapses. He was engaged throughout dinner in animated talk with my wife, a conversation devoted to pictures, books, and golf. Eisenhower told her of the relaxation and pleasure he took from his morning painting sessions and showed interest in the Canadian pictures we had on the embassy walls. My wife introduced him to *The Reason Why* by Cecil Woodham-Smith and next morning he sent round to her *The Fremantle Diary* with a typically generous note: 'I think that you and your husband will like it. I hope so. Your party was delightful – both Mrs Eisenhower and I had a wonderful time.'

Not long after Massey's visit I met the President again at the formal signing of the long delayed St Lawrence Seaway bill. It was a pure publicity stunt, the senators and congressmen pressing round the President straining for the spotlight. Senator Alexander Wiley and Representative George Dondero, the principal sponsors of the bill, managed to get into the front row where, somewhat to my embarrassment (because the Canadian government and people were then having second thoughts about a seaway under joint auspices), I was invited to join them for the inevitable press photographs. By this time the President was calling me 'Heeney' instead of 'Mr Ambassador,' which I took to be evidence of progress.

I never really got used to the peculiarly heavy Washington weather. One very hot and humid morning in early summer, with the other Commonwealth ambassadors, I went out early to the airport to meet Winston Churchill and Anthony Eden who were arriving for talks with Eisenhower and Dulles. Without warning, minutes after we had been lined up on the tarmac, I felt the airport spinning about me. Then, as from a great distance, I heard the voice of my British colleague's wife who was next to me in line: 'Take the Canadian Ambassador out.' I was removed from the scene in time to avoid disgrace. It was a most unpleasant experience, particularly as Canadian reporters having observed my precipitate departure included a reference to my 'collapse' in the stories they wired home. The fact is I never learned to like or do more than barely support the Washington climate, though from that early occasion the judicious use of salt kept me upright.

That was the summer of the greatest difficulty between our two major allies on the subject of China and the offshore islands. The British seemed unable to get the depth of American antagonism into their heads. When I called on Bedell Smith in mid-September 1954 to say goodbye to him on his retirement as undersecretary, he kept me for over an hour of exceptionally interesting and frank talk. He told me that there was a difference of opinion within the administration as to whether or not the Chinese communists would launch an attack on Quemoy. The advice of the Central Intelligence Agency Director, Allen Dulles, based on the latest intelligence, was that the Chinese did not intend to attack the island. But Bedell could not agree. There was every reason why they would want to take the island and, in his opinion, it would be a perfectly feasible operation. Any foggy night, powered junks could get across the two-and-one-half miles of water intervening. And why should the Chinese allow an island off their principal port in that area to remain in nationalist hands? The loss of a hundred thousand men would be an acceptable sacrifice to Peking in return for such a prize. Notwithstanding such anxieties I had the impression, and reported to Ottawa, that neither Bedell Smith nor the President favoured full-scale intervention by the United States if an attack did take place. On the other hand an invasion of Formosa would be quite another matter.

At that time the Americans were feeling depressed about the collapse of the European Defence Community and, on that account, were irritated with the French; so much so that the concept of a 'peripheral' strategy omitting the French altogether had gained a good many adherents especially in the Pentagon. When I called on Smith that September he had developed this concept at some length. Heaving France out involved building an immense allied beach-head based on the Low Countries and reaching down through western Germany into Austria. To the northeast this beach-head would be supported by the British Isles and to the southwest and south by the Iberian Peninsula and North Africa. Thence, the allied line would run north and east through Turkey and on to Iran and Iraq, the two last of which he said were soon to fall into the Turkey-Pakistan 'axis.' Such a strategy, Bedell pointed out, would enable the allies to make use of the soft underbelly beloved of Churchill.

The whole idea of a NATO without France seemed to me fantastic and dangerous in the extreme, and I told Bedell so. I asked him if he thought it would be feasible to establish and maintain forces on northern and southern lines, facing west, with the whole vast area and population and resources of metropolitan France at our backs and neutral at the best. I had always assumed that France was geographically essential to any defence of western Europe. It seemed to me nonsense to talk of a coalition to be consolidated and maintained by the simultaneous embrace of Germany and desertion of France. Bedell replied that, while we would all prefer to have France with us, the joint chiefs of staff questioned that nation's political reliability. In the light of the history of the past ten or fifteen years, could he honestly advise them that their fears were without foundation? We might indeed have to do without France as we had before. In that event some alternative strategy would have to be adopted before it was too late. Furthermore, he went on, it was to be noted that the United States was retaining the principle of fighting as far to the east as possible even if they had to do so without France. Some years later General de Gaulle did pull France out of NATO.

Late in September 1954 the new Canadian Minister of Finance, Walter Harris, came to Washington for the annual meeting of the International Monetary Fund and the Commonwealth finance ministers. He stayed at the embassy and, by a combination of early planning and good luck, I had managed to get the Chancellor of the Exchequer, R.A. Butler, the US Secretary of the Treasury, George Humphrey, and the chief members of the financial hierarchies of the US and Britain for dinner at the embassy. While Harris reluctantly accepted the wisdom or necessity of such an occasion, it was perfectly obvious that he really did not enjoy it. He thought little or nothing of the social comings and goings that characterize such annual international gatherings and was impatient to get back to Ottawa where he said that he had many important things to do. In fact he refused to stay for the Commonwealth finance ministers meeting and left Washington after the fund sessions, to the discomfiture of the Canadian delegation and the unconcealed irritation of Butler. At that time there was a sharp difference of opinion between our Department of Finance and the British Treasury over sterling, and the failure of Butler and Harris to get along together complicated the situation. Harris was not prepared

to go to a Commonwealth 'family party' based on a leave-it-to-father principle. So he returned to Ottawa and that was that. It was a disappointing experience for an ambassador who had carefully set the stage upon which personal relations between his own Minister and the British authorities, as well
as those of the United States, could develop.[4]

As November 1954 approached political columnists and speculators were
preoccupied with the number one question: Would Eisenhower run for a second term? I remember being at the White House for lunch during a Washington visit by C.D. Howe where there was a good deal of chaff about what the
President would do next. Eisenhower said that whatever job he did take on,
he didn't want it to be a 'big one – about the size of one of George Humphrey's duck blinds.' But by then there was little doubt what the Republicans
wanted Eisenhower to do. My friend Brownell told me that I could 'put this
in my book': the President would not only run again; he would be re-elected.
The party was counting on him as their greatest asset and their hope for a successful election in 1956. They were making the strongest possible appeal to
Eisenhower's conscience.

At the beginning of 1955 Canada-United States relations were in good
shape. McCarthyism, one of the sources of ill-feeling in Canada, had declined.
The Korean war had ended and there were signs that President Eisenhower
was firmly in control and willing to exercise his great personal authority at
home and abroad. As the year matured, however, our problems with Washington multiplied.

By the end of January the situation in the Formosa Straits had become
difficult, and I was frequently in the State Department expressing Canadian
concern and urging caution. There was increasing confidence in the President's
own desire for peaceful solutions and some evidence that he was willing to
exercise his authority to that end. Nevertheless the attitudes of such men as
Senator William Knowland and Walter Robertson, the assistant secretary in
charge of Far East affairs, and the rest of the extreme Chaing Kai-shek group
caused concern. On 28 January I saw Dulles and Merchant to explain the
Canadian position on Formosa and to make it clear that we would have to
oppose openly any extreme US policies. Dulles called Pearson directly on the

4 In his personal journal for 30 September 1954 ADPH comments on Harris and Butler
   and their relationship on this visit: 'Harris and Butler have not hit it off at all – at least
   H. has clearly found B. patronizing and less than frank with him ... Harris himself is
   not bitter or harsh, but it will take a good deal now to re-establish Butler in his opinion. This might have quite serious implications for Canada-U.K. relations. Harris himself is quiet, modest, and pretty impressive. His temperate habits and distaste for parties has, of course, been an element in his reactions here. I confess that tonight I found
   Butler sublimely self-confident and pretty patronizing – in the nicest possible way. I
   am very disappointed in him.' Editor's note.

telephone in my presence and gave him a long and reassuring statement on their intentions. In my subsequent assessment for Ottawa, I said that, while I was convinced that the United States would fight for Formosa, I thought their present actions were calculated primarily to prevent the communist Chinese concluding the reverse; at the same time they were conscious of the danger that Chou En-lai might conclude that the United States was set on aggression.

Later the same spring I accompanied John Foster Dulles to Ottawa for an 'official' visit. As we were passing over the eastern end of Lake Ontario, he became quite excited; looking down, he was able to identify his beloved Duck Island amid the ice floes of Sackets Harbor. In such moments he brightened and became attractive and, as I was to learn later, he was capable, in such moods, of exercising considerable personal charm. But Dulles was generally unattractive in manner and, on most occasions, lacking or spurning any of the social graces. He often appeared strange, almost gauche, a difficult dinner companion with little 'give' and no charm. Yet he was certainly intelligent and gave every evidence of commitment to his country's interests as he saw them. I sensed in him a strong personal ambition to be a 'great secretary of state,' but I could not believe then, nor indeed did I later when I got to know him better, that he had the quality of greatness.

Although that visit to Ottawa was marred for me by worry over father's condition, I was able to participate fully in the round of meetings and other occasions which had been arranged for Dulles' visit. A lunch was given by the Prime Minister at which the conversation was kept in motion by Pearson or by St Laurent himself. Dulles seemed tired and distant. Dinner at the US embassy was much the same. Yet in the cabinet Dulles made a good presentation of the United States position in the Pacific and undoubtedly impressed the Canadian ministers. Unfortunately there was no time for real discussion, although Pearson did indicate our different view. When the visit was over I felt that it had done some good, chiefly in giving our ministers an understanding of the aims and motives of the United States. At a final lunch at the Country Club Dulles surprised me again and a great many other people by his witty post-prandial remarks referring to his own 'off-shore island' in Lake Ontario.

During the Dulles visit I had a good chat with C.D. Howe whom I wanted to consult especially about the speech that I was to make in Texas on the subject of energy and continental oil policy. After approving of the line that I proposed to take, he went on to speak nostalgically of the old days when Mackenzie King was at the head of the cabinet table. He and St Laurent were now of another generation from that of their present colleagues. There were for him too many new faces around the table now. Walter Harris was not like Abbott; Pearson was the right man for the leadership, but 'he'd have to raise a finger himself.'

Soon after my return to Washington my wife and I set out on our first visit to the southern states. Based on a visit to our Consul General at New Orleans, which was our first stop, we went on to Dallas, Fort Worth, Austin, and Houston. At each of our stops there were the inevitable speeches, receptions, and dinners; and we were impressed by the welcome given us by the warm and hospitable inhabitants. My attempts to strengthen the historic link between Louisiana and New France were, I fear, something less than spectacular. When I began my speech in New Orleans in French I received great applause. When I continued, however, my large audience went rapidly blank, so that I quickly switched back to English.

Both my wife and I were fascinated by Texas. It was all that we had heard and read about and a great deal more. As we approached Dallas I thought the country had much the aspect of southern Manitoba. The morning was clear and cool and the farm buildings were covered with white frost. On the other hand, the standard of luxury in hotels and banks and in clubs and private homes was quite beyond our previous experience. I remember being told that the banking chamber in the Republic National Bank of Dallas, where we were entertained at lunch, had more square feet of gold leaf than any other building in the world. The table on that occasion was adorned by no less than five hundred American Beauty roses – our Consul General had counted them during my 'few words' after the luncheon. The Baptist Church, the current pastor told me, was the biggest in the world with a 'plant' covering more than a city block, built at a cost of some six million dollars.

At Fort Worth we were put up in the 'Will Rogers Memorial Suite' of the Texas Hotel as guests of Sid Richardson, the oil tycoon who had large interests in Canada. The first evening we dined at our host's home amid a collection of modern French impressionist and post-impressionist paintings. Our hostess had not only collected the art which surrounded us but personally 'managed' no less than six ranches and owned and flew her own airplane. She was a genuine Texan with a rather tough and brassy exterior who on acquaintance proved to be a warm, pleasant, active, and intelligent person.

On the way back to the hotel that evening I expressed to Richardson our concern in Canada at the restrictionist tendencies of United States policy particularly in regard to oil and gas. Next morning he telephoned me to say that he had 'got to thinking' about what I had said. His view of what Canada should do in the circumstances was simply that of 'a country boy down here' but one who was interested in Canada and very friendly (if he were then in his twenties he would settle in Canada because of the bright future he felt that we had). What he would do if he were in our position would be to accept the fact that, in the short term, the prospects for substantial increases in exports to the United States market were not good. The United States industry was not going to accept the present sharply limited levels of production from its own wells and at the same time have foreign sources pouring thousands of barrels a day into the American market. In our situation, he would adopt a policy of protecting and exploiting our own domestic market. Richardson's views were shared by most people I talked to in Texas, and by that time I had talked to scores of oil men and people interested in oil and gas. They had no desire to exclude Canadian imports as such, but the US market had to be restricted. That was all there was to it.

Soon after our return to Washington from Texas, Mother telephoned me from Ottawa to say that father, whose health had been failing, was near the end. Shortly afterwards on the same afternoon, Colonel Pat Edwards called to say that father had just died. My sister and I flew to Ottawa immediately, where we found Mother extraordinarily calm and confident. On Saturday, 16 April 1955 the funeral service was conducted at Christ Church Cathedral by the Bishop of Ottawa, Ernest Reed, who had been a dear and good friend of all of us from Winnipeg days. Then the familiar journey to Danford and the little church on the hill which was filled with local friends and relatives who had known father and the family over the years. Finally the coffin was lowered into the sandy soil under the pine tree in view of God's Hill and the scene father had known from his birth; indeed, his grave was within a few hundred yards of where he had been born. For me it was a moving occasion but not a tragic one. Nevertheless with father's disappearance there ended too a distinct period in my own life, one in which he had to the end played such an important part.

Washington spring moved quickly into summer. The hours at the Chancery were long, the crises in US relations recurred and were dealt with one way or another, and the extracurricular activities went on without cease. During that summer of 1955 we dined at the Swedish embassy in honour of the Secretary of State and his wife, and I observed for the first time how Dulles' manner constituted a barrier to communication. Dag Hammarskjold was at the dinner that night, and with him Dulles was at his most abrupt, his most gauche. As a result Hammarskjold's English suffered, and he became increasingly difficult to understand. There was no meeting of these minds and no sympathy between them. After Dulles had left, Hammarskjold was quite openly critical of him in talking to me. He spoke bitterly of Dulles preventing him from getting direct access to the President, and the 'colouring' given all his communications to Eisenhower by the Lodge-Robertson-Dulles screen through which they had to pass. It was a depressing incident altogether, but one I was to see virtually repeated in the same surroundings a year later.

That summer I was back to Ottawa on several occasions partly to discuss with the Prime Minister, Pearson, and others the proposal which was then developing rapidly that I should return to take over the chairmanship of the

Civil Service Commission. These trips also served the purpose of refreshing my understanding of government views on relations with the United States. At that time Walter Gordon was in the process of developing the basis for a new national policy in his Royal Commission on Canada's Economic Prospects. In April he had taken away from his post at the embassy my friend and chief economic adviser, Douglas Lepan, to be his director of studies. I noted after a talk with Gordon that under his leadership the commission seemed to be moving in a distinctly protectionist direction. He appeared to be convinced that, for the maintenance of employment and an acceptable standard of living, Canada would have to desert simon pure liberal doctrines. It was on the whole, I thought, a healthy bias so long as it did not go too far. At any rate I found it preferable to the customs union ideas which had been current in Ottawa some years before.

On these journeys back to Ottawa I saw Pearson and had good talks with him. His views were always fresh and imaginative and he seemed to me then to be at the height of his international usefulness.[5] It was good to get back to Canada and to be with old friends like Pearson, Jack Pickersgill, R.B. Bryce, and the others who had been my colleagues during the war and postwar years. I knew I would be happy when the time came for me to return. In fact two years after my arrival in Washington I was looking forward with satisfaction to accepting a posting home in a year or eighteen months' time. The Washington experience was stimulating, fascinating, and challenging. But I would be happy to merge into my native background leaving behind the prominence, the luxury, and the generally exotic elements of ambassadorial life.

In the autumn of 1955 the Canada-US ministerial Joint Committee on Trade and Economic Affairs met in Ottawa. This session involved Dulles, secretary of state, Humphrey, secretary of the treasury, Benson, secretary of agriculture, and Weeks, secretary of commerce, on the United States side, and on our side Pearson, secretary of state for external affairs, Howe, minister of trade and commerce, Harris, minister of finance, and Gardiner, minister of agriculture. Once more a meeting with the American top brass went all too smoothly. The US secretaries were frank enough and made it abundantly clear that we could hope for nothing from them beyond what US domestic political realities would permit: 'the facts of life' approach. That implied at the best proceeding at a snail's pace towards the admittedly desirable objectives of a

---

5 In his personal journal for 24 September 1955, on one of these visits to Ottawa, ADPH wrote of Pearson: 'LBP is in fair form, and full of his impending trip to Russia of course. He continues to be constantly vigorous and interested and stimulating and cheerful. But over the years, although consistently friendly and satisfactory with me, he is increasingly impersonal – a deep one whose secret self very few, if any, can know.' Editor's note.

more liberal trading and payments system between the two countries. Once more, on the other hand, the Canadian ministers were relatively silent and reserved on the issues of chief current concern to us so that I felt the American members were entitled to conclude from this reticence that Canadians had no worries about their economic relations with the United States. Howe, it was true, was categorical in his condemnation of United States wheat sales methods; but otherwise the Canadian ministers made no effective rebuttal of the US views. In such circumstances officials were virtually powerless. I could not help feeling that we would have to stand up for ourselves and show some independence in these meetings if we were not to be dragged round by the Americans, friendly as they were.

My own personal treatment in Washington by the US cabinet members could not have been better. On one occasion, for example, I remember the Secretary of Defence and Mrs Wilson including my wife and me, the only foreigners present, at a dinner where the talk among the Americans was almost embarrassingly frank. This attitude on the part of US officials towards Canadian representatives was personally pleasant but often embarrassing professionally. Their informal, friendly manner did not mean they would yield one inch to our persuasions simply because they liked us and found us agreeable, especially when Humphrey's 'facts of life' pressed them in another direction. Perhaps, in a curious way, they were too friendly, personally, for Canada's real good. It would be less comfortable for us but perhaps more effective towards the achievement of our ends if we were treated otherwise by US officials. We should aim at their regarding Canadian reactions as realities, facts of their political lives with which they must reckon. This might require Canadian representatives, at the ministerial as well as diplomatic level, to have less pleasant encounters with their American opposite numbers.

It was in the same autumn of 1955 that Dulles put the Canadian embassy in Washington on the carpet. The occasion was a Canadian proposal, a 'package deal,' to add sixteen new members to the UN, including Outer Mongolia. British and United States delegates at the UN had offered considerable resistance to this effort. As I learned later, Dulles himself first heard of the Canadian proposal when driving to the Madrid airport, and then from a Spanish foreign office official! By that time the Canadian initiative had reached an advanced stage. He was furious and, when he arrived back in Washington next day, he summoned the Canadian minister in charge, George Glazebrook (I was in New York), and hauled him over the coals over our failure to consult the United States. In fact, we had consulted the State Department, but the senior US officer who had been informed of the Canadian intentions had apparently failed to get his message through to the Secretary of State or had thought it of insufficient importance to bother him. In any event, poor Glazebrook was unable to get a word in to respond to the Secretary's outburst. Dulles should have known of our intentions long before; but admittedly the inclusion of Outer Mongolia, especially without notice, was hard for him to swallow. I am bound to add that later, when Dulles was told of our previous approach to the State Department, he had the grace to apologize for his outrageous conduct. In fact as soon as I got back to Washington from New York, I called on the State Department and made clear our irritation at the way he had treated Glazebrook.

The consequences of the UN incident over the package deal on new members were favourable to the Canadian position. The handsome apology from the Secretary of State was an unusual dividend. In the weeks that followed, although the United States remained critical of our position, my contacts with senior officials at the State Department were notably warm. Just before Christmas I made another call on the Secretary himself. He was most cordial. Though he still believed we were wrong on the issue, our fully documented rebuttal to his complaint regarding consultation had had its effect. At any rate officials of the State Department became sensitive to the need for consultation with Canada, making it clear that we could expect a good deal more attention in the future. My own guess, subsequently confirmed, was that it was unlikely that this sensitivity to Canadian views would endure.

The year 1956 began with no indication that it was to be critical in relations between the United States and Britain. The Middle East was uneasy, certainly, but then it usually was. We had no reason to suspect that before the year was out the British and their French allies would have committed themselves to a course of military action which would produce between our two great allies the most painful episode of the generation.

Before the first month of the year had gone by we dined again at the Dulles' to find the Secretary in excellent form, attentive to his guests, and quite charming. Again I thought what a pity that he could not show this side of himself on his public occasions. He took me aside after dinner to tell me that the President was going to propose that our Prime Minister and the Mexican President visit him before long in some suitable out-of-town location. Eisenhower had no particular purpose in mind, just 'wanted to have neighbours in.' Indeed he did just this at White Sulphur Springs in the month of March. Dulles went on to talk about disarmament (he thought that 'our side' must get out of the position of always raising well-based technological objections) and the peaceful uses of atomic energy (where he was not too hopeful).

In February I was up in Ottawa again to see the department. The Governor General invited me 'to stay,' and Government House under Massey proved both elegant and comfortable. I had a good opportunity to see our first Canadian Governor General in the environment which suited him so well and which he enjoyed so much. I had a long talk with Pearson whom I thought not entirely comfortable in a ministry which seemed no longer to have the cohesion of earlier days. Once more, however, I felt in my bones that he would stick it out. There was no doubt that he had private longings for release as the shadow of having to stand for the leadership, with all that that involved, became deeper. If that were to come he hoped that he would be offered the post unopposed as he shrank from the sort of personal competition which other candidacies would involve. On that same visit I saw the Prime Minister. He said he had no enthusiasm for Eisenhower's proposed meeting with the Mexicans though he would go. He spoke very nicely of my performance in Washington, said that 'they' felt confident with me there; 'the succession would be a problem.'

That spring I headed the Canadian delegation to the twelve-nation negotiations in Washington to prepare a draft statute for an international atomic energy agency. It was an interesting experience and it resulted in the establishment of the present agency in Vienna. In the course of the discussions I remember having a good deal more trouble with Percy Spender, my Australian colleague, than with the representatives of the Soviet Union, the chief of whom was my old friend Zaroubin.

The White Sulphur Springs 'conference' took place at the end of March. It was a strange affair related by the cynics directly to the publicity which was beginning to build up for the Republican campaign. Before we took off for the meeting I was able to gather a group in the embassy for conversation with my Minister, including some of the best US journalists, among them Walter Lippman and James Reston. The journalists expressed serious concern over Eisenhower's almost total insulation from 'outside' information. The conference began on Monday, 26 March in the garish surroundings of the Green Briar Hotel, which must be one of the largest enclosed acreages of bad taste in the world. That evening we dined with the President who as usual was friendly and relaxed. Although he appeared in good health physically, he seemed to be living in the past as he related stories of Marshal Zhukov and the last months of the war. St Laurent, on the other hand, was weary and withdrawn, both then and throughout the entire meeting. This threw the principal burden for Canadian participation on Pearson who, despite the silence of his chief, handled the situation with his usual skill.

The tripartite meetings the next morning in the President's sitting room were hardly notable. Dulles made an able tour d'horizon which was followed by a bright commentary by Pearson. It seemed to me that one of the American motives for the meeting was the desire to impress upon the Mexicans the danger of communist subversion in the hemisphere. If so, they did not get much help from us; nor indeed do I think they made much impression upon the President of Mexico. During the two days of the conference we came to realize that the US administration had hardened further in its attitude towards Peking. A year before, it had seemed faintly possible that the United States would move gradually towards recognition or at least acceptance of communist China, despite Walter Robertson and the other hard-liners. But at White Sulphur Springs the President himself put an end to any such speculation by stating that he would never recognize men 'with blood on their hands.'

St Laurent came up to the embassy for a brief visit on his way home. He was gracious as always, but seemed almost suddenly to have become an old man. He had none of the accustomed sparkle in his black eyes, and any response seemed an effort. My own feeling was that he was bone tired and worried deeply about the present and the future. I then realized how very difficult things were for Pearson.

In the House of Commons in Ottawa the disastrous pipeline debate was moving to a climax. The government was losing control of the conduct of affairs. The Prime Minister, more withdrawn than ever, seemed to be listless, to have lost all desire to lead. It was a wretched time for Pearson. Small wonder that he was strongly tempted to take the secretary generalship of NATO which the British and others were urging on him. When he came to Washington in late March, however, Pearson soon sloughed off his political fatigue. It was obvious then that he recoiled from many of the petty aspects of public life. That Sunday he went off with Roger Makins to a ball game, his favourite form of relaxation.

At the end of August 1956, after one of the best family holidays at Danford, I left sultry Washington for the University of Rochester to speak, along with Livingston Merchant, then US ambassador in Canada, to the university's Canada-US conference. As always I had good talks with Merchant upon the affairs of our two countries. He then thought that for the immediate future there were three things likely to cause friction. First, the Columbia Basin and all questions about the use of water to which this development would give rise. The second was China. He had chosen quite deliberately to make it the subject of his first public speech in Canada. Evidently he was considerably apprehensive about what Ottawa intended to do about recognition and UN membership. The third topic of potential continuing trouble lay in our economic-commercial relations. He felt that US companies could do many things to take the edge off Canadian nationalistic criticism and I encouraged him in his intention to carry this message back to his fellow countrymen.

That autumn my wife and I visited Louisville, Kentucky, for the opening of an exhibit of Canadian 'non-representational' paintings. We managed to coincide with the President speaking in Lexington that same evening and with Billy Graham who was conducting a crusade in the city. Nevertheless there was a fair turnout at the Art Gallery. We were royally entertained and as on certain other similar occasions observed that 'the Queen of England' was dragged into the conversation a good deal, not excluding the grace at dinner pronounced by an affected little 'English' parson. The 'members opening' at the gallery was a strange affair consisting for the most part of elderly men and women unalterably opposed to anyone and anything after Constable. In fact so many people asked me to 'explain' the pictures that, to my wife's horror, I scrapped my prepared speech and tried my hand at a somewhat simplified exposition of abstract art.

That October I paid a visit to the headquarters of the US Air Forces Strategic Air Command at Omaha, Nebraska, where my host was the legendary General Curtis Lemay. Arriving with senior members of my joint staff in an unimpressive RCAF Dakota (I had insisted on Canadian transport), I was greeted by a guard of honour, ruffles, national anthems, and the works. Lemay met me at the ramp and 'hosted' a dinner in my honour that evening where he made a speech which left no doubt as to his own concept of the SAC mission and of his capability to carry it out. In fact I was sure that one of the reasons for the warmth of my welcome was that the United States at that period wanted permission to establish tanker bases in Canada which would provide a ten-fold increase in the range of their B-47s and a four hour saving on operations. The briefings were slanted that way and there was little question of the value they set upon a northern facility.

As always a closer association with the nuclear striking arm of the United States posed political problems for Canada. Once more we were encountering the issue of effective participation in the ultimate decision to use these weapons. I thought perhaps this current request for tanker facilities might give us opportunity to clarify and re-emphasize our right to hear and be heard and the political necessity for our doing so. The practical implications and the working out of this proposition were difficult. I myself saw no way to avoid co-operation in this matter if we were to participate in the joint defence of the continent. Subsequently the facilities were permitted.

That autumn I had word from the Prime Minister that he wanted me to take over the Civil Service Commission early in the New Year. Pearson had agreed that I should go, and over the next several months there was much talk back and forth between Ottawa and Washington about the details of the move. But such administrative matters were soon driven from our minds by developments in the Middle East.

The crisis broke over our heads at the beginning of November. From the beginning the worst feature for Canadians was the shocking strain it imposed first upon the Anglo-United States alliance, second on the Commonwealth, and third upon the North Atlantic community. Before his sudden operation for stomach cancer on 4 November, I had been in close touch with Dulles on the various moves that preceded the fatal British-French decision to move into the canal zone. With Dulles in hospital, Herbert Hoover, the undersecretary, became acting secretary of state. From that time on I was to see him regularly throughout the crisis not because Canada was in any sense a principal (except in the United Nations where Pearson had a primary role), but because of the virtual cessation of communication between Washington and London.

Much has been written about the Suez affair. Much more will be written. For us in the Canadian embassy the most shocking aspect of Eden's decision to deliver the ultimatum to Egypt was that it was taken without any consultation at all with the Commonwealth governments or with the United States. Indeed Roger Makins, the British ambassador, had just left Washington to be replaced by Harold Caccia, then en route by sea to the United States. Makins had been kept entirely in the dark about the Suez plans, as had most senior British officials. Dulles, to the exasperation of Hammarskjold, was devious and, it was felt by many, inconsistent and wobbling.

Pending the arrival of the new British ambassador I was able to act as a kind of go-between, seeing the Acting Secretary frequently and the British Chargé d'affaires, John Coulson, to acquaint him with the United States position as it developed. When poor Caccia finally did arrive the atmosphere was still calculated to discourage even one of such sanguine temperament. He found himself virtually 'in Coventry.' The Secretary, who had returned to the State Department after his operation in remarkably short order, conveyed a message to Caccia that for the present it would be better if they (Dulles and Caccia) were not seen together. 'How then,' Caccia inquired of me, 'am I to fulfil my mission?' The day before Christmas, and in the privacy of the Secretary's home, however, Dulles did see him and stressed the need for 'patience' on the part of the British. They should not expect rapid developments in United States policy. The administration would have to wait and see how the new Congress reacted to Suez and to the United Kingdom's financial troubles. Meantime, events should be allowed to work themselves out. At the same time, Dulles intimated that he wished to remain in close consultation with the British ambassador though it was essential, in the interests of effective co-operation, not to give colour to any suspicion of collusion. Caccia had been disposed, perhaps, to exaggerate Dulles' negative attitude, but I felt sure that he would be reporting in such terms to the Foreign Office. I did what I could to explain the rationale of Dulles' position vis-à-vis Congress, pointing out the real risk involved for any US administration in such circumstances was that they would find themselves too far ahead of congressional opinion. As the year ended there was no doubt that the gap between London and Washington remained wide. I felt it would be some time yet before the old intimacy and confidence could be restored, a sad state of affairs for Canada.

The year 1957 opened with the social and ceremonial activities connected with the second inauguration of Eisenhower. While my wife and I were able to avoid some of the items on the program we were still overwhelmed by the necessary minimum attendances. The inauguration itself, with Eisenhower very serious and severe, went off as planned. The diplomatic corps fought for their cold buffet before the inaugural ceremony. After the event the long and disorganized procession customary on these occasions wound its weary way along Pennsylvania Avenue, one of the final participants being the Wide-Awake Club of Bergen County, New Jersey. My wife and I managed to escape before four pm. Finally the inauguration balls (that at the Armory was attended by some nine thousand people) ground to a halt, and the new administration was in office.

On 16 March 1957 the announcement of my appointment to the Civil Service Commission was made in Ottawa, almost seventeen years to the day since my first permanent Civil Service appointment. We had our first farewell dinner at the British embassy very soon after. The same day I made my last speech as ambassador to the National War College. But our planned departure from Washington was delayed by the repercussions of the Norman case.

On 4 April I was awakened at 7:15 by Bob Farquarharson, my information counsellor, calling me to tell me that that morning Herbert Norman, our ambassador in Cairo, had jumped to his death. There seemed little doubt that the tragedy had resulted from the renewed outrageous and cruel publicity given by the Senate Subcommittee on Internal Security to the old 1951 charges against Norman. Six years previously these accusations of disloyalty had infuriated Canadians who had reacted strongly then against the activities of the committee. This time the senators' activities produced a wave of anti-Americanism in Canada which Pearson told me exceeded anything in his experience. The pre-election tension in Canada intensified the crisis. The opposition could not resist the temptation to turn on him, implying that he and the department had for some sinister reason hidden the Norman case from the public and from Parliament. Memories of the events of 1951 when we had had to cope with the first senatorial airing of this tangled tale came back to me vividly. At that time Pearson had courageously taken the responsibility of expressing in the House full confidence in Norman's loyalty. But it was not possible to produce irrefutable proof. Now, six years later, the same unsubstantiated suspicions cast a dark shadow on the dealings between the two countries.

I took the Norman case up promptly with the State Department from Christian Herter on down (Dulles ironically was on Duck Island). All were sympathetic. Yet they were virtually powerless, themselves primary targets of the Senate red-baiters. Herter, as acting secretary, was direct, honest, intelligent and fair. When on 9 April I presented our angry note threatening to suspend our security exchange arrangements with the United States, Robert Murphy and Burke Elbrick, upon whom I called for the purpose, tried to be helpful. But they admitted frankly to being apprehensive as to the consequence of State Department intervention on the Hill.

On 10 April when I called on the President to say goodbye he raised the issue of security and explained his own position. He expressed himself as genuinely concerned at the deterioration in Canadian-US relations and extended his personal sympathy on the death of Herbert Norman. When I said that Canadian opinion was angry, he said he understood that. Yet he would not openly criticize Jenner and the other senators involved; that, he thought, was just what they wanted. Jenner himself was 'nuts,' but look what had happened to McCarthy. The same fate, he assured me, would eventually overtake Jenner and company. It was not a very satisfactory reaction to my representations; nor could I quite fathom Eisenhower's thinking in the matter. I had hoped for some public condemnation. When I came out of the White House that morning after seeing the President and after a chat with Sherman Adams, I was immediately surrounded by the press, photographers, and television cameras. I left them in no doubt as to the anger of the Canadian people and their stories reflected this view. It was an unnecessary tragedy, the direct result of the most irresponsible senatorial conduct which the administration failed to prevent.

On 26 April I called on Dulles for the last time. He was relaxed, friendly, and in excellent spirits, showing no evidence that he was an overworked man of seventy who had had recent surgery for intestinal cancer. Yet his unpopularity abroad and at home had grown apace. With justice, he was regarded as being singularly rigid and inept. The public image had hardened with the years. Nevertheless I left Washington with a personal liking for him and a respect which was not dispelled by his obstinacy and rudeness. He served his country according to his lights with great industry and devotion. Vain and complicated, often less than frank in his dealings, he could be, and often was, infuriating. Nor did I ever expect him to go out on a limb for Canada, for Pearson or for the ambassador.

On Friday, 9 May 1957, my wife and I crossed the border at Windsor at 5:30 in the afternoon. I was no longer ambassador to the United States. The following day, at midnight, I ceased to be a foreign service officer, and became in fact and in law chairman of the Civil Service Commission of Canada.

11

Canadian horizons
Reform in the Civil Service

My return to Ottawa in the spring of 1957 projected me into the new and very different world of the personnel management of the Civil Service. My interest in the business of public administration and the machinery of government dated from my experience in the Privy Council Office during the periods of war and reconstruction. I was then close to the final stages in the decision-making processes of government, and it became evident to me that the efficiency of management, particularly in personnel administration, left a good deal to be desired. No one in a position to observe the daily course of executive government could fail to be impressed with the vital importance of the relationship between the top professional Civil Service advisers on the one hand, and the ministers of state, especially the prime minister, on the other.

Rumours of an overhaul of the service had been current for some years. Accordingly, in 1954, when it was reported that I was about to be named 'czar' of the Civil Service 'in a drastic shakeup,' the speculation was not wholly without some prophetic content. It was not, however, until the following year that St Laurent asked me if, at the end of my Washington posting, I would be interested in the appointment of chairman of the Civil Service Commission for the specific purposes of reviewing the existing legislative and conventional framework of the service and preparing recommendations to the government for revision and reform. My response to this proposal was favourable.

By 1957 all political parties had committed themselves publicly to Civil Service reform. For the purpose of the inquiry I was to head a brand new commission, untrammelled by traditional methods of operation, the only limitation upon my freedom of choice being the specific undertaking given by St Laurent that one of the three Civil Service commissioners should be a woman and one a French-speaking Canadian. While I was still in Washington, Robert Bryce, the secretary to the cabinet, and I proceeded to select my fellow commissioners. Ruth Addison confirmed the good opinion we had had of her, and we were equally agreed on Paul Pelletier. We easily avoided the various partisan suggestions we had received and which an earlier tradition of patronage might have encouraged had the Prime Minister not given us his full backing. By the middle of March the names of the new commissioners were made public and by that summer all three of us were in office and at work.

For my wife and me it was heartwarming that spring to get back to Ottawa and into our own home. It was frankly a relief to be facing a more Canadian task in the familiar Canadian environment. The two years which followed were full of interest. In the commission I had quickly to accustom myself to a totally new role. Fortunately once again I found myself surrounded by devoted and able people willing and anxious to respond to a new situation which our appearance seemed to afford. All three of us had a great deal to learn. Even the vocabulary was in large part new, for the commission's staff had been infected by much that was at best dubious in the lexicon, as also in the techniques, of modern personnel management.

Concentrated in Ottawa, but with offices across the country, the commission's staff was imbued with its responsibility as the guardians of the inviolable rule that merit alone should be the criterion of appointment and preferment. If many of them cherished and revered excessively the intricacies of the regulatory system which had been built up to maintain the principle and prevent abuse, the motive and origins of their zeal and even their rigidity were not only respectable but admirable. The victory of 1918 over the forces of patronage and the lesser triumphs which studded the record of the commission in the years that followed, constituted a formidable chronicle of battle honours. It was hardly surprising that in the process some of the traditional sins of bureaucracy had developed.

It did not take long for my colleagues and I to identify the central issue. The problem, as we put it later in our report, was 'how to provide the freedom and flexibility required to enable the administrator to do the job and, at the same time, maintain the measure of central control necessary to ensure a career service based on the merit principle and governed by uniform standards.' Defence of ancient victories was not enough to meet the demands of the totally new situation and the burgeoning of the service which had taken place over the preceding forty years. Before long we were labouring to design a total system which, without sacrificing the virtues of the old, would provide the flexibility and simplicity necessary to allow for efficient management. Half a century before, the need was for a Civil Service free from what Sir Robert Borden had called 'the malign influence of patronage.' Barriers to this danger had been erected which were more than sufficient. Without allowing them to be breached it was for us to devise means to enable those who had the responsibility for management to exercise the powers necessary for effective performance.

In addition to responsibility for the inquiry and review committed to us, the commissioners had also to discharge the normal day-to-day task of administering the service. I made a point of visiting all of the commission's regional offices and brought together the chief federal civil servants in all of the major centres to discuss problems of personnel management. I also visited many of the universities which were our principal sources of officer recruitment. These trips in Canada were among the most rewarding of my experiences during those two years in the commission. On the whole, I was impressed by the quality of the people that we had in the government's employ. Of course, there were laggards and incompetents amongst them, as I believe there are in all large organizations, but by and large I was impressed with the attitudes and degree of competence and the enthusiasm I encountered.

As time went on I spoke to organizations of citizens and service clubs about the country. I quoted Adlai Stevenson, 'your public servants serve you right!' I harangued the Rotary Club of Vancouver on 'Canada's Biggest Employer.' I addressed the Canadian Club in Winnipeg on 'Your Civil Service: A National Institution.' I went down to the maritimes and entitled my address in Halifax, 'Pride or Prejudice – Canadians Look at their Civil Service.' I discussed the issue with academics in various places and, at Edmonton, addressed the Canadian Political Science Association on 'Civil Service Reform, 1958.' As my experience grew I found myself becoming more and more evangelical, and my conviction strengthened that in the Civil Service we had an institution of great and virtually unknown potential in the continuing effort to build and maintain a united Canada.

The defeat of the St Laurent government in June 1957, and the assumption of office by the first Conservative government in nearly a quarter of a century, caused some uneasiness among civil servants. In certain quarters it was confidently predicted that there would be drastic changes, that the new ministers would not be long in taking advantage of an opportunity long deferred to deal with the nest of Liberal appointees with which, they were alleged to feel, the departments and agencies of government were thoroughly infested. Others felt, and freely expressed the opinion, that the merit system and the tradition of professionalism were so firmly established in law and custom that there would be little change. Neither extreme view proved accurate. There were mutterings, of course, and a very few instances in which partisan considerations could justly be said to have determined appointments even to senior posts where the government had a free hand, but in general the principles of merit and permanency endured. I believe the experience of the 1957 election and the subsequent change of government proved a healthy and constructive event in the history of the Canadian Public Service.

I myself experienced little anxiety, perhaps rather less than was justified by the circumstances. The three commissioners of the CSC were all recent appointees of the St Laurent government. We might, then, have anticipated some degree of coolness in ministerial quarters, if not a failure of the cooperation required for effective personnel administration. We had, of course, the bulwark of the existing Civil Service legislation behind which to shelter; but, in practice, a suspicious, unsympathetic minister can do much to frustrate the law if he is determined to do so. In addition, where the law offered no protection, namely in the appointment of deputy ministers and other senior officials, there was no legal barrier to patronage but only the sanctions of persuasion and convention. Although we did not fully appreciate the situation at the time, I believe it was an open question among the new ministers in the summer of 1957 whether the American principle would be introduced and radical changes made in the semi-administrative posts or whether the British principle should continue to prevail. Despite some dissatisfaction among politicians, and notwithstanding a few exceptions, the Diefenbaker government confirmed our appointments. Indeed, on 18 December Howard Green, as acting prime minister, defended the senior civil servants against a charge of Liberal partisanship, referring to the 'splendid co-operation' the new government had received from senior officials. He went on to observe that 'it would have been quite impossible for a new government to have taken over the leadership of the country without great upset had it not been for the loyal cooperation given to us by the senior civil servants.'[1]

Earlier than this, I had expressed my own confidence in the intentions of the new government:

Apart from a handful of personal assistants to the new Ministers in the Capital, the Prime Minister and his colleagues [have] contributed the sole, if very important, variant to the familiar picture. Now three months later, the same officers, clerks and employees who served under the previous government, carry on in the same way. And, subject only to normal human wastage, they will still be doing so – a year, five, ten years from now – whatever may happen, meantime, on the national political scene.

Yet, as I went on to point out, there were problems:

Particularly at the top ... for the Deputy Ministers and other senior officials and advisers, there must necessarily be serious adjustments. In the first place there will be the kinds of human adjustments which are involved in any altera-

1 House of Commons, *Debates*, 18 December 1957, p 2515.

tion of close personal relationships, in any sphere. Personalities vary and there will be changes of methods and habits of work. Further, at this high level of government, there will certainly be distinctions in viewpoint between the new government and the old. And, most important of all, there will be new policies and programmes to be administered by the old hands.[2]

There was one celebrated clash of personalities and attitudes which led to the departure of a talented senior deputy minister from the service and his eventual re-emergence into government as a Liberal politician. Gordon Churchill had been given the portfolio of Trade and Commerce; the deputy minister was Mitchell Sharp. Churchill was a vigorous and vocal partisan and one of those who made no secret of his suspicions concerning the willingness and fitness of senior officials appointed by Liberal governments to serve the new government effectively. Sharp, with a western Canadian background, had been in the Civil Service for many years where he rightly enjoyed a reputation for intelligence, ability, and integrity. He had been closely associated with J.L. Ilsley and D.C. Abbott in the Department of Finance and most recently as C.D. Howe's deputy minister of trade and commerce. He was certainly one of the nuclear group upon whom ministers had relied in the formulation as well as in the execution of policy, especially on the economic side.

I had known Sharp well since he came to Ottawa early in the war. His career was that of a professional servant of the state and he wished no other. After the change of government in 1957, I am confident that he intended to devote his talents and his abounding energy to the service in the same way that he had done under previous Liberal administrations. Indeed, a speech he made in Toronto the following year indicated clearly his attachment to the orthodox view of the senior official's non-partisan status.[3] But Churchill's suspicions were too deep and the clash of personalities between the minister and his deputy too bitter to permit any accommodation. It soon became impossible for them to combine effectively in the administration of an important department of state. As chairman of the Civil Service Commission, and as Sharp's friend, I tried to find another suitable post in which he could continue to serve. But to no avail. The damage had been done, and Sharp resigned from the service in regret and depression, going on to an important and lucrative position in industry from which some years later he emerged to embrace a successful political career. Gordon Churchill had created Mitchell Sharp the politician.

2 A.D.P. Heeney, 'Permanence and Progress in the Civil Service.' Address in Montreal, 3 October 1957.

3 Mitchell Sharp, 'Reflections of a Former Civil Servant.' Address in Toronto, 14 November 1955.

With our renewed mandate to review Civil Service legislation and examine the role of the commission in the machinery of government my colleagues and I set out to identify and define the principles which we thought should govern personnel administration in the Public Service in the sixties and to relate them to a legal and conventional regime which the new circumstances seemed to require. In the course of our work we reviewed at some length the United States situation and that prevailing in the United Kingdom. By the late autumn of 1958 our task was completed and just before Christmas we called upon the Prime Minister to present our report.[4]

This is not the place to describe our recommendations in any detail. They were aimed at providing a larger degree of independence in administration, decentralizing much of management, providing common standards throughout the service, and introducing a means of employee participation in pay determination; in fact at bringing the service up to date, and all of this without derogating the merit system. We were reasonably satisfied with the result. Although governments did not choose to implement all our proposals, notably those regarding pay determination, the report nevertheless formed the basis for many, if not most, of the reforms effected in the administration of the service during the Diefenbaker and Pearson administrations.

The Prime Minister received us cordially, although not at length, and listened to our brief exposition of our proposals. Since, to say the least, Diefenbaker was known to have no passion for administrative problems, I was surprised and pleased that as we left he said that he would like to see me again during the next week. I assumed that Diefenbaker intended to reflect upon our recommendations and to discuss with me at greater leisure their legislative and executive implications. It was not to be. In fact, my career as an administrative reformer was about to be rudely interrupted.

As it turned out, however, I again became involved in the process of administrative reform of the Public Service after I returned from my second tour in Washington in 1962. By that time both of the major political parties, and the New Democratic party long before, had committed themselves to the introduction of some form of collective bargaining into the Public Service. The suggestions which the commission had put forward in the report of 1958 involved a form of arbitration for the determination of pay and conditions of service in which the commission itself would have the independent third party role. In the intervening years such a solution had been overtaken by events. All the Public Service associations were by then committed to more radical courses, and there was great and growing dissatisfaction among government

4 *Personnel Administration in the Public Service: Report of the Civil Service Commission of Canada* (Ottawa 1958).

employees generally with the arbitrary and paternalistic system which continued to prevail, especially in the means of determining rates of pay. In these circumstances, Prime Minister Pearson asked me whether I would be willing to head an inquiry to determine what form collective bargaining should take in the Public Service and to recommend the legislative measures which the government might introduce in Parliament to put such a system into effect. This was the genesis of the Preparatory Committee on Collective Bargaining in the Public Service which was set up by the Pearson government in August of 1963. Two years later it produced the document which provided the foundation for the system which was subsequently established by law.[5]

Composed entirely of senior officials having broad administrative experience, the preparatory committee proved to be a practical and flexible alternative to the more cumbrous and costly expedient of a royal commission. Its task was to 'make preparations for the introduction into the Public Service of an appropriate form of collective bargaining and arbitration, and to examine the need for reforms in the systems of classification and pay applying to civil servants and prevailing rate employees.' It was asked to 'consult with employee organizations and other interested parties, and to make recommendations to the Cabinet.' In my years of association with governmental committees and commissions I have not known a body which discharged its function with greater efficiency and despatch. This was due not only to the personnel of the preparatory committee itself, although this was an essential factor, but also to the staff which we were able to assemble both from the Public Service and from outside sources. We were ably assisted by the excellent work of Douglas Love, the secretary of the preparatory committee and director of the staff, Sylvain Cloutier, his associate and successor, and their colleagues. Another important factor in enabling us to produce a coherent report was the procedure which we adopted for consultation with the employees' organizations as well as with consultants and experts from academic life and from labour unions. When our report was submitted to the government in July 1965 and tabled in Parliament, it contained not only a statement of principle but also much of the detail necessary to design a system suitable to Canadian conditions.

The preparatory committee had been directed, in effect, to devise a system of arbitration for the determination of pay and conditions. We recommended that arbitration awards be binding on employees and employee organizations and, subject always to the availability of funds provided by Parliament, on the employer, the government itself. Some of the employee organizations which

5 *Report of the Preparatory Committee on Collective Bargaining in the Public Service* (Ottawa 1965), p 1.

had come before us, although not the majority, opposed arbitration, taking the traditional union attitude that compulsory arbitration was essentially inconsistent with the principles of free collective bargaining. Yet when the report was made public the auspices for its reception on both sides seemed good.

On the subject of strikes, our report contained a passage described a few months later, on the outbreak of a crippling post office strike, as 'famous last words.' After rejecting the idea of a statutory prohibition against strikes in the service our report had gone on: 'Looking at the recent history of the Public Service, we concluded that it would be difficult to justify a prohibition on grounds of demonstrated need.'[6]

The government had set up an ad hoc committee of cabinet to examine the preparatory committee's report and to prepare legislation to place before Parliament. I was asked to work with the cabinet committee along with other officials, and a few months later the Prime Minister introduced the Collective Bargaining Bill into the House of Commons where it received good initial reactions from all parties and was referred to a special parliamentary committee for final study.

In the process of cabinet committee consideration, and in the light of the Post Office strike, the model legislation which accompanied the preparatory committee's report was changed in one important particular. Bargaining agents for the employees were to be given the option of arbitration or, alternatively, the more traditional procedure of conciliation and, with certain limitations, the accompanying right to strike. In the end the associations representing the majority of civil servants chose the former route in spite of prophesies of a number of politicians and labour leaders to the contrary. As yet it is far from clear that this situation will continue, and as time goes on and experience is accumulated I have no doubt that further changes will be made in the model we designed in the preparatory committee.

Altogether I found my experience in this special area of collective bargaining and in the formulation of related measures affecting the Civil Service both enjoyable and rewarding. When the Public Service Staff Relations Act received royal assent on 23 February 1967, we felt that a veritable administrative revolution had been accomplished.

The durability and effectiveness of these reforms have still to be proven and will depend upon the willingness of government and public servants in good faith to make them work. They will depend too upon the quality of the individuals and groups selected and elected on both sides to discharge the various functions contemplated by the new law. Furthermore, it is inevitable that

6 *Ibid.*, p 6.

weaknesses in the system will be uncovered as time goes on and will have to be corrected. Indeed, the process has already begun. Nevertheless, it is possible to say as I write, that in 1966 the Canadian Public Service entered a new era from which not only government employees but the country as a whole stands to gain.

12

Washington reprise

When, with my fellow commissioners of the Civil Service Commission, I called on the Prime Minister on 30 December 1958 to present our report, the embassy in Washington had for three months been operating under a chargé d'affaires. Norman Robertson, who had succeeded me as ambassador in 1957, had been recalled in October 1958 to become undersecretary. In Parliament the opposition had begun to question the government on the succession and a good deal of public criticism of the Prime Minister focused on the delay in the appointment of an ambassador. There had also been the usual rumours as to whom Diefenbaker had in mind.

No suspicion that the Prime Minister wanted to see me on the week following presentation of our report for some purpose unconnected with that report crossed my mind. My wife, on the other hand, when she heard that Diefenbaker had asked me to call on him again, at once concluded that he intended to ask us to return to Washington. As it turned out, this was exactly what he wanted. When we met, he observed that he had given a great deal of thought to the succession to Robertson, although he had as yet consulted no one on the subject. It had been suggested to him that someone from outside the service should be appointed, but he felt otherwise. Furthermore, none of the names which had been mentioned publicly seemed to him to be suitable at this time. Would I be 'willing to return to Washington?' He saw no reason why acceptance of the embassy need interfere with my participation in the parliamentary consideration of the commission's report and in preparation of the legislation which would be based upon it.

I responded quite frankly that I would much prefer to remain where I was. My wife and I enjoyed living in Ottawa; my work with the commission was interesting and much remained to be done there. On the other hand I did not feel that I could refuse if on further reflection the Prime Minister asked me to return. As I had always taken the view that the civil servant did what he was told by the government I could make no other reply. I appreciated the fact that the Prime Minister's proposal constituted an expression of confidence, and for this I was grateful. Finally, if the Prime Minister decided to ask me to go back, I hoped that it would not be for longer than the remainder of the Eisenhower administration. A week after the turn of the year I saw Diefenbaker again. On 8 January 1959 he asked me to come to Sussex Street (he was in bed with a heavy cold) and we talked for more than an hour. He began by saying that he remained of the same mind; the embassy in Washington was the best place for my services; he was in no doubt whatever about that.

Neither my wife nor I was at all anxious to return to our old stand. What we wanted for ourselves was to settle down in Ottawa and live a more normal family life. When Diefenbaker referred to the matter I repeated that I was certainly not seeking the appointment, although I would waive my personal preferences if the government concluded that we should go back. Diefenbaker persisted. He was quite willing to meet our personal convenience as to the date of our removal and our wish not to remain beyond the termination of the Eisenhower administration. However, it was most important that a public announcement be made as soon as possible after the opening of Parliament, which was to be within a few days. I should discuss the dates and details with Sydney Smith, Diefenbaker's secretary of state for external affairs, who had not yet heard of the Prime Minister's intention. So it was settled between us. He phoned Smith upon whom I called immediately, and who gave me a warm welcome back to the department. He agreed with the Prime Minister that the important thing from the government's point of view was to be able to announce my appointment promptly. Dates were secondary. My name would be put before the cabinet and the submission made to the Queen for communication to the White House without any delay. All of this was flattering; but it was very upsetting to our personal plans and hopes.

On 16 January the order-in-council for my reappointment was passed and the announcement was made by the Prime Minister in the House a few days later when the usual formal preliminaries had been fulfilled. Once more we were launched upon a familiar course and the multitudinous and detailed arrangements for our removal from Ottawa and the assumption again of ambassadorial functions in the United States got under way.

In selecting me, the Prime Minister no doubt had in mind stilling the criticism which had arisen in Parliament and in the country over the continued vacancy at the head of our most important embassy. My reappointment would be a safe move. Certainly the opposition could hardly complain, for Pearson himself had first recommended my appointment eight years previously – not that I thought Diefenbaker insincere in his judgment of my suitability for the post. Over the years that followed I had no reason to question his confidence in me. Before I left Ottawa he telephoned me one morning at 8:30 to say that he had just seen a newspaper statement that the Washington embassy had been offered to George Drew, possibly others, before I was appointed. He wanted me to know that there was not 'a scintilla of truth' in such reports, that the appointment had been offered to no one other than myself, either indirectly, directly, or 'even by implication.' He wanted me to know that and that I could tell this to 'anybody I liked.'

My friend and former colleague at the embassy, A.E. Ritchie, had been in charge since Norman Robertson's departure, so that I knew our affairs had been in good hands. In addition to welcoming me back, he and the other officers of the mission had completed efficiently all the arrangements required for my formal reception and takeover. It had been agreed that my appointment should become effective at the beginning of February and that, as soon as possible after that date, I should go to Washington for the presentation of my credentials to the President and for my formal call on the Secretary of State. In fact it did not prove possible for the President to receive me until 2 March.

When I did call on Eisenhower to repeat the performance of 1953, he greeted me warmly. As I reported to the department that afternoon he had every appearance of good health and vigour and was in a relaxed mood, inquiring about my work over the past two years in the Civil Service Commission and commenting from his own experience in personnel selection methods in the United States Army. He made it evident that he was aware of the trading difficulties which existed between our two countries, mentioning specifically oil, lead, and zinc which were then very much to the fore. In such matters, he said, I could count on his administration trying to ease the Canadian difficulties but, as I would know, there were serious problems involved with Congress and local US interests. He referred to pleasant and satisfactory conversations he had had with the Prime Minister and spoke of his forthcoming visit to Canada for the opening of the St Lawrence Seaway. It was clear that he was taking a personal interest in the arrangements for the ceremony at Montreal. Altogether, there was every evidence of warmth and friendliness in his welcome as I formally resumed my mission.

It was a curious experience going back six years later to the familiar surroundings and the same responsibilities. In many ways it was a continuing state of déjà vu. The old Washington friends were generous in their welcome. Our own people at the chancery and in the joint staff had changed but could not have been more helpful. There had, of course, been many developments in the subject matter of our daily work at the embassy since my departure. But the categories of our troubles were mostly the same: joint defence of the continent, trade restrictions by the United States, Canadian anxieties over real or imagined sabre rattling in the Pentagon, and so forth. I felt, however, that there had been a deterioration in the cordiality and mutual confidence between the two governments, largely for reasons which originated north of the border. The excesses of general election oratory had been partly to blame for Canadian suspicions of United States motives. Canadians resented American lack of understanding of our problems and were indignant over certain United States actions which were taken without apparent concern for Canadian interests. The worsening of Canada-US relations was also due to a widespread Canadian ignorance of US institutions and conventions and a lack of appreciation by Canadians of US problems, both domestic and international.

This 'anti-Americanism,' as it was beginning to be called openly, was to dog my diplomatic footsteps throughout my whole second term. It penetrated into the highest quarters in government and into Parliament, the press, and the Canadian people. As the months went by I could not avoid the conclusion that many of my fellow countrymen tended to equate criticism of the United States with Canadian patriotism. In many things Canadians were smug and self-satisfied, convinced that somehow they had managed to combine the best qualities of Britain and America, and perhaps France as well. It was sobering to reflect that our mixed heritage could equally well lead us to embody some of the least attractive characteristics of our triple inheritance. Now, in addition to the chronic difficulties and the familiar problems such as production-sharing and commercial relations, there had developed an atmosphere not of ill-will but of combined asperity and cockiness on our part which I felt would make mutually satisfactory solutions hard to achieve.

The Americans continued, as always, to be personally charming and generous but at the same time officially unpredictable and frightening. Dulles, who by that time was making a gallant and stubborn fight against the cancer which would bring about his death three months later, had received me before I saw the President. It was clear that before long I would be dealing with another Secretary of State. Many of my old friends, including Sherman Adams, had gone from the White House as had Gabriel Hauge, the President's chief economic adviser. While Eisenhower himself seemed reinvigorated, I had the suspicion that he was not really capable of the sustained effort required of his office. At the State Department, too, many of those who were friends and colleagues during my first tour had left, either to return to private life or to posts elsewhere. As the situation in Berlin moved relentlessly towards what seemed certain to be another crisis, I could not help but feel that the western alliance was not in a position to deal firmly with what seemed likely to befall.

On 27 May we buried John Foster Dulles. Courageous, obstinate, industrious to a degree, he was nonetheless awkward and insensitive to the point of genius. In my dealings with him he was almost always satisfactory and fair, and in our personal relations I had even become fond of him. Rightly or wrongly, I suspected that he had had something to do with my return to Washington. His funeral service at the National Cathedral was impressive in its beauty and dignity and in the rank and variety of the official attendance. It was not only a reflection of the power and prestige of the United States; it was also a tribute to the determination and devotion of the dour Secretary and to his courage during those last weeks and months. To see Adenauer and Madame Chaing Kai-shek both solemn in total black standing beside one another, Gromyko and the other world leaders of that generation seated together in the south transept, the President and his family in the nave, with the diplomatic corps in the north transept, each group facing inward towards the bier clothed in the stars and stripes, was a singularly moving spectacle. One seemed to be present at the ceremonial ending of an era.

In June of that year I went on up to Ottawa to visit the department and to have talks with Diefenbaker and Howard Green on the subject of my mission. I was able to run over quickly with the Prime Minister the present state of our affairs with Washington. At that date there were no important outstanding economic issues between the two countries. Indeed I had reached the conclusion that there had been a conscious US decision at a high level to meet our requests whenever possible. Diefenbaker appreciated this. However, he was worried by the number of US requests for defence co-operation. Not all could be dealt with favourably in the way they were put forward. As the Prime Minister was leaving for cabinet I had time only to observe that where such 'requests' were suggestions for action to improve the joint defence of North America, which commended themselves as such to our judgment, surely we should meet them. As I left, I realized that the whole area of defence co-operation was going to be a delicate and difficult one.

Later that same day I saw the Minister, Howard Green, and we went over a good many subjects – Berlin and Germany, the de Gaulle-Adenauer axis, NATO and a number of other current matters. Green referred to the forthcoming visit of the new Secretary of State, Christian Herter, whom he thought a fine person and one that he could trust. Smiling, he said that he was 'beginning to think that, after all, the Americans may be easier to deal with than the British.' I told Green, as I had told the Prime Minister, that I had been increasingly convinced during the last six months or so that a high-level decision had been taken in Washington to meet reasonable Canadian demands. The Americans fully appreciated the value to them of favourable Canadian opinion. They were following Canadian events more closely than in the past and I was conscious of an anxiety in administration quarters as to the courses and policies Canada might follow. I thought it important from the Canadian point of view that Washington should have confidence in Ottawa and vice versa and I was worried about certain expressions of opinion in Canada on the subject of neutralism, the weakening of faith in the western alliance, and relations with the United States.

The Minister was disturbed, as the Prime Minister had been, about the number of defence requests being received from Washington. The Americans, he thought, should not be given all that they asked for. Because of the attitude he had adopted when in opposition and in the recent election campaign, he felt a special responsibility to safeguard Canadian sovereignty.

I assured Green that I understood his political difficulties. But I pressed my view that the military problem was a joint US-Canadian one, and that American 'requests' were suggestions for improvement in our joint defence, not manifestations of foreign interference. Canadian sovereignty, after all, must be protected from the north as well as from the south. I pointed out that in certain quarters he was regarded as prejudiced against the United States, even anti-American. He agreed with me that this impression should be dispelled and that a visit to Washington might help to do this.

I left Ottawa with a real sense of foreboding. Both the Prime Minister and the Minister had been frank in their talks with me. Both had agreed on the importance of good relations with Washington and had expressed respect and good feeling for the American administration and the President in particular. Nevertheless I was anxious about their assessment of Canadian attitudes to the United States. As the months and years went by such anxieties proved to be more than justified.

Personally, the next few months were not very happy ones for me. On 10 October, after a short illness, mother died without pain or any sign of discomfort and, I am sure, with utterly no fear. Two weeks later, 24 October, I flew to Paris with Howard Green and his party for a meeting of our heads of posts in Europe and the Middle East. One morning, shortly after our arrival, I woke with the symptoms of an illness which was to lay me low and affect my vigour of mind and body for many months. Not until the end of the following January was I able to look forward to the return of normal health. In the interim I spent my days and nights under the care of doctors and nurses. Physically the experience was unpleasant and painful, although no more so than many others have had to support. Psychologically it had a strange effect, at times seeming to induce quite strange aberrations, not all fully unpleasant. For some time after I had been certified to return to work, strange indefinite apprehensions would assail me for no apparent reason and I would be subject to anxious fears of no rational origin. While I was in hospital with this kidney ailment and during my convalescence I was naturally concerned with the future of the embassy and my own relationship to it. I believed that I could still manage to discharge my duties, and in accordance with my understanding with the Prime Minister, stay on until the end of the Eisenhower administration, provided that the government were prepared to have me do so within the limitations which my illness had imposed. Both Diefenbaker and Green had been solicitous and kind during my illness and, when I saw them in Ottawa on my next visit, they were anxious that I should continue as ambassador until the end of the Eisenhower era. It was thought possible that afterwards I might succeed General McNaughton as chairman of the Canadian section of the International Joint Commission.

In February 1960 my wife and I attended the Winter Olympics in the strikingly beautiful surroundings of Squaw Valley. For Canadians, the victory of Anne Heggteveit in the women's skiing was thrilling; our skaters in every class were a credit to their country and very popular. Hockey, however, was another story. Our players managed to make themselves singularly unpopular with the spectators from all nations; they, in turn, clearly resented the attitude of the crowd. It was a curious and unpleasant sensation for us to sit in a predominantly American crowd thoroughly hostile to Canadian players not only during the game with the United States, but during that against Sweden and, more astonishing, that with the USSR. At the time I certainly did not blame the boys on the team. They were doing what came naturally, putting into practice the style and tactics of the National Hockey League. I think they were probably as surprised as we were at the result. Nevertheless, the Canadians provided the only lapse in sportmanship I saw in all the games. When I communicated my disappointment at this to the Canadian Press I was severely criticized by the Canadian Amateur Hockey Association. As to the respective merits of the Olympic regime and the rules of the National Hockey League I had, and have, no judgment to make. But as a representative of my country abroad, I left Squaw Valley with absolutely no doubt of the unfavourable image which our brand of hockey was projecting upon the world scene. As one Canadian editor put it 'money could not buy that kind of an audience to look upon Canada with such concentration. But here we were under the spotlight and lousing it up.' Subsequent efforts to improve the situation, largely those of Father Bauer, did much to raise the bearing and conduct of our players, although unhappily their skill did not improve.

In April Howard Green and his wife visited the embassy. He was there with other foreign ministers of the NATO countries and there was little doubt that he enjoyed the visit. Vice President Nixon, who was then beginning to square off with John Kennedy for the November elections, had the ministers and their ambassadors out to his house where he proceeded to give a very able and surprisingly objective analysis of the political situation. As we drove back to the embassy, Green virtually reproached me for not having warned him that Nixon was such an intelligent and fair-minded person. To this I could only reply that not all Americans had horns. A Senate lunch was given in his honour, where his chief mentor and guide was Senator George Aiken of Vermont. The lunch went well enough and Green made an excellent speech, in effect telling his hosts not to worry too much about public criticism of the United States in Canada; they were all politicians and understood what it was sometimes necessary to say in the course of political campaigns. His crowning pleasure was when he and I were introduced by Aiken onto the floor of the Senate and he heard one senator after another praise in fulsome phrases their 'great neighbour to the North' and its foreign minister. Only with great difficulty was I able to restrain him from responding in kind. When I said goodbye to him as he left for Ottawa soon after, I felt that something had been done to dilute if not dissolve his inbred suspicion of Americans and of United States intentions. Alas, although Green's sincerity was never in question, his fundamental attitudes and prejudices remained unchanged.

In early June we had our first visit from the Prime Minister and his wife who came down at the President's invitation to spend an afternoon and evening with him. The White House dinner in the Prime Minister's honour went well and Diefenbaker made a very suitable speech in response to the President's toast to the Queen. The event was only slightly marred by the strange inclusion of two references to the 'republic' of Canada in the speech read by Eisenhower. After their visit I noted in my diary that Diefenbaker did well.

No doubt [he is] an able, shrewd politician – very pleasant with me ... But I am pretty apprehensive about the course of the government in international affairs. Green, the most pleasant of good simple men, is an innocent abroad, and what is more, obstinate and underneath inclined to a sort of *pacific-isolationism*. [Diefenbaker] is much more hard-headed, but ruled ultimately (and quite credibly) by political factors. I can work with them at this distance, but it would be harder in close contact.

Unhappily, in a matter of weeks the friendly atmosphere began to change for the worse. Early in July my holiday at Tadoussac was interrupted by my having to attend a meeting of the Canada-United States ministerial Joint Committee on Defence at the Seigniory Club. This was the meeting at which the Americans first raised with Canadian ministers their proposal for co-operation in an intended economic embargo of Castro's Cuba. This was the meeting from which, despite differences which had developed between the two sides in the course of discussing defence co-operation, the US secretaries departed feeling that they had achieved essential agreement on the delicate question of the use of nuclear weapons. On the matter of the embargo there had been no diplomatic preparation whatever and Canadian ministers reacted coldly. Cuba remained a subject upon which Ottawa and Washington ultimately agreed to differ; until 1962, and the Kennedy-Castro confrontation, the problem of our differing policies could be handled without undue friction. Nuclear arms and North American defence were matters which caused increasing irritation on both sides, largely I believe because of the oversimplification of the issue by the United States and the unwillingness of the Canadian government to make a clearcut decision one way or the other. The meeting was not helped by the crude intervention of one of the United States military advisers whose 'appreciation' of Soviet intentions and of the capabilities of the United States deterrent was to shock Howard Green and confirm his worst suspicions of the malign influence of the Pentagon.

From the time of the Seigniory Club meeting onwards, relations between Ottawa and Washington deteriorated, and by autumn my mission had become more difficult and delicate than at any previous period. When I saw the Prime Minister in Ottawa at the end of August he spoke to me in the gravest terms of the 'anti-Americanism' which was developing in Canada. In his judgment it was worse than at any time in his lifetime or mine. It was growing to the proportions of an 'avalanche.' It was causing him the greatest concern and he would like the President to know his assessment of its gravity, for he was anxious that nothing should be done during the remainder of the Eisenhower administration to exacerbate relations. Diefenbaker told me that he attributed this baleful development to the widespread impression that the United States was 'pushing other people around,' to distrust of the US military and anxiety over the Pentagon's real intentions, to the economic aggressiveness of US interests, and finally to the adverse trading position. Furthermore, Canadians resented the lack of any appreciable notice of Canadian affairs in the US press, radio, and television. American press representatives in Canada were second rate and tended to file only critical pieces on Canada and Canadian policies. Diefenbaker went on to tell me that he based his assessment of Canadian sentiment on his own extensive correspondence and on the opinions of members of parliament. All evidence from these sources pointed to an accumulation of resentment and criticism of the United States which would, he repeated, assume unprecedented proportions. At the next session of Parliament he would probably have to introduce legislation to compel US-owned corporations to disclose financial statements. He hoped that he would not have to initiate other measures aimed at the United States.

Naturally I expressed alarm at all this. I was, of course, aware of differences and criticism in Parliament and in the press. But I had no idea that anti-Americanism had reached such a level in Canada. Generally speaking, economic and commercial relations between the two countries continued to be good. There would, I thought, be no serious difficulty in Washington about restrictive legislation of an economic character such as the Prime Minister had mentioned. The most serious issues in my opinion arose in relation to joint defence where the US was currently worried about our co-operation and puzzled by our hesitancy to go along with such matters as nuclear storage. As the Canadian ambassador in the United States I could not be but disturbed by the Prime Minister's assessment. I regarded the Canadian-US alliance as our most precious international asset, the loss or erosion of which would be tragic for Canada. What could I do on my return to the United States to counteract the developments of which Diefenbaker had been speaking?

The Prime Minister reverted to the topic when I called on him the following day. There would be serious difficulties for the government if it did not take greater account of the widespread anxiety and dissatisfaction felt by Canadians about US nuclear policies and economic aggressiveness. Again there was reference to his correspondence from which he read me substantial excerpts. Many of these were highly emotional and abusive of the United States. He then went on to point to the criticisms in the press and in Parliament, from the official opposition, and from the members of other parties. Many of the critics to whom he referred were advocating a non-committed, even neutralist, policy for Canada. He wanted me to understand and appreciate this outburst of feeling and, further, he wanted the US administration to be aware of it. When I asked whether he wished me to express his estimate of these developments to those in authority in Washington he said certainly.

I repeated that I was not especially concerned about measures in the economic field such as laws requiring disclosure of financial information by American-owned undertakings in Canada or even measures for safeguarding industrial operations in Canada. If I were instructed in advance I anticipated no serious difficulty in explaining such actions in Washington. Our attitudes on joint defence and on the western alliance were much more serious matters. My nightmare was that the buffetings and criticisms of her allies, and what Americans regarded as the failure of support from other nations, would push the United States into a neo-isolationist policy. Recent and prospective technological developments made the concept of 'fortress America' plausible again; the same need for US troops and installations overseas would not endure much longer and a policy of armed isolation for the United States again became feasible. It would be tragic if this came about as a result of the disintegration of the alliance, and doubly so if we had any part in bringing about such a result. Finally, in my twenty-two years of connection with Canada-US affairs, there had never been an administration in Washington which knew more about Canada and Canadian affairs or tried harder to meet Canadian wishes. This was true of the President himself, of the Secretary of State, of the Secretary of the Treasury, and of the principal official involved, Livingston Merchant. In January there would be a new administration in the US capital. Whichever party won we would be confronted by those 'who knew not Joseph.' Inevitably they would be more difficult to deal with.

It had been a rather shattering interview. Nevertheless, as I left, the Prime Minister said that he valued these personal talks with me. He invited me to write him personally and privately when I had had an opportunity to assess the position after my return to Washington.

As Undersecretary of State for Political Affairs, Livingston Merchant was the principal official, aside from the Secretary of State, who dealt with Canada-US relations. Soon after my return to Washington following my talk with the Prime Minister I arranged to meet him privately as a preliminary to seeking an interview with the Secretary of State. I told Merchant fully the substance of what had passed between the Prime Minister and me and that Diefenbaker had asked me to inform US authorities of his grave concern about the situation which had developed in Canadian opinion. I added a number of personal observations. In the first place I said that, despite current critical attitudes, I thought most Canadians assumed that relations between our two countries were basically sound and friendly and would continue to be so. The present discontent seemed to me to arise from two main sources: first, genuine anxiety at the possibility of nuclear war and, in that context, worry, even distrust, over US military intentions; second, the extent to which US interests were acquiring ownership of key sectors of the Canadian economy. There was perhaps little or nothing that the US government could be expected to do about the latter; the process was essentially one of private funds finding their way into attractive investments of one kind and another. Nevertheless this economic 'invasion' had given rise to genuine alarm in Canada and to demands for counter-measures. As to the military threat, Canadians were not alone in criticizing actions and attitudes in the United States which seemed provocative and which tended to increase the likelihood of nuclear disaster. I did not ask Merchant to make any comment immediately upon my message; but I did ask him to speak to the Secretary and to get in touch with me again.

Merchant was evidently impressed and worried that the Prime Minister should have reached the conclusion that I had described. Yet he said he was not entirely surprised because of the reports they had had from their ambassador in Ottawa and from State Department reading of Canadian press comment. Merchant himself took a very serious view of the divergence between Ottawa and Washington. The revival of opposition to present administration policies in the US press and in the Congress was a danger to which recent and current allied attitudes, including Canada's, was contributing materially. There was a real risk of a strong resurgence of isolationist sentiment in the country. Merchant went on to say that he would certainly communicate my message at once to the Secretary of State and I could be quite certain that both Herter and the President would be deeply concerned at the Prime Minister's assessment of current Canadian sentiment. The problem was 'what could be done about it?'

One thing that could be done was to get Green and Herter together while they were both at the United Nations. This meeting was arranged for 20 September. The night before I spent about two hours with Green recounting to him my two conversations with the Prime Minister, commenting so as to illustrate my own estimate of United States policies and intentions, and emphasizing my anxiety as to the grave effects for Canada, the United States, and the Atlantic alliance of further weakening of the Canada-US relationship. I then described to Green my conversation with Merchant. Green listened closely, occasionally interrupting to examine in more detail points which I had raised. He regarded the Prime Minister's estimate of the extent and depth of anti-Americanism in Canada as 'exaggerated'; on the other hand he pointed out that Diefenbaker was very good at appraising public sentiment and had sources which had proved reliable in the past.

We then went on to discuss the defence problem. It was clear that Green's instinctive revulsion from any nuclear involvement was at the base of his own negative attitude. After we had gone into the matter of storage of nuclear weapons in Canada and a current proposal for an exchange of aircraft which was then to the fore, I came back to the general question of principle. I said that my anxiety derived from the fact that we continued publicly to support the principle of joint North American defence but there was or seemed to be a gap between our professions and our performance. Our frequently stated public position was that the US nuclear capability, Strategic Air Command (SAC), was the deterrent upon which we and the rest of the free world depended. Our contribution to joint defence was to the protection of that deterrent. It seemed to follow that we should do what was necessary to maintain the efficiency of our element in the joint defence arrangement. Did this not imply doing what was held to be necessary for the effectiveness of these arrangements including in due course the arming of Canadian forces with nuclear defensive weapons? It seemed to me that the only alternatives to this policy were either to stand aside altogether in some sort of neutralist role or to confine ourselves to supplementary conventional arms and leave the defence of North America to the United States.

Green would not accept this proposition. On the other hand, he insisted he was no neutralist. Only recently in public speeches in British Columbia he had repudiated a policy of neutrality for Canada because 'it would not be in accord with Canadian tradition.' Look at 1914 and 1939. Worse, 'it would be bad for the Canadian character.' He had received a good deal of applause for this sentiment; Canadians were not in any danger of espousing a neutralist attitude. I asked Green whether it would not be politically possible in Canada to launch a spirited public defence of United States policies, at least in terms of the general objectives. Green thought that such an initiative would be very damaging in the present state of Canadian public opinion. At the same time he agreed there had been and remained much that was commendable in US policies and behaviour. When I suggested that perhaps I might undertake myself one or two public speeches in Canada on this theme he was at first rather favourable to the idea. On second thought, however, he felt that I should clear any such proposal with the Prime Minister as it was he who had raised the problem with me.

The following day, at noon, Green called on the Secretary of State at his suite in the Waldorf Towers. Charles Ritchie, our permanent delegate to the United Nations, and I accompanied him; Merchant and Foy Kohler, assistant secretary for European affairs, were with Herter. After some preliminary talk about the UN Assembly, the Secretary raised the subject of Canadian opinion. His reports indicated that among Canadians there was antipathy and antagonism to the United States. If this were accurate, it disturbed him greatly, particularly at a time when the United States was being battered about by those in other parts of the world who did not understand the situation so well. In a kindly, but nevertheless quite pointed fashion, he went on to say that he hoped that Canadian political parties would not enter into a competition in anti-Americanism but that the tendency in that direction would be checked in Canada and by Canadian leaders.

Green responded by saying that he did not think that things were so bad as the Secretary had been led to believe. Certainly there had been and continued to be a good deal of criticism in Canada of the United States and of Americans. This had always been more or less a feature of Canadian life. It was to be attributed to our being a small nation living up against a powerful neighbour and to the resultant fear by Canadians of 'American domination.' After referring to the economic difficulties which he attributed to the extent and nature of private investment rather than to government policy, Green went on to say that he thought that our current difficulties arose from another cause. Canadians 'were not nearly so worried about the Russians' as were Americans. This was an important distinction between public opinion in the two countries as witness the fact that both parties in the current US election campaign were harping on defence while in Canada there was no support at all for increased military expenditure. Further, he continued, the US administration's estimate of the actual risk of war seemed to be much gloomier than that of the Canadian government. Canadians felt that nuclear war must be avoided. The US Defence Department was thought by some to be courting disaster by provocative words and actions. Canada had no desire to become another nuclear power, and the government was opposed to the spread of nuclear military capabilities. His own personal view was that Canadian forces should not be armed with nuclear weapons, and he thought this was a position widely shared in Canada. Notwithstanding these difficulties the Minister agreed that relations between the two countries were 'as friendly and intimate' as it was possible for those of any two countries to be. He found that he could talk to US officials as he could talk to those of no other country, 'even the British.' Canadians assumed close friendly relations with Americans as a matter of course. He would not worry too much about reports of anti-Americanism in Canada. The Conservatives had criticized the Liberal government when in power for not standing up to the United States; now that the Liberals were in opposition they were taking the same tack.

As we left the Secretary said to me that after he returned to Washington he would like to discuss the whole subject with me privately. It was clear that Merchant had passed on to him the substance of our own conversation.

As Green and I walked away he expressed the greatest admiration for Herter. He was a fine man 'completely the opposite of what Canadians expect Americans to be.' 'What a pity,' he went on, 'that there were not other Americans like him!' The Prime Minister had exaggerated the situation. It was not as bad as that. He should not have got 'these people all upset.' Before I left New York Green again expressed his concern that the Americans were 'all upset.' When, after speaking to Merchant, I was in a position to leave him in no doubt that the Secretary of State was indeed genuinely disturbed, Green demurred. Herter had seemed to him not to be unduly disquieted. I disagreed; we had not heard the last of it I felt sure.

A final episode in this unhappy series of conversations occurred when the Minister of Finance, Donald Fleming, was staying at the embassy during meetings of the World Bank. I told Fleming of my talks with the Prime Minister and the Minister and with the Secretary of State and Livie Merchant. Fleming was concerned about this development and took the view that the government had some responsibility for setting public opinion aright. He raised the question himself in a meeting with Robert Anderson, then secretary to the US Treasury, asking whether he was worried on this score. His own judgment was that the current manifestations of anti-American sentiment in Canada were mostly superficial 'froth and foam.' They should not be taken as affecting seriously the basic soundness of our relationship. But it was evident that Anderson was familiar with the recent growth of Canadian criticism of the United States, particularly in its military policy. He said he was not sure that there was not as well a pretty wide divergence between strategic and political concepts in Ottawa and Washington where it was generally thought that if war were to come it would be an all out business involving the whole nation with full employment of nuclear weapons. Many Americans, the Secretary went on, were getting weary of bearing the major part of the defence effort for the free world; in such circumstances criticism from allies, in particular Canada, tended to arouse resentment and bad feeling. It was, in Anderson's judgment, essential that senior officials of the two governments maintain the closest and frankest relations with one another with the object of meeting and dealing with differences before they became enlarged and inflamed and harder to dispose of. Personally he attached the greatest importance to the maintenance of our traditionally close and friendly association and to the continuance of genuine confidence between the two governments. Finally, in reply, Fleming said that he wanted the Secretary to know that in his judgment recent Canadian public criticism of the United States and of us policy was largely the result of ignorance of the facts. Fundamentally the friendly feelings of Canadians towards Americans remained.

When I reported to Diefenbaker on what had transpired as a result of his instructions, I left him in no doubt that the assessment which he had asked me to convey to higher us authorities of the current state of Canadian opinion had caused them serious anxiety and some bewilderment. My long private talk with Merchant and Green's talk with Herter had made this clear. Back in Washington, at the end of September, reflecting on what had happened, I made an attempt to define the issues and the options in defence policy as I saw them then.[1] Rereading it ten years later I am bound to say I find the situation very little changed and the political solutions almost equally elusive.

Meantime the us election campaign moved on to its climax in November. The celebrated Nixon-Kennedy television debates took place and, as the Prime Minister remarked to me when I saw him after the election, there was little doubt that they had harmed the Republican candidate. Diefenbaker felt that the 'ins' were bound to lose on such a deal. Neither of the protagonists had distinguished himself, but Kennedy had certainly profited. We had a dinner party at the embassy the evening of the first debate and after it had concluded I polled our guests on who had been the winner. My recollection is that it was a draw with my casting vote in favour of Nixon! And when I was in Ottawa late in October or early November, the Prime Minister asked me about the policies that could be anticipated from the new administration and my expectations concerning high appointments. I had nothing much new to say because it was too early to prophesy with any confidence, but I doubted that Canadian relations would be much affected. There had been no mention at all of Canada in the campaign. Certainly we would lose a number of our best informed friends in office whoever won.

Diefenbaker said that, as he had anticipated, anti-American sentiment had continued to develop in Canada. He referred to statements made by the Leader of the Opposition and other parliamentarians including Walter Gordon

1 See appendix B.

('what he says is the Liberal gospel according to St Mark') on the dangers of unbridled US investment, and said he would introduce certain measures in Parliament to offset these developments in the Canadian economy. When I mentioned the importance I attached to being given opportunity to inform US officials in advance and confidentially of such measures, he agreed again and promised to keep the point in mind. On the question of nuclear storage in Canada the Prime Minister told me that he had been deferring approval until there could be satisfactory agreement on the 'joint control' of the use of nuclear weapons. This was an exceedingly difficult matter altogether, and there was a great deal of sentiment in Canada against any Canadian involvement with nuclear weapons. The Liberal party was opposed and so was the CCF, a totally unrealistic attitude in his opinion. Ultimately Canadian forces would have to be armed with nuclear weapons but there must be satisfactory arrangements for joint control of use. The issue would have to be determined before long.

When I saw Green later that same day I found him as strongly opposed as ever to any involvement with nuclear weapons. It would, he thought, destroy the Canadian position on disarmament talks and at the United Nations. The Canadian public was against Canada having anything to do with nuclear arms. It might be possible to allow storage on US bases in Canada for their own use, but otherwise he would not agree to having any nuclear weapons in Canada. As to any arrangements for joint control he thought the United States would never give us satisfaction. In any event the cabinet had not reached a decision.

When I said that the United States government might quite easily agree to a satisfactory formula for joint control, indeed thought that it had reached one in July, Green protested. What, then, was I to say in Washington? US authorities were totally mystified as to our position. Their proposals had been before us for a long time. Was I to say that there had been a change in Canadian policy? It was important for the maintenance of our relations that I should be able to tell the United States where we stood. Green agreed that my position was awkward and that the major issue would have to be deliberated upon and decided in cabinet before much longer.

In fact the Canadian decision was put off, although the Minister of National Defence, Douglas Harkness, visited Washington later that same month (November) and had meetings with Thomas Gates, the deputy secretary of defence. Green cautioned me to emphasize to Harkness how strongly he, Green, felt that there should be no commitment with respect to the arming of Canadian forces with nuclear weapons or the stationing of nuclear arms in Canada. In saying goodbye to me Green smiled and again expressed sympathy with the embarrassment of my position in Washington. I could only reply that I guessed I could take it 'for a few months more.'

My departure from Washington and the names of various favourites for the succession were rumoured spasmodically in the press as the year drew to a close. An irritating personal aspect to some of these stories was that my retirement was related to my failing health, whereas in fact by that time I was fully recovered. I remained determined that my return to Ottawa should not be long delayed after the change of administration but I fully intended to continue in the service. In fact I took steps to remind the authorities in Ottawa that it had been agreed at the highest level that my United States mission would terminate soon after Eisenhower left the presidency. I must say that the Prime Minister remained considerate of my wishes in this respect and took occasion to make it clear to the press that I had now completely recovered and that upon my leaving Washington he felt sure there would be many fields of public service open to me. He also spoke generously of the job that I was doing as ambassador.

On the eve of his departure from office, President Eisenhower invited the Prime Minister to come to Washington to sign the Columbia Treaty. This was duly accomplished in the White House on 16 January 1961, the Canadian signatories being Diefenbaker, Davie Fulton, and myself. As it happened I had had nothing to do with the negotiation of that controversial instrument, the signing of which was accompanied by the usual fanfare on the American side. Eisenhower made it one of his last official acts and the dinner he gave that evening in honour of the Prime Minister was his last official meal in the White House. As I sat on his left I found him easy, confident, and happy. Kennedy might well prove to be a better President, I reflected, but it was small wonder that people were saying that the American people would have chosen Ike again if they had had the option.

The Prime Minister responded that evening most appropriately and humourously. In fact his bearing towards the Americans was in every way friendly. I wondered whether I had helped to soften him up a bit and whether the critical attitude he adopted in Canada about the United States was only political and not personal. I wondered too whether it could ever be possible for a Canadian politician to gain political kudos by saying something good about Uncle Sam. Perhaps we would be witnessing a new spirit of co-operation in the relationship between the two countries as well as in other things when Kennedy took over. The new team had already been selected and of them everything was expected. Why not an improvement in Canadian-American relations as well?

On 9 January I had had an interview with Dean Rusk, Kennedy's secretary of state. He had begun by asking me how I could justify the 'special relationship' which I had claimed between our two countries. Could it be maintained without arousing suspicion or resentment on the part of other close allies of the United States? Given the opportunity, I was able to enlarge upon the current areas in which the principles of partnership, which had a long and respectable lineage, should be maintained in the mutual interest. In joint defence and in economic matters this surely was self-evident, and I did not believe that in such a relationship there were difficulties for other allies. Our dealings were essentially informal and intimate and over the years we had developed a good deal of machinery for conducting our joint affairs on many subjects and at various levels without arousing unfavourable attention elsewhere. The ties between our two countries were numerous and strong so that the danger of any really serious divergence in major matters was not critical. Nevertheless, within this generally satisfactory framework of friendship there had developed, in recent years especially, points of difference which had caused difficulty and which had given rise to misunderstandings and criticisms on both sides of the border. I then went on to reiterate the much-repeated problems of US economic domination of Canada and the Canadian distrust of US military intentions, the latter especially as they related to the worsening situation in Laos and the advent of communist government in Cuba. Finally, I mentioned disarmament and the very high importance which we in Canada attached to an affirmative approach on the part of Washington.

Before I left, Rusk said that he was glad to have had the chance of a good informal chat with me on these matters. Apart from the normal diplomatic contacts and those through the joint bodies I had mentioned, the fact that he and his son customarily went to Canada to fish might provide occasions for informal conversations with Canadian officials. He might arrange to drop in to Ottawa quietly on such an expedition. To my surprise and disappointment when I passed this suggestion on to Ottawa it was dismissed as one more indication that the Americans thought of Canada only as a place for fishing and hunting.

This was the beginning of an official and personal relationship with Rusk which continued during my remaining time in Washington. He was unfailingly friendly and put much time and effort into Canadian affairs. Although his schedule became increasingly heavy, he and his wife came on a number of occasions to the embassy for informal evenings. He never failed to see me at the State Department when I asked him to do so on matters of business. He was not always, even often, persuaded to our view; but he did act as if he had already known the answer to his own first question of me concerning the special relationship, and he accepted as a fact of geography and history that our two countries were bound together.

My wife and I had met the attractive young junior Senator from Massachusetts and his wife some months earlier. But, like most other diplomats in Washington, I suspect, it was not until after the Los Angeles convention, more especially until after the television debates with Nixon, that we had any real inkling of the Kennedy phenomenon. The story of the inauguration on 20 January 1961 has been told many times by many witnesses. But to my mind no one has been able to convey adequately the sense of excitement which affected all of us who stood round that young man that winter day as, putting aside his overcoat, he took the solemn oath of the presidency and delivered the speech that has passed into American history. The familiar setting of the Capitol was itself unusual that morning for it had snowed eight inches during the night and, by Washington standards, it was very cold. But the sky was blue and the sun was brilliant. Despite the confusion, delay, and uncertainty which seem inseparable from all United States ceremonials, on this occasion the climax was dramatic and impressive. The main reason was the young man himself, tall, serious, and strong. From where I sat I was able to see his face and Eisenhower's turned together towards the rostrum in the centre of the gathering. After the long and tedious prayers pronounced by Cardinal Cushing and others, Kennedy was sworn in, and then he spoke. When he did so he raised the occasion as much by the manner of his delivery as by the content of his text. As we heard the words they sounded, as indeed they read later, worthy to rank with the great presidential inaugurals. What I had thought of as certain to be an uncomfortable and tiresome affair turned out to be one of the memorable moments in my years in the United States capital.

That evening my wife and I were fortunate to be among the very few foreign guests at a dinner given for the new President and Mrs Kennedy before the inaugural balls. Kennedy was there with most of his new cabinet. Unfortunately Jacqueline, who was expecting a baby, was absent. The atmosphere was imbued with the enthusiasm of youth. Victory had been won; the new heaven and the new earth were at hand. My wife and I were participating in the first flush of excitement. I was fortunate in being seated next to the President's mother-in-law, a charming and cultivated woman. Thus I was able to begin my indoctrination with the new group with whom I would have to do business. When we went back to the embassy that night, we had no doubt in our minds that Washington was in for rapid change on all fronts.

Not long after Kennedy had taken office, I recall sitting at dinner at the home of the then senior Canadian Minister at our embassy, Saul Rae. He had been a university contemporary of three or four of the brightest stars of the new administration who were fellow guests that evening. One of the new men, whose name was soon to become a household word, suggested that the comparison between the Kennedy administration and its predecessor must be fascinating to me, who had had the opportunity of observing the beginnings of both. What was my impression? Partly, but not wholly, in mischief I replied that the thing that struck me most was not the contrast but the similarity between the Washington of 1961 and that of 1953. There were in both the same enthusiasm and optimism, the same determination to reform old ways and initiate new; in both one was everywhere impressed by the will of those in authority to 'get the country moving again.' The reaction about the table to these observations was a mixture of surprise and incredulity. The men around Kennedy found it impossible to believe they had anything at all in common with those that had been about Eisenhower when he had taken office eight years earlier.

Late in January I was in Ottawa and able to make my first personal report upon the attitudes to be expected of the new United States administration. The absence as yet of any personal relationship between the Prime Minister and the new President had introduced an incalculable factor into relations with the United States. Furthermore, the Prime Minister seemed to have formed somewhat unfavourable early impressions of the new administration. However, this situation was sharply reversed as a result of Diefenbaker receiving from Kennedy soon afterwards an invitation to come down for a chat and for lunch. I think that the invitation arose from the quite simple desire to make the acquaintance of the head of government of a neighbouring country, the attitude of which on a number of problems must have been reported to him as diverging from that of the United States. At that time we had differences over Cuba, the application of the Treasury regulations on trade with communist countries, and the persistent and unsolved question of nuclear weapons.

Whatever the motives, Diefenbaker was very happy about his first contact with the President. The morning of his arrival we went straight to the White House and, without any formalities whatever, the two principals engaged in a quite unrehearsed and frank discussion. Howard Green and I accompanied Diefenbaker, and Rusk and Livingston Merchant, who had recently been reappointed as ambassador to Canada, were with the President. The talk went on over the lunch table and afterwards Kennedy took Diefenbaker out by the front steps and walked along with him, surrounded by the press, to our car waiting in front of the presidential offices. As we drove to the airport, the Prime Minister enthusiastically expressed his pleasure at the informal and genuine atmosphere which the President had created. Here he said was a man whom he understood and with whom he could do business. He was a politician and he understood how to deal with those of Kennedy's background. He felt that he could understand Kennedy completely. Altogether the short visit appeared to have been an auspicious beginning to relations between the two governments. True, nothing of great importance had been settled, but Diefenbaker had had an opportunity of explaining face to face, and in his own particular way, some of the difficulties which he himself was encountering in relation to the us connection.

The promise of that encounter seemed to be confirmed when the President decided that his first visit outside the United States should be to 'our nearest neighbour.' The Prime Minister was delighted and in May 1961 the Kennedys were in Ottawa. Following diplomatic custom my wife and I travelled to Canada in the presidential plane, participated in the events of the interesting days which followed, and returned to Washington with the President and Mrs Kennedy. A good deal has been written about that visit. The public occasions unquestionably were a great success for the President and his wife. Their reception by the population of Ottawa was as enthusiastic as was to be expected for an attractive couple about whom the aura which had developed in the United States had travelled rapidly northward. Kennedy's speech to the parliamentarians was well delivered and well received. The other items on the program passed off satisfactorily and the farewell ceremonies were warm and friendly.

It was only later that there was criticism of Kennedy's deportment in Canada, in particular of the openly expressed wish in his speech to Parliament that Canada should consider favourably joining the Organization of American States. In fact the reference to that traditional bugbear of Canadian foreign policy seemed to me to have been couched in delicate, indeed flattering terms, calculated to avoid disturbing Canadian sensibilities. In fact, when Walt Rostow, one of Kennedy's advisers, had some weeks previously consulted me on what the President might include in his speech, I had not hesitated to say that a reference, appropriately expressed, to a United States welcome to the OAS would not be taken amiss. But as I found out later I had miscalculated; for both the Prime Minister and the Minister subsequently gave that reference as an example of pressure from Washington. Whether they would have done so had there been no fruther contretemps is another matter.

In the course of this visit private talks took place in the Prime Minister's office at which only two or three advisers accompanied Kennedy and Diefenbaker. Here occurred the notorious incident of the 'secret paper.' After the meeting a single page memorandum prepared for the President and indicating topics to be taken up with the Prime Minister was discovered. Some considerable time later, the existence of this paper, which allegedly contained in the margin an offensive comment on Diefenbaker and a reference to 'pushing' the Canadian authorities on certain issues, became known publicly.

There are dramatic explanations of the celebrated 'paper' incident. My own is that it was intended solely as an aide-memoire to the President and that too much significance should not have been given, therefore, to such verbs as 'push' or 'press,' if indeed these terms were employed. The fact was, however, that there were other reasons, quite distinct from the 'secret paper,' for the government's adoption of a strong line against the United States. Furthermore, as the acquaintance between Kennedy and Diefenbaker developed it became evident that there was little personal ground for the kind of intimacy, perhaps even mutual respect, which at first had seemed to exist.

As I talked with the Prime Minister later that year it became evident that the friendly feelings Diefenbaker earlier had entertained for the President had disappeared. He expressed little confidence in the US administration and resented its failure to take effective account of what he regarded as legitimate Canadian interests. As for the President, the Prime Minister resented (that is not too strong a word) what he regarded as a series of personal slights, failure to acknowledge messages, or to do so personally or promptly. As the date for the Canadian election approached, Diefenbaker's criticisms of the United States became overt and the campaign which followed was marked by the kind of anti-Americanism which I could only deplore.

These developments were baleful from my point of view as ambassador in Washington. The Prime Minister did not conceal from me the fact that he intended to make public use of the Rostow memorandum 'at the proper time' if United States pressures in such matters as the OAS continued. The results in Canada, he implied, would be explosive. He was very critical of Rostow and of his influence upon Kennedy. My attempts to explain to him the President's position seemed to have little effect. I was deeply disturbed; at the time I noted that I had rarely, if ever, been so distressed by a conversation with the head of a Canadian government. My mission to the United States, which the Prime Minister and the Minister were now determined I should continue at least until the end of 1961, seemed in serious jeopardy.

On a number of occasions that spring and early summer the Prime Minister discussed with me the question of the succession in Washington. Repeating always that he intended to release me in accordance with our understanding, he nevertheless hesitated to make the only decision which would relieve me. When he invited my advice as to a successor I urged the importance of selecting someone of national reputation and above all someone in whom he had personal confidence. At his request I suggested two or three persons who I believed could discharge the mission well. When I inquired whether he would not consider one of his own colleagues, which would be some public measure of the importance he attached to the post, his response was 'Which one?' When pressed I even suggested one or two names in that exalted category. But he dismissed the idea. I do know that he made one serious effort at least to find an appropriate nominee. No doubt there were others. But for whatever cause the months went by and when early in June 1961 my wife and I left for our summer holiday, it was understood that I would remain at my post until the end of the year.

It was on Latin American policy that I had my first brush with Dean Rusk. Sitting next to me at the annual Gridiron dinner in 1961, he told me that the

US government was about to apply to Cuba its Trading with the Enemy Regulations. They expected to provide an exemption for US subsidiaries in Canada and hoped that in return we would agree to prevent shipment of mill and refinery parts and vehicle replacements and parts. I replied that this move would certainly not be well received in Canada. Apart from such arrangements as might be made between us regarding Canadian trade in strategic items and transshipment, the fact was that we in Canada questioned the wisdom and efficacy of the measures proposed for the purpose for which they were intended, namely to prevent Cuba going communist. We had felt this way about their export embargo and their breaking off diplomatic relations. Where was all this getting them?

Rusk's response became quite heated. The United States was simply not going to have a communist base established in Cuba and would do whatever had to be done to prevent it including, if necessary, sending in troops. This was a rendition of the Munroe doctrine with a vengeance. Furthermore, US policy was not going to be altered because Canada didn't like it. Had we any alternative to suggest? I replied I had no alternative but I still thought their policy unwise. Then I added that everything went well between us when Canadians agreed with the US government; it seemed to be another matter when we had a different opinion. Incidentally, what would the other Latin American countries do about the intensification of economic measures against Cuba? Rusk could say little in reply. He did, however, permit himself to add that the US public was becoming critical of our position. That, I replied, was unfortunate, but it was not going to determine what we did. Altogether it was an exchange characterized more by heat than by light; but it indicated a new asperity in the relations between Ottawa and Washington.

After a long, happy holiday in Ireland touring through the land of my ancestors, August in the Canadian embassy in Washington was a marked contrast. It was very hot and very humid. And as I resumed my responsibilities the active files seemed all the same – Indochina, Berlin, Cuba, economic policy, defence, and Latin America with particular emphasis on Cuba. That month the chancery was picketed by anti-Castro Cubans and I had the unusual experience of receiving a delegation of somewhat inarticulate Latinos who were under the impression that Canada was in the arms of Castro and Khrushchev.

Altogether the latter part of the summer was grim. The Kennedy confrontation with Khrushchev at Vienna had failed to open the slightest chink of hope for exploratory talks between the two great powers. The Soviet Union's position on Berlin was totally unacceptable to the United States and vice versa. At an informal dinner towards the end of August for a colleague from Europe, the guest of honour was left with the impression from half a dozen of the principal architects of United States foreign policy, including the Secretary himself, that the administration had virtually given up the idea of any modus vivendi with the USSR, that they were totally fed up with their allies and with the uncommitted countries, and that they were going to drive right ahead with their own policies whatever the results on the alliance. The principal topic on that occasion was the Berlin situation. While I did not share my guest's black pessimism as to the attitude of the US administration, I did understand how he had obtained his impression from the conversation that evening. The following day McGeorge Bundy, who had been among the most articulate of our guests, confirmed in a letter my own less pessimistic conclusion:

The discussion [at dinner] was certainly lively. As you remarked toward the end, our problem is largely one of the difficulty that is imposed by our demands on each other – you really don't think of us as Germans or Russians – and you must never suppose that we think of you as appeasers. If we can agree on the facts, I think we can agree on the main ways and means of dealing with them ... The difference last night was not in purpose but in estimates of the situation and we should be very happy to be wrong.[2]

That autumn Blair Fraser, the Ottawa editor of *Maclean's*, visited me. He too went away with what I thought was an exaggerated judgment of the rigidities of the United States position. But after he left he wrote to me that it had been 'an extremely useful and illuminating experience and I certainly did come away convinced that the Kennedy Administration has been far more responsible, flexible and forthcoming in private than it had seemed to be in its public pronouncements.'

Howard Green was increasingly depressed by the turn of events. Genuine and obstinate in his conviction that what was required more than anything else was decent and honourable behaviour between nations, he allowed himself to drift into the role of one who would have peace at almost any price. At about this time an indiscreet remark of his to correspondents on a flight from Norway to Geneva exaggerated this impression. Deeply concerned at the Cuban crisis, Green had allowed it to be inferred that Canada would be willing to 'mediate' the issues between Havana and Washington. That same evening the Washington papers had carried a despatch reporting the incident. My wife and I were dining with a small group of the inner circle of the administration. After the ladies had left the table, I was immediately set upon, notably by Arthur Schlesinger who asked with unrestrained sarcasm whether we had arrived at the position where we put Castro and Kennedy on the same footing, with us in the role of 'conciliator.' Then much more to the same effect from

2 Letter from McGeorge Bundy to ADPH, 24 August 1961.

those about the table. I reacted vigorously and suggested that the attitude taken by my critics was one more example of the United States taking a flimsy, unconfirmed newspaper report and erecting upon it an interpretation of the foreign policy of one of its closest allies; and, in this case, an ally that had stood them in pretty good stead over the years. That same week *Time* magazine carried a highly coloured account of this episode which, in the mysterious ways of Washington, had got about widely the following day.

The year 1961 drew to a close with no assurance yet as to the time of our deliverance. I was frankly weary. My second term had proved a trying one, and I felt that my usefulness in the United States was wearing thin. It was not that the place and the job were ever lacking in interesting and challenging employment of mind and body, nor that our life there was too burdensome or boring. Quite the contrary, for the final years of the Eisenhower administration possessed their own faded fascination and the first months of the new frontier were especially stimulating and exciting.

Furthermore, I realized even in those last weary months that I had been fortunate not to be in the East Block during a period of exceptional malaise and discouragement. The Prime Minister's relations with External Affairs were not good. He seemed to have little confidence in the department, and was thought to be suspicious of the loyalty of senior officers identified permanently with the Pearson regime. The consequences of this distrust were demoralizing and tended to induce – or so it seemed to me – the very attitude which Diefenbaker apprehended. The result was a widening failure of confident official communication and a marked deterioration in the process of arriving at decisions in foreign policy. Another result was to weaken further the influence of the department in external policy formation, particularly in economic affairs for which the Minister had neither liking nor aptitude. Through it all, however, because of his personal qualities, Howard Green continued to retain the loyalty, even the affection, of those in the department who worked with him, and often disagreed with him. His relations with the Prime Minister never seemed close to me, yet there was a foundation of mutual political confidence between the two men even when they differed. In a curious way too many of Green's attitudes and prejudices combined with Norman Robertson's cosmic anxieties – notably in our defence relationships where nuclear shadows were cast – to produce a strongly negative force when decisions were being sought. The magic of Howard Green, the disarmer and the peacemaker, was unquestionably a party asset of which the Prime Minister could not be unaware. Yet in the atmosphere of 1961 and 1962 it did not long endure outside of Canada. Green was one of the 'nicest' and most decent of men, whose friendship I continue to cherish, but I can only conclude that he was sadly miscast in his office.

Although increasingly conscious of the gulf between the Prime Minister and the department, I had nothing to complain of in my own relations with Diefenbaker during my Washington mission. Throughout my second tour he saw me frequently and encouraged me to communicate with him directly, an invitation of which I took full advantage, though I always took care to keep the department informed. To the end of my mission he always appeared to have confidence in me and to deal with me frankly and freely. In public and in private he was consistent in his commendation of my conduct of the embassy and I had no reason to doubt his sincerity. Nevertheless, I had little evidence that Diefenbaker was much influenced by my advice on Canadian policies towards the United States. As we moved into 1962 I became increasingly anxious about the attitude of the government.

While I was in this sombre mood early in 1962 I was approached by the Chancellor of McGill University to inquire whether I would be interested in succeeding to the principalship. My first reaction was favourable. Meantime the Prime Minister had talked to me about the possibility of my succeeding General McNaughton as chairman of the International Joint Commission after the General reached his seventy-fifth birthday in February. I had expressed interest not only because it would mean returning to Ottawa but also because the work of the commission would seem to fit in well with my experience in the United States. The McGill proposal developed favourably. After speaking to Diefenbaker, and after an interview with representatives of the Board of Governors in New York, I said I would be willing to accept appointment as principal for a period of five years, provided the support of the faculty was assured. However, the university machinery moved slowly. When the Prime Minister telephoned me early one morning that McNaughton's chairmanship of the IJC was not being renewed (as the General put it publicly, he was being dismissed 'by the arbitrary action of a dictator'), he asked me to tell him by six o'clock that evening if I wished to accept the succession. On communicating with McGill I found that it would be impossible for the university to give me immediate assurance of full faculty support. Such assurance would require a meeting of the Senate, and that could not be convened without due notice. In the circumstances I said I would have to decline the university's offer and accept appointment to the IJC. The die was cast.

In the previous November the Prime Minister, in response to press enquiries occasioned by a fresh crop of rumours that I would be leaving the embassy, had said that he expected I would be returning to Ottawa soon to take up a position there. He had also said that my return was not connected with the resignation of Leslie Frost from the premiership of Ontario (Frost had been rumoured as my successor). By February the decision that Charles Ritchie, then our permanent representative to the United Nations, should succeed me had been taken and the changeover time was fixed for April. The announcement of Ritchie's appointment followed on 12 February. Once more there were tributes in the House of Commons by the Prime Minister and the Leader of the Opposition. The time for my going home had finally and irrevocably been fixed.

From the date of the announcement of my successor until our actual departure in April, my wife and I had to endure once more the exhausting process of diplomatic farewell. Not that we were unappreciative of the generosity and kindness shown us by our Washington friends and by our diplomatic colleagues. Indeed some of the farewell occasions were as memorable as any that we have attended. I recall in particular the dinner arranged by Felix Frankfurter, the distinguished justice of the Supreme Court of the United States and a dear friend from our early days in Washington. It was a very small but elegant affair at his own house. The only other guests were the indestructable Alice Longworth, Elizabeth Niebuhr, daughter of the celebrated theologian Reinhold Niebuhr, and Carter Brown, who was to become director of the National Gallery. After we had enjoyed our meal and the sparkling conversation which never flagged under the stimulus of our host and Mrs Longworth, Frankfurter rose to his feet and in his special brand of careful moving eloquence bade us goodbye. My wife and I were both deeply moved. By any standard Frankfurter was one of the great Americans of his generation as well as being one of the sweetest of human beings. We never saw him again for he died not long after we left Washington. Those last weeks were long and exhausting; but neither my wife nor I will ever forget the generosity and friendship showed us then by our American friends.

As we left the embassy in our little car at noon on Wednesday 25 April, the Raes were there to see us off. We drove back to Canada via Wheeling, West Virginia, to see my wife's sister and by Detroit to visit my own. On 30 April 1962 we crossed the border at Windsor. My ambassadorial career was at an end.

13

Canada and the United States
Independence and partnership

For the last eight years of my public life I was engaged in the affairs of the International Joint Commission. I had been named to that body on 10 April 1962, and it was to that position that I went immediately on our return from Washington to Ottawa later that month. For me, the change from diplomatic life in Washington to the chairmanship of the Canadian section of the IJC provided a welcome contrast. My wife and I were able to move into our own home again, resume life among our friends in Ottawa, and be in more frequent touch with our children. Our son Brian, having acquired his D PHIL in history at Oxford, established himself at Edmonton, first as Anglican chaplain at the University of Alberta teaching British history, and later as a full member of the Department of History. Our daughter and son-in-law had settled in Montreal. As the years went by our grandparental activities and satisfactions increased. Despite the attractions and privileges of diplomatic life, neither of us found many occasions to regret our return to the normal simplicities of our family existence. I continued, of course, to be engaged in the conduct of affairs between Canada and the United States, first in the commission itself and in my project with Livingston Merchant, and later in the work of the Permanent Joint Board on Defence, of which I was appointed Canadian chairman in 1967. However, most of my time and efforts were, in fact, devoted to the IJC.

On 7 May 1962, at my first meeting with my colleagues of the Canadian section, Donald Stephens of Winnipeg and René Dupuis of Montreal, I was duly elected chairman.[1] I had, of course, known of the IJC for many years. In the early days of the Department of External Affairs the commission had occupied a somewhat mysterious but nevertheless prestigious place. Mackenzie

---

1 The two chairmen of the IJC are not appointed as such by their respective governments, but simply appointed commissioners, with salary, on the understanding that their election will be forthcoming.

King frequently referred to it as the kind of civilized institution which nations should be able to establish for the disposition of disputes between them, without recourse to violence and open disagreement. In King's mind, I think, the IJC was equated in some way with his own notions of conciliation in industrial disputes, a dubious parallel at the best. When in office his appointments to the Canadian section did not always support the lip service he gave to the importance of the institution.

Within External Affairs, however, the commission was highly regarded both by senior officials such as O.D. Skelton and John Read as well as by more junior colleagues who had a good deal to do with references to the commission over the years. I myself had heard much about the commission's work from my friend and predecessor A.G.L. McNaughton, whose own career as chairman had been characterized by that total and passionate devotion which, throughout his whole life, he gave to whatever post he occupied. Each spring, when the commission came to Washington, and while I was at the embassy, I would have a long talk with McNaughton – or rather he would have a long talk with me. The chief subject of our conversation over those years was always the Columbia River. From the chair of the Canadian section he had fought the battle of what he conceived to be the Canadian interest. Upon his retirement he continued the fight by every means at his command.

The International Joint Commission is the most venerable of joint organisms established for the conduct and disposition of certain phases of the multitudinous relationships between Canada and the United States. It is the only joint mechanism based upon a treaty the provisions of which constitute the law of both countries. Within its jurisdiction it complements and to some degree replaces the normal diplomatic machinery. It is a permanent body and was established to deal with problems arising 'along the common frontier.' In the course of its half century history it has dealt particularly with water resources common to the two countries; latterly boundary air rights have taken an increasing proportion of its attention.

The story of the negotiation of the Boundary Waters Treaty by which the commission was established is an interesting and instructive one to anyone concerned about the development of relations between the two countries. When at the time of its signature in 1909 pessimists prophesied that it would be a short-lived experiment, Elihu Root, who had earlier signed the treaty as secretary of state, retorted in the US Senate: 'Not so! I do not anticipate that the time will ever come when this Commission will not be needed.' Despite many ups and downs, despite periods of inactivity and reduced competence, despite the ebb and flow of governmental support on both sides, Root's prediction has on the whole been justified. The IJC has fulfilled the expectations of its original sponsors, especially those who laboured long in Ottawa and

Washington to give it the unique character it possesses among international institutions. Of these, on the Canadian side, George Gibbons of London, Ontario, deserves the principal place of honour.

The unique features of the International Joint Commission are its composition and its method of operation as well as its flexibility and its capacity to adjust to change. It was the conviction of the negotiators of the treaty that solutions to boundary problems should be sought not in the normal bilateral negotiations of diplomacy, but in the deliberations of a permanent tribunal composed equally of Canadians and Americans. To this principle the treaty gave its sanction; to it the commission has sought to adhere. The commissioners act not as delegates striving for national advantage under instructions from their respective governments, but as members of a single body seeking solutions to common problems in the common interest.

The treaty was signed on 11 January 1909 by Elihu Root, for the United States, and by Lord Bryce for Great Britain, for Canada was as yet in Britain's tutelage in foreign affairs. By 1912 the commission was in business with a full complement consisting of five lawyers and one engineer, an interesting contrast to the present composition of three lawyers, two engineers, and one economist. Gibbons, alas, was not to realize his cherished expectation of becoming the first Canadian chairman. Following the general election of 1911 and the defeat of his patron, Sir Wilfrid Laurier, he was banished to the political wilderness.

The cases which have come before the commission so far have all concerned matters along the boundary. Air pollution was the subject of the precedent-setting Trail Smelter reference of 1928, as well as of a reference in 1949. It has again come before the commission in a broader context and with graver implications under a reference made in 1966. Undoubtedly the problem of air pollution will become of increasing concern to both countries as population and industrial plants burgeon in border areas. To date, however, the bulk of IJC business has had to do with the use of our common water resources, from Passamaquoddy Bay to the Straits of Juan de Fuca. It has included questions of domestic and sanitary supply, navigation, power development, irrigation, recreation, scenic beauty, and pollution. Water problems examined have varied in nature and extent from the extraction of maximum benefit from small prairie streams to multimillion dollar developments on our rivers.

To conduct its investigations and for technical advice, the commission requires substantial assistance from experts, notably engineers, hydrologists, and economists. So far the commission has been able to meet suitable and sufficient personnel requirements without recruiting more than a minimum staff in each of its own offices. The reason for this is that, with each problem referred to it, the two sections of the commission are authorized by the governments to call upon the services of the best qualified officials in their departments and agencies. The commission is also given full access to such information and technical data as may have been acquired, or as may be acquired, by such agencies during the course of its investigations. With the upsurge of public interest in water and air pollution in recent years, however, I would expect some increase in the commission staff on both sides, especially in the United States where the commission has had to carry on so far with a corporal's guard.

As I write, water pollution has become the most important preoccupation of the IJC. Reports of the increasing pollution of North America's water resources and the fearful prospects of critical shortages of clean water in some regions have given rise to increasing public anxiety in both Canada and the United States. This concern has been manifested in a spate of international, national, and local conferences and in seminars and studies under both private and public auspices. Pollution is no respecter of political boundaries, and the consequences of pollution in lakes and rivers which straddle the international border is more than likely to affect health and property on both sides of the line. The thousands of miles of water frontier between the two countries, the scores of rivers and streams which flow across the boundary, all in some degree open to misuse, are, in this context, potential sources of friction and dispute. Here the International Joint Commission has no direct jurisdiction. But article 4 of the treaty does prohibit pollution of boundary and transboundary waters 'on either side to the injury of health or property on the other.'

Following its first investigation in 1918 of water pollution from the Lake of the Woods to the St John River in New Brunswick, the commission reported that the situation in parts of the Great Lakes was 'generally chaotic, everywhere perilous, and in some cases disgraceful.'[2] Even such forceful language fell on deaf ears. North Americans in those days still believed that their supplies of fresh clean water were inexhaustible. The contrast with the present state of public opinion is striking. The vast and detailed investigations now being carried on to their conclusion in the Great Lakes Basin under commission auspices have not only aroused public interest but are in large measure the direct response to public pressures upon local and federal governments on both sides of the boundary. I will be much surprised if the issue of the commission's comprehensive report does not increase the pressure on all governments to get on with the huge projects required to correct the situation, despite the cost involved.

2 *Final Report of the International Joint Commission on the Pollution of Boundary Waters Reference* (Washington, DC, 1918).

In the other types of cases which come before the commission, including the control of levels and flows in boundary lakes and rivers, the commission's record of acceptable solutions to problems between the two countries is substantial and sound. Indeed it can be said that the commission's history in this area has demonstrated that the machinery devised by the authors of the Boundary Waters Treaty is capable of reaching mutually acceptable solutions. It is not surprising, therefore, that from time to time proposals have been advanced for extending the commission's field of action, or at least its method, to areas other than those 'along the common frontier,' as set out in article 9. There is no barrier in the treaty to such development. Indeed, article 10, contemplating an arbitral role for the IJC, does not limit the commission's jurisdiction to boundary questions. But this article has never been invoked.

From time to time proposals have been made that matters such as other energy resources, civil aviation, specific trade matters, continental shelf resources, and perhaps even continental water resources should be included within the scope of the IJC for study and report. In particular, in our *Principles for Partnership* study Merchant and I proposed a consideration of 'some extension of the Commission's functions.' Another suggestion which has gained some currency would have the present commission converted into or replaced by a supranatural institution, and endowed with authority to manage all aspects of boundary waters, or at least those of the Great Lakes Basin. Such an institution would apparently have powers comparable to a domestic administrative or regulatory body, including the powers to license and presumably to enforce. It is seen as a solution to problems posed by the multiplicity of government agencies in both Canada and the United States which now have responsibilities over water and its uses, for it would provide greater concentration of authority. It also originates in understandable impatience with allegedly slow and complicated procedures, and the absence of any mandatory character in the commission's conclusions, for IJC recommendations become effective only when adopted and carried out by other bodies.

Such proposals as this last have done credit to the zeal and social conscience of their sponsors but somewhat less to their sense of present reality and their judgment of what is possible in international, let alone national, affairs. If the International Joint Commission is to assume this new guise, there would, of course, have to be a new and radically different treaty. For the whole philosophy of the Boundary Waters Treaty is quite opposed to the concept of an international body with administrative or enforcement authority and functions. As General McNaughton had occasion to observe when he was chairman of the Canadian section, the very reason the IJC was not given policing powers, as had been proposed in the commission's first report on water pollution, was to prevent its becoming a superpower with authority beyond that of the national governments. The commission, as presently constituted, is dedicated to the proposition that equitable solutions to common problems can be worked out by close co-operation between jurisdictions – local, national, and international – under agreed principles and upon a foundation of mutual confidence.

I was not long in the commission before it became clear to me that the IJC method of finding solutions to problems between the two countries was different from that to which I had been accustomed. Whereas in normal diplomacy the representatives of each side, under instruction from their respective governments, strove for their national advantage as a buyer and seller in a commercial transaction, the six commissioners of the IJC approached the problems put before them with the object of reaching solutions which would be to the mutual advantage of both nations. This was the intent of the treaty which provided the commission with its basic law; and, despite some lapses, it has been the unbroken tradition of the commission throughout its long existence. As I got to know my colleagues, American and Canadian, I gradually came to appreciate the fact that the commission possessed internal dynamics of its own. The commissioners cherished their considerable measure of independence from their governments and appeared to find no difficulty in approaching as a single body the various problems put before them. As the months went on and my experience grew I realized that the commission, within its limited ambit, operated in a new dimension of international dealing.

Not long after I assumed the chairmanship I recall receiving a preemptory and, I thought, offensive telegram from Robert Moses on behalf of the New York Power Authority demanding the release of more St Lawrence water at Cornwall for the purpose of power production. That year the water level of the St Lawrence River was low and the competition for allocation of water between power and navigation was, to say the least, spirited. The Port of Montreal was insisting on higher levels in the harbour and the commission's Board of Control was having a very difficult time trying to advise the IJC on its weekly pattern of optimum levels for Lake Ontario and flows in the international section of the St Lawrence River. The manner in which the commission was advised by the mixed team of officials, American and Canadian, and the way in which the commissioners were able to provide acceptable solutions on the basis of the treaty, provided me with one of my first lessons in the value of the joint mechanism devised by the negotiators of the Boundary Waters Treaty over fifty years before.

The development of the common life of the commission and its unity of purpose and procedure was greatly facilitated by the amicable personal relationships among the six of us as we engaged in informal discussions, travelled, and lived together at various points on each side of the boundary in the conduct of our hearings and meetings. As our investigations of such widely separated and different problems as the development of the Pembina River in Manitoba and North Dakota, the feasibility of a Champlain Waterway from the state of New York to the province of Quebec, and the pollution of the St Croix River in Maine and New Brunswick went forward, so I found the independent life of the commission taking on new strength and effectiveness. When, in our off time, we were together in hotel and motel rooms along the border, our talk was shop talk. When we sat in the presence of those in the various localities whose interests were directly concerned in our decisions, we did so as one body to hear with judicial impartiality the Americans and Canadians who came to express themselves. During my time on the commission I can remember no occasion upon which the commissioners divided in their opinion on national lines.

There were, of course, contrasts between American and Canadian traditions and ways of doing things. Our United States colleagues, reared in the traditions of congressional government and republican democracy, sometimes found it difficult to understand proposals which to us on the Canadian side seemed normal consequences of our own parliamentary system. Interesting, too, was the quite noticeable difference in the character of the public hearings on the two sides of the border. I recall, for example, the contrast between a grave, orderly, and low-key meeting that we held in southern Manitoba on the Pembina development and, only a few hours later, the rounds of applause which followed the intervention of the more popular witnesses at our meeting on the same topic in Walhalla, North Dakota. On another occasion, in northern New York, I remember a large and enthusiastic audience in the local high school greeting the observations of my United States co-chairman with prolonged and vociferous booing. In the same case the following day our Sorel public maintained throughout a respectful and dignified mien.

It has been an interesting and encouraging experience to have been part of the commission over these years. Interesting, partly because of the ingenuity of the administrative apparatus and the opportunities it has afforded for taking part in the actual working out of practical problems between the two countries, and partly, of course, for the human relationships which have developed in the process. The encouragement has derived from the commission's success, as a body composed of appointees of two nations, in working out acceptable solutions to the mutual advantage of both. For this method to be successful, however, it is essential that the principles upon which such solutions are to be found must be agreed in advance, as they were in the Boundary Waters Treaty. It is essential too that the commissioners accept and be moved by the conception of the common advantage. There have been occasions in which the commissioners on the two sides have assumed the normal diplomatic posture of representatives of their respective governments. Usually this was the result of their having taken positions on the questions at issue in advance. Consistently the result of such procedure has been to thwart solutions. The reason for this is quite simple: once the unity of the commission is broken, the commissioners inevitably resolve themselves into two teams of national negotiators in a stance of confrontation. In fact examples of such breakdown have been extremely rare. I know of only three cases. One of them, however, was a very large and controversial one, the Columbia River Reference for which the commissioners were unable to carry the matter further than the enunciation of what were called 'principles' for any joint development and the treaty had to be worked out between governments. In that case, the Canadian Chairman believed that his sole and sacred duty was to advance the Canadian interest; this he did in public as in private, an admirable and patriotic attitude characteristic of McNaughton, but in my judgment totally inconsistent with the basic precepts which must govern the IJC if it is to be effective.

No other joint Canada-United States entities which have come into existence in the past thirty years have the same legal and conventional foundations as those possessed by the IJC. All of them differ from the IJC in that they are essentially institutions for bilateral negotiation on special subjects, carried on by continuing delegations from the two governments. Some are at the ministerial or cabinet level, such as the Committee on Joint Defence and the Committee on Trade and Economic Affairs; most are at the official level, such as the Permanent Joint Board on Defence; two or three have executive or quasi-executive functions. All of them vary in their effectiveness with the general climate of the relationship between Ottawa and Washington and according to the current state of affairs in their various areas of concern. When things are going well cabinet committees will meet to confirm arrangements already negotiated by officials and provide some political spotlight for agreements. Occasionally a cabinet committee may be employed to deal with a situation of urgency, even emergency. But this is rare. When relations between the two governments are cool, cabinet committees will not meet at all, even though there are outstanding questions of importance between Ottawa and Washington.

Two years after my return to Ottawa I became concerned with the general problem of the conduct of business between Canada and the United States. This new involvement began with a meeting between President Johnson and Prime Minister Pearson in Washington on 21 and 22 January 1964. After their talks they issued a communiqué which contained the following paragraph:

The Prime Minister and the President discussed at some length the practicability and desirability of working out acceptable principles which would make it easier to avoid divergencies in economic and other policies of interest to each other. They appreciated that any such principles would have to take full account of the interests of other countries and of existing international arrangements. The President and the Prime Minister considered that it would be worth while to have the possibilities examined. Accordingly, they are arranging to establish a Working Group, at a senior level, to study the matter and to submit a progress report to the April meeting of the Joint Committee [the ministerial Joint Committee on Trade and Economic Affairs].[3]

The idea of such a 'statement of principles' was not new. In February 1959, as leader of the opposition, Pearson had floated the idea in the course of debate in the House of Commons.[4] Four years later the ministerial Joint Committee on Trade and Economic Affairs heard a more precise proposal from George Ball, the US undersecretary of state, who tabled a document which he suggested be issued in conjunction with the communiqué at the close of the meeting. The principles which Ball proposed were two: first, that both countries should have maximum opportunity to profit from the proximity of their economies; and second, that conflicts of national interests should be reconciled expeditiously as they arose by the use of special procedures and machinery if necessary. At that time he suggested the establishment of working parties on joint energy problems, on the balance of payments, and on the extraterritorial application of economic statutes.

Although they were not opposed to the idea of a statement of principles, the Canadian ministers were not prepared to accept Ball's version and the joint communiqué which was issued on 21 September 1963 was confined to an expression of agreement 'that early consideration would be given by the two governments to the best means of elaborating and strengthening the basic principles of economic cooperation between Canada and the United States.' In the year which followed, as economic difficulties increased – especially over balance of payments questions – official Canadian opinion became more favourable to the idea of a declaration, provided the Americans would go well beyond Ball's original suggestion in order to protect special Canadian interests.

This, then, was the background to the Johnson–Pearson statement of January 1964. In the following month it was announced that the working group referred to in the communiqué would consist of Livingston T. Merchant and myself. The press releases from the White House and the Prime Minister's Of-

3 A.D.P. Heeney and Livingston T. Merchant, *Canada and the United States: Principles for Partnership* (Ottawa: Queen's Printer, 1965), annex A.
4 Canada, House of Commons, *Debates,* 1959, II, p 1410.

fice made some play with the co-incidence that Merchant had served two times as US ambassador to Canada and I twice as Canadian ambassador to the United States. It was a great satisfaction for me to learn of Merchant's appointment, for I had known him well and in a variety of places and circumstances over some eight years, and had learned to respect as well as to like him. I knew that he possessed a broad and deep knowledge of Canada, that personally he attached high importance to good relations between the two countries, that I could count upon his total fairness and understanding, and that I would be able to work with him in full frankness. I doubt that I would have accepted appointment had it not been for the President's selection of someone of Merchant's calibre and experience. His appointment was an indication of the seriousness the US administration attached to the endeavour.

After consultation with the principal officials in Ottawa who had to do with United States affairs, chiefly on the economic side, I made my first working contacts with Merchant and was happy, though not wholly surprised, to find that his view of what could be done and how we should set about it coincided closely with my own. We agreed that we would not feel bound by earlier studies or documents, whatever their origin, although we would of course make use of relevant previous experience. As a practical modus operandi we decided to have fresh examination made of a number of agreed 'cases' where there had been difficulty between Washington and Ottawa in recent years. While we expected to have available to us the normal governmental machinery on each side, we regarded ourselves as quite independent for the purposes of the study. Neither Merchant nor I had any intention of adding to our working group. We were, perhaps, the smallest task force on record. At the outset we agreed that 'consultation' lay at the root of our problem; and, when I insisted that consultation, to be valid, could not stop at 'advice and consent,' Merchant readily concurred. We both understood that 'if agreement upon mutually satisfactory solutions or accommodations could not be reached, each government should be free to follow its own course, without recrimination.'

In April, when the ministerial Joint Committee on Trade and Economic Affairs met in Ottawa, I was able to submit a progress report. By that time we had had several meetings and considerable correspondence, and we reported that our preliminary examination confirmed the usefulness of the project. We had already begun the re-examination and analysis of cases in recent experience. Consideration of any new machinery for consultation would be deferred until we were in a position to estimate with confidence whether a statement of acceptable principles was likely to prove feasible.

The topics for our case studies were selected arbitrarily, each of us taking turns in naming one until a total of twelve was reached. They included principally subjects of economic and commercial policy: the US interest equalization tax, trade with Cuba, wheat marketing, oil and gas export, and others. We also added politically significant and difficult subjects, for example, nuclear weapons, the extraterritorial implications of domestic legislation, and American magazines in Canada.

Our next move was to consult, each on his own side, officials who had been directly involved with the subjects chosen. Assuring the authors of complete anonymity, we requested brief, informal, personal, and private papers, concerning not only historical surveys but also analytical discussions of the issues and evaluations of how they had been handled. We wanted to know whether consultative procedures other than those actually followed, or earlier agreed 'principles' of co-operation, might have eased difficulties or avoided divergencies; alternatively, we were interested to discover what consultative procedures or principles of co-operation or other favourable factors contributed to the satisfactory resolution of the issues involved.

The response to these requests of ours for individual help and unfettered guidance was prompt and, in most cases, of a high calibre. As they were received from their authors Merchant and I read and exchanged them, and in November I attempted an analysis of all twenty-four papers received from both Canadian and US sources. I sought to find out whether there had been adequate consultation in each case and whether solutions had been achieved which were regarded as satisfactory or tolerable from either or both points of view. I discovered that, of the eleven bilateral cases examined (relations in the multilateral context were omitted), there had been adequate consultation on six and no prior consultation on one; satisfactory solutions had been reached on three, tolerable results on five, and no solution on three. In other words satisfactory or tolerable solutions had been reached on eight of the eleven cases, but only on three out of the eleven could they be characterized as really satisfactory by both governments. In each instance the judgment was made on the basis of both the Canadian and United States papers. Admittedly this was a rather subjective exercise, but when I sent my results to Merchant, I discovered that his response did not vary greatly from my own assessment. I cannot contend that either of us put much weight on this element in our exercise, but it was I think worthwhile in pointing to the kinds of things with which the two governments had to contend when dealing with one another on bilateral problems.

Some months previously, just before the ministerial joint committee had met, George Ball had spoken about the basis of the US-Canada relationship. Although he was regarded as a hardliner in his dealings with Canada (Howard Green later regarded him as the really 'tough guy' on the American side), it was evident from his speech that he had given a good deal of thought to means of providing for that combination of interdependence and independence which was basic to the alliance.

The desire of our Canadian friends to safeguard the identity of their national market apparently stems from the belief that the nation and people may lose something of their national political independence if their economy is too closely meshed with that of other nations and particularly the United States.

The maintenance of political independence, however, depends more on the state of the national will than on economic relationships. Certainly, neither Canada nor the United States is interested in yielding or compromising its own freedom of political decision. In fact, on both sides of the border there is a fierce desire to resist any steps in that direction. I do not believe, therefore, that as between Canada and the United States there is any basis for assuming an automatic and parallel relation between increased economic interdependence and the loss of independence in political life.[5]

In the same address Ball spoke of the importance of seeking 'a basic philosophical approach to the purposes that should govern our relations' and said that the work in which Merchant and I were engaged provided an opportunity to achieve such a result.

Later, in his book *The Discipline of Power* (1968), Ball went a good deal further and expressed the opinion that the growing economic interdependence of the two countries provided little ultimate hope for the kind of political independence which Canadians wanted. This later conclusion was widely criticized in Canada. But in 1964 and 1965 it was only Walter Gordon and the more vocal economic nationalists who confronted him directly.

During the first year of our appointment Merchant and I had met half a dozen times and had submitted an interim statement to the joint committee. By spring of 1965 we had begun the final report, exchanging drafts of various portions based on a skeleton outline upon which we had already agreed. Merchant was quick to grasp the peculiarly Canadian considerations which bore upon specific issues and to appreciate Canadian sensitivity to the vast power of the United States and its pervasive influence in every aspect of Canadian life. Without neglecting the interests of his own country, Merchant nevertheless accepted what I regarded as the basic realities of the enduring Canadian national position: partnership on agreed and well understood conditions, yes; erosion of political independence, no.

By the beginning of June we were ready for the ultimate stage in the preparation of our report. We met in a long hard session for four days at the Seigniory Club. At the end of that month we were in a position to submit our agreed document to our respective principals under the title *Canada and the United States: Principles for Partnership*. On 12 July 1965 the Prime Minister

5 Address to the American Assembly, Harriman, NY, 25 April 1964, in Department of State, *Bulletin*, L (18 May 1964), p 773.

and the President simultaneously released the report with suitable expressions of gratitude to Merchant and myself and indications that the report would be carefully studied by the two governments.

What followed is common knowledge. Public reaction in Canada focused on paragraph 81 which read in part: 'It is in the abiding interest of both countries that, wherever possible, divergent views between the two governments should be expressed and if possible resolved in private, through diplomatic channels.' Critics leaped to the conclusion that this emphasis on what they described as 'quiet diplomacy,' on the avoidance of public disagreement, was a proposal to gag the Canadian government and to prevent Canadian public criticism of American external policies. Approval of such a principle would be taken as acceptance by Canada of satellite status. Headlines in the Canadian press and comment by Canadian columnists employed such terms as 'lap dog.' I was charged with having been 'conned' by Merchant into recommending a shackling of the legitimate expression of Canadian views. 'Quiet diplomacy' became a term of abuse.

In those first days after the report's publication I found this and similar criticisms rather hard to take. They were all on the same theme. 'Taisez-vous et tout ira bien!' was the way the Montreal *Métro-Express* summed it up on 13 July. The *Montreal Star* (14 July) had an equally facile interpretation: 'The bureaucrats' dream. Keep it quiet, boys, work it out, we will all keep out of trouble and things will go smoothly. That is its purport.' Charles Lynch wrote: 'That old devil compromise has become part of Mr. Heeney's nature by now. Mr. Heeney has many of the characteristics of Lester B. Pearson – in fact he is the kind of man Mr. Pearson might have become had Mr. Pearson stayed out of politics.' He went on: 'If the Heeney-Merchant doctrine catches on, it seems certain to confirm our lackey status.'[6] Some newspapers went so far as to suggest that the proposition put forward by the report was that the Canadian government 'should refrain from public criticism of U.S. foreign policy and in return the United States should refrain from rocking Canada's economic boat.'[7] One of Canada's ablest cartoonists showed me being rushed into a kind of padded cell by Merchant whose triumphant expression was explained by the legend: 'We will now retire to our private, top-secret, hush-hush, sound-proof, leak-proof chambers and discuss our divergent views.'[8]

The majority of Canadian newspaper comment seemed to be negative and concentrated on one element in the report, and that in isolation. However, there were a number of journals which went deeper, drawing attention to the balancing paragraphs which followed and to the reciprocal nature of the obli-

6 Charles Lynch, Southam News Service, 14 July 1965.
7 *Globe and Mail*, 14 July 1965.
8 *Montreal Star*, 14 July 1965.

gations suggested for restraint in public controversy. When a former Canadian Minister of Agriculture, Alvin Hamilton, asserted that the report's suggestions 'would make Canada a "lap dog" to the U.S. and be "a complete surrender of our sovereignty,"' the *Ottawa Journal* (16 July) asked whether there was no limit to the permissible degree of exaggeration in public discussion:

One wonders if the critics of the report read it. They appear to be saying that even where it is possible to settle divergent Canadian-American policies quietly it is better to settle them noisily before the cameras and microphones of the world of which a good part would revel and prosper on our apparent disunity.

Bruce Hutchison observed that the Merchant-Heeney 'code lends itself to easy misrepresentation and cheap sneers. You might suppose from some of the Canadian oratory that they were plotting the surrender of Canada's independence through their intentions were precisely the opposite.'[9] As the weeks went by and there was time for thought and reflection more positive public comment began to balance the first critical fusillade. Blair Fraser emphasized our point about the advantages of persuasion in private and remarked that this did not mean Canadian representatives should never 'speak out against the policies of friendly nations.' Rather, he went on, 'such speaking out is not an attempt at persuasion. It's a sign that persuasion has failed.'[10]

One unfortunate feature of some of the criticism directed at our report was that it was related, quite wrongly, to a speech which the Prime Minister had made in April 1965 at Temple University in Philadelphia. In his address Pearson had suggested that the United States halt air strikes on North Vietnam to see whether peace feelers might possibly ensue from the other side. This had irritated President Johnson and cast a pall over his meeting with Pearson which followed shortly afterward. In fact Merchant and I could not have had the Pearson speech in mind, for it had not been delivered until after those portions of the report on the advantages between friends of quiet rather than noisy diplomacy had been drafted in their final form. Nevertheless, the myth persisted especially in the United States where it was accepted by many that we intended a public rebuke of the Prime Minister.

Our report received a good deal of attention in Britain where our High Commissioner reported that comment was widespread. Once more attention was concentrated upon the recommendation that public criticism of United States policies should be avoided except where Canadian interests were directly involved. Leonard Beaton in the *Guardian* (14 July 1965) stated cate-

9 *Winnipeg Free Press*, 22 July 1965.
10 *Maclean's*, 21 August 1965.

gorically that our 'high level proposal that the Canadian Government should no longer take public stands against American world policy' was 'undoubtedly a result' of 'Mr. Johnson's extreme irritation with Mr. Pearson's speech' on American soil with regard to cessation of North Vietnam bombing. He went on to suggest that the report would lead to a major political controversy in Canada and concluded by expressing surprise at the 'political simplicity of the proposal.'

Comment in the United States press was less extensive. A few editorialists highlighted our conclusion that the United States should always consult Canada before framing policies bound to affect us. Otherwise the principal point emphasized was that we had taken Pearson to task for speaking out in the United States on Vietnam. There was no disagreement with the general proposition for continuous and frank diplomatic consultation. Amicable settlement in private was given none of the sinister implications accorded it by Canadian wiseacres.

I confess that I felt somewhat bruised by the initial treatment the report received and in particular, I suppose, by the implications drawn by a number of commentators that Merchant had taken advantage of his friendship with me to persuade me into a betrayal of Canadian interests. In a letter to Merchant on 19 July, after drawing attention to the effect of many newspapers taking out of context or distorting paragraphs 80 and 81 so as to create the effect that we had recommended a gag on Canadian government comment on US policy, I went on:

With the advantage of hindsight, I think paragraph 80 might have been better expressed. Nevertheless, the very fact that it has aroused a rumpus up here (particularly because U.S. journalists as well as some of our own have related what we said to the P.M.'s Philadelphia speech) may result in our report receiving more attention than it otherwise would have done. I hope that U.S. officials will not interpret wrongly our suggestions on this point – it could be damaging if they did.

The words of the Canadian critics still tingling I concluded:

At this point I tend to be philosophical and optimistic. Certainly we cannot complain that our report has been ignored. Even in Britain it got wide newspaper attention and our heads of posts are being sent guidance and instructions on how they should deal with it. I expect the 'Merchant-Heeney' report, as it is now called here, will be around for quite a long time.

The Prime Minister had been generous and genuine in his comment. He read the report as soon as he received it and immediately telephoned me. 'There is only one addition that I would make,' he told me, though I assume it is too late to make any change. Where you speak of Canadian authorities having regard for the United States government's position, avoiding so far as possible public disagreement in the absence of special Canadian interests and so on, you state that the Canadian Government 'cannot renounce its right to independent judgment and decision'. If you were to add the two words 'and pronouncement' or words to that effect it would be an improvement.

I replied that of course 'pronouncement' was intended to be implied as was surely logical. Nevertheless, he said, its absence would cause us some trouble. And so it did. Subsequently, when asked his own opinion of the offending paragraph at a press conference he answered precisely the same way. There was never any doubt as to where Pearson stood on the main conclusions of the report. He was in favour of them and said so, even though it caused him some personal and official embarrassment.

Personal reactions from friends and associates were on the whole encouraging. Mitchell Sharp concurred publicly as well as privately and without qualification. Walter Gordon did not like many of the recommendations, or indeed the central philosophy, but he was generous in his personal references. Others were more reserved. Vincent Massey wrote me a long letter, favourable in his commendation of much the report contained but reserved and quietly critical where, indeed, I would have expected. He had been worried by the reference to restraint on the part of Canadian authorities in situations where 'her neighbour adopts policies which might lead to a situation in which she [Canada] herself would be heavily involved.' He was deeply anxious too, lest 'Canada's views on American foreign policy be muted as a result of economic measures, our silence purchased, to put it crudely, by the power of the purse.' Canadians generally would not agree with an attitude so supine as those who suggested that 'you shouldn't be rude to a rich uncle.' Finally, he feared economic union which he felt very strongly 'could only lead to political union' and, reverting to an earlier view, could not refrain from referring to 'the Canadian tariff as a bulwark of Canadian nationhood.' Massey's letter was a good and one I greatly appreciated, but it was sad to find that he too had misread and misunderstood what Merchant and I had tried to say.

The following autumn I had an opportunity to enter a public defence of the report at the Third Annual Banff Conference on World Development.[11] Still pretty hot under the collar and refreshed by a good summer holiday I felt justified in taking the offensive. Needless to say my Banff speech and my subsequent comments in reply to questions by reporters did not dispose of

11 A.D.P. Heeney, 'Dealing With Uncle Sam,' in J. King Gordon (ed), *Canada's Role as a Middle Power* (Toronto 1966), p 87.

the matter, and I am under no illusion that our report as such is ever likely to become a popular statement of ideal Canadian-United States relations in Canadian eyes. I suspect the document upon which Merchant and I laboured over those eighteen months will remain associated in the minds of many, perhaps most, Canadians not with the actual proposals which it recommended but with what it was thought to contain, and reported to have contained, on quiet diplomacy. I think that paragraph 80 might have been better expressed, yet I doubt that it was really a problem of draftsmanship at all. As the months of criticism went by I began to wonder whether spasms of emotional outburst among Canadians against their big neighbour were not endemic, an inevitable aspect of our national psychology. This was a proposition we had optimistically, yet categorically, discarded in our report.

Despite the sorry evidence provided by the critical reception of the report in Canada, I continue to believe that it is possible to reconcile a Canadian position of influence and authority in Washington well beyond that of Canada's deployable material resources with a consistent and self-respecting Canadian nationalism. Given the obvious, inevitable, and increasing interdependence of the economies of the two countries, the manifest decreasing significance of sovereignty in its narrow construction in the affairs between all nations, and given the impossibility – to say nothing of the undesirability – of a policy of political isolation and economic autarchy, I believe we have no self-respecting option but to seek the expression of our Canadianism in the kind of limited partnership which Merchant and I tried to describe in our report. The desire of Canadians for an independent foreign policy for Canada is understandable in the sense that all nations would like to be untrammelled to express their special identities in the world in their own particular ways. But total national independence in foreign policy is as impossible as is total independence for an individual in organized society. The trick is to achieve and maintain that sufficiency of freedom of action which will enable the nation, and the individual, to contribute best to its own and to world society. In the Canadian situation there is no alternative to partnership with the United States, provided always that the terms of that partnership give the necessary minimum protection for Canadian independence and that the international policy of the United States, not in detail but in general, is not hostile to Canadian national objectives.

Such being my view I believe that those in authority on both sides of the border should continue the search for an agreed framework for the relationship. The conduct of Canadian affairs with the United States will continue to be primarily a pragmatic process. But, if Ottawa were able, in any difficulty, to appeal to agreed principles, I believe substantial practical diplomatic advantage might result. It goes without saying that a document embodying such principles would reserve, emphasize, and underline the right of the Canadian (and, incidentally, the United States) government to take its own line on any situation whatever, privately, publicly, and in any way it saw fit. Nevertheless the first Canadian objective surely should be to influence American decision-making, for US decisions over the whole range of international affairs have more importance for Canadians, as well as for the rest of humanity, than those taken in any other capital of the world, including Ottawa. If all the legitimate devices of quiet diplomacy fail – and they can fail – then by all means let us take to the rooftops. But let no one think that therein is a victory; for we will have achieved no more than hollow and transient release for our emotions. The problems will almost certainly endure in form and conditions more difficult than ever.

My participation in the IJC and the Merchant-Heeney affair were not the only ways in which I was involved in North American diplomacy in the years after I left Washington. For three years after 1967 I was Canadian chairman of the Permanent Joint Board on Defence, a body set up purely by executive act (and a very informal one at that) of Mackenzie King and Franklin Roosevelt in August 1940 to consider in the broad sense the defence of the northern half of the western hemisphere. It was the intention of the Prime Minister and the President that this board should be more than temporary; indeed it was meant to deal with a continuing problem. Consisting of military and civilian representatives, and chaired jointly by nominees of prime ministers and presidents, the PJBD is divided into two national sections on the pattern of the IJC, which may well have been in Mackenzie King's mind at Ogdensburg. During its early life in the war years the board was largely concerned with the details of the sea, land, and air defences of North America and the activities of United States forces on Canadian soil. In more recent years, including my time as chairman of the Canadian section, its principal preoccupation has been air defence; and in 1967 and 1968 it was deeply involved in the negotiations for renewal of the NORAD agreement.

I found the work of the defence board both stimulating and familiar. It carried me back to the range of political-military problems and the association with the principal staff officers of the Canadian forces to which I had become accustomed in the Cabinet Office during and immediately after the war. It brought me into close touch too with the ministers chiefly concerned and the cabinet committees which dealt with mixed questions of foreign and defence policy. One great virtue of the board as an institution for consideration of Canada-United States questions was this mixed military-civil membership which made for really frank exchanges across departmental as well as national frontiers, and enabled short cuts to be taken in important advice to governments without having to resort to the frustration and delays of 'channels.' Meeting customarily for four days three times a year on military bases in Canada and the United States, the members of the board and their principal assistants have been able to achieve a measure of mutual confidence and informality which I believe to have been of value to both countries and particularly to Canada. As long as we remain in alliance with the United States and as long as it is the policy of the government of Canada to co-operate with the government of the United States in the defence of North America, the board will have an important role to play.

14

And in conclusion

Although the retirement age for both the commission and the board was never equated with that of other branches of the Public Service, it seemed evident to me from many points of view that I should make the posts available to someone of a younger generation. Accordingly, in January 1970, I informed the Prime Minister of my wish to vacate both posts. When I did so, I outlined what I considered to be desirable characteristics in a successor.

Now that I am at the end of my life in the Public Service, I am anxious that the duties of my two posts be taken seriously in the future. In speaking of the IJC I have drawn attention to the validity of the mechanism set up in 1909, and to the possibilities for its development. Its role in dealing with water and air pollution, only beginning to be understood, is obviously of deep concern to Canada. The problem of air pollution is particularly acute, and governments should make every effort to meet the rising demand for action along our boundaries. Governments at every level have risked disaster by their neglect of the potentialities of the IJC in these fields, and the facility with which this unique mechanism may be applied readily and informally. The PJBD has also discharged important responsibilities in the past; and I believe its role in the future defence relationships between the two countries could be further developed to the mutual advantage of Canada and the United States, unless we are to make some very radical change in the direction of our foreign policy.

In my experience of Canadian-American negotiations, which stretches over thirty years, Canadian delegations have, in most cases, been outmanoeuvered by those on the US side of the table. It is a great virtue of a joint agency on the IJC pattern, that the inherent inequality in our relations with our giant neighbour is reduced to a minimum. In the PJBD, as in the IJC, Canada can discuss and settle mutual problems with the United States without being over-whelmed and crushed.

From the first time that I visited Washington with Mackenzie King in November 1938 for the signature of the Trade Agreement, I have been continually involved in greater or lesser degree in Canadian-American affairs. Some might say that this has distorted my vision. But when one thinks of the degree of Canadian attention habitually directed southwards, there is, perhaps, some solid justification for this preoccupation. The nations of the world, both in the East and the West, have for a generation been fascinated by the politics of power in which the United States has been the centre of the western alliance. Interest and concern in American affairs necessarily involves understanding the attitudes of other nations, so that my professional concerns have been almost as varied as the world itself.

There is great personal reward in the sense of public service; and at the end of a long time in that service it is hard for me to imagine myself finding a comparable reward in the world of private business. This personal satisfaction comes largely from knowing the importance of the work to which I have given my life.

In recent years there has been a tendency to substitute temporary for permanent advisers to government: to institute in Ottawa, as elsewhere, a cadre of experts and confidantes devoted to particular policies and politicians rather than to the permanent service of the state. In a rapidly changing society this is probably inevitable. It is no longer likely that a professional Civil Service, however competent, can remain wholly in tune with the political and social situation of contemporary Canada. The prime minister must be free to accept advice and appoint advisers from outside the ranks of the regular public service.

Yet there are dangers in this trend. There is the danger of a return to patronage, a bypassing of the carefully developed non-political service recruited on merit alone. Will able men and women be content to join a service for life knowing that they may have no chance of rising to its most sensitive and demanding posts? There is also the danger that the importance of administration and expertise continuing through changes in political power, the traditional role of the civil service, may be underrated.

The Public Service is not autonomous. It exists only to serve the government and the people. Nevertheless, in itself, it embodies the principle of national unity which remains the greatest political aim of government in this land. In the Civil Service men and women from all parts of Canada work together and share a common direct responsibility and direct loyalty to the federal government. The federal Civil Service is a professional microcosm of Canada itself. Obviously this expression of national unity is of particular importance as Canada seeks to become a genuinely bilingual community. The implementation of the recommendations of the B and B Commission with respect to the Civil Service will be a long and difficult process. But it has begun; and the measure of its success is of great significance to the future of Canada.

In a complex society which makes ever-increasing demands on government, a large and complicated public service is inevitable. Great size and complexity carry with them terrible dangers, chiefly, of course, the dangers commonly associated with the word 'bureaucracy.' Individual civil servants may well lose – or may never acquire – the sense of vocation which is so important to the quality of human achievement. They may well feel themselves to be without purpose in a massive government machine. Should this happen, able men and women will not be persuaded to enter the Public Service. To prevent this happening should be the continual care, not only of government, but of all Canadians.

Appendix A

Personal memorandum

1   Would the post be 'political,' i.e. concerned with partisan activities? As I see it, the position should not involve participation in the activities of the Liberal or Conservative (or other) parties as such. Irrespective of the 'secretary's' personal sympathies or previous allegiance he should, upon being appointed, discontinue connection with any political party and should thereafter be called upon to perform no duties of a partisan character. He should, therefore, have no association with party whips, caucuses or offices of national or local party organizations.

2   What should the relationship be to the Prime Minister? Intimate contact with the Prime Minister obviously constitutes one of the principal features of the position, indeed its greatest attraction. In my opinion, however, such contact should be clearly an association in the conduct of the business of the Cabinet and the administration of the country's affairs; it should not in any sense relate to the management of the party nor should the position constitute an adjunct to the Prime Minister's personal staff. The future of the position will depend upon this distinction and if the occupant can, after a brief apprenticeship, perform the function of a secretary to the Cabinet, divorced from party politics, his office will tend in time to be regarded as an integral part of the permanent public service.

3   What would be the duties?

a   Would the 'secretary' assist the Prime Minister in the preparation of agenda for meetings of the Cabinet?
b   Would he be·concerned to see that Ministers and their Departments provided memoranda upon business to be brought before the Cabinet and arrange for their circulation to interested colleagues and officials?

c   Would he attend all Cabinet meetings?

d   Would he record 'conclusions' or minutes and circulate them to members of the Cabinet?

e   What is the present practice in Canada in these respects?

The position of Secretary to the Cabinet in the UK involves all of these functions and derives its importance and utility chiefly therefrom. In fact under Hankey a 'Cabinet Office' was gradually built up, the business conducted therein now forming an essential part of the machinery of government. It relieves the Prime Minister of the day of much of the complicated routine in preparing for, recording and, in collaboration with the responsible Ministers and their Departments, attending to the carrying out of the decisions reached in Cabinet meetings. It is a nerve centre co-ordinating the work of the Cabinet under the Prime Minister's direction.

4   What would the title be? On the English precedent and from the point of view of accuracy, 'Secretary to the Cabinet' seems most appropriate. 'Principal Secretary to the Prime Minister' is open to the objection that in the public mind at least it is likely to be confused with principal *private* secretary; it seems to indicate attachment to the person of the Prime Minister rather than an office in the public service proper. It might, for obvious reasons, be difficult to make use of the English term at once but its introduction might prove easy after 'the secretary' had served a brief innominate apprenticeship.

5   What would be the relationship to Ministers and Heads of Departments? The suggestion that the position should be somewhat analogous to that of a Deputy Minister is of considerable practical importance. 'The secretary's' status, and hence his opportunities of performing the functions contemplated, would be much enhanced if he were free to confer with, consult and make suggestions to Ministers and the higher officers of the Civil Service on a plane of equality – at least without any reason for any sense of subordination. If this were not the case there would be danger of the position degenerating into that of a mere agency of communication for the Prime Minister and there would be little or no possibility of 'the secretary's' initiative being exercised.

6   What would be the relationship to the Prime Minister's office? To his personal staff? Insofar as the Prime Minister's office is a 'Cabinet' office I presume that 'the secretary' would exercise a general oversight thereof. He should, however, in my opinion have no official connection with the Prime Minister's private secretaries or personal staff.

7 What steps could be taken to assist in the development of such a position, i.e. that of a Secretary to the Cabinet? Although it is no doubt true that the position would develop only if its occupant has the ability, energy and initiative to make use of his opportunities, it is probably true also that the Prime Minister could do much by discussing the matter with, and explaining the intention to, the other Ministers, possibly the Leader of the Opposition when occasion arose and particularly the permanent heads of departments and higher officials of the service.

Hankey was first included in 1916 on a temporary basis. His successor now occupies a post which under Hankey became permanent.

8 What preparation could be had before 'the secretary' undertook the actual performance of the duties of his office? It would clearly be unwise, if not impossible, for a person unfamiliar with the operation of the public service, and without experience in the performance of the routine duties of administration, to undertake the important and responsible tasks involved without some preparation. Such a person should be given the opportunity of familiarizing himself with the whole administrative machinery. He should have a chance of getting to know the Ministers and the permanent officials. He should, in fact, for some time after his appointment, be an observer of the machinery in motion.

Some assistance might be had from study of administrative law and practice in combination with a period (of perhaps two months) of actual observation ... Possibly a few weeks attached to the Cabinet office in London under the present Secretary and the opportunity of interviewing Hankey himself at some length would be useful and equip the prospective Secretary for Canada with certain special knowledge which would be of practical value and assist him in establishing the position on a permanent foundation in the Canadian system.

Apart from the foregoing considerations which are of paramount importance in that they have to do with the nature and scope of the position, there remain the following 'baser' questions of a personal and material nature which cannot be ignored:

i   While under the Prime Minister or attached to the Cabinet what would be the situation with respect to –
   1 Possible increases in salary in course of time?
   2 Pension?
   3 Travelling required and expenses connected therewith?
   4 Vacations?
   5 Assistance, e.g. would there likely be a Deputy or Ass't.?

II If under External Affairs what would be the situation with respect to –
1   Seniority?
2   Other members of the Dept.?
3   Advancement?
4   Post abroad?
5   Pension?
6   Leaves?

Montreal
July 26, 1938   A.D.P.H.

Appendix B

Thoughts on Canadian defence policy

1   It seems to me that there are three directions in which Canadian defence policy might logically develop. These can be defined roughly as follows:

First, a *neutralist policy*. This would involve renouncing our traditional joint defence arrangements with the United States, leaving NATO and sharply reducing our defence expenditures. Under such a policy, Canadian defence forces could be restricted to 'coast guard' operations and patrols, probably sea, land, and air, which would have no military significance.

Second, a *limited policy*, based upon the denial to Canadian forces of nuclear weapons of any kind or training for nuclear weapons with concentration on conventional defences. Such a policy could be accompanied by full and public acceptance (or reaffirmation) of the Canadian reliance on the US nuclear deterrent and, as a corollary to this, willingness to do everything necessary or desirable to improve not only the defence of the deterrent but also its effectiveness. So, for example, while Canadian forces at the disposition of a joint Canada-United States command, NATO, and the UN would be strictly conventional, Canada would contribute directly to the efficiency of the nuclear deterrent by the provision of bases, storage, refuelling points, and so forth for SAC as well as for NORAD.

Third, *continuation of the present policy*, as developed since 1940, Ogdensburg. Ostensibly this involves full co-operation with the United States in North American defence, in the protection of the deterrent, facilitation of US strategic nuclear power *and* the preparation and training of Canadian forces for nuclear armament. In fact, this has tended more and more to mean 'integration' of Canadian elements with those of the United States, at any rate in North America. The process has been slow and spasmodic and, though based upon fairly consistent 'doctrine,' has led to criticism within and outside government circles in Canada.

2   The first policy, with variations and additions, is not far from the CCF or the new party platform as I understand it. The second may have some features

in common with the new Liberal position although this is far from clear. The third policy is that which has been followed by Canadian governments, Liberal and Conservative, since before Pearl Harbour. Practice has tended increasingly to diverge from official profession, not only where Canadian 'sovereignty' appears to be involved but especially where there is some nuclear element in the mix.

3   An important advantage which might be claimed for a policy along the second line would be that it would tend to withdraw the poison from recent Canada-US defence relationships. It would enable the Canadian government to be frank and co-operative in its dealings with the United States. It would enormously facilitate the use of Canadian geography for North American defence and it would enable Canadian (conventional) forces to be fitted in precisely with those of the United States while, at the same time, retaining, I think, a larger measure of national identity. In this conception, Canadian forces would be tailored to tasks for the North American Alliance, for NATO and for the UN to which they were suited. Another considerable advantage would be the contribution of such a policy by Canada to restricting to the US and the Soviet Union the use of the nuclear weapon. Such a policy would not and should not involve any reduction in Canadian defence expenditure.

4   The third 'traditional' policy has become greatly confused in the public mind and, I believe, in the minds of those who have to operate within it on both sides of the border as nuclear and other technology has developed. The special public distaste for Canadian involvement in anything to do with the nuclear weapon has been partly responsible for this and the rigidities of US law have added to the difficulty. Consequently it has not been possible for Canadian governments to accept the full implications of agreed principles and the tendency has been to delay and even refuse proposals involving Canadian action even though such actions are clearly implicit in professed policies and recommended by the military advisers of both nations. If the traditional policy is to be continued, there would be advantage in having it restated fully and frankly and it seems to me the government could minimize rather than add to their difficulties at home by a reaffirmation of closest military partnership and frank admission of what that involved in terms of integration and joint command.

5   There are obvious difficulties in any one of these three courses, both practical and political, domestic, bilateral and multilateral. Nevertheless, I am inclined to the opinion that, unless an attempt is made soon to develop a coherent line, the situation at home and in our relations with the United States is

likely to become worse rather than better. The first step would be a serious and certainly 'agonizing' reappraisal in Ottawa on a political and military level. It would also be necessary to have very private conversations with US authorities before anything final were decided. Such an undertaking, even if it did not result in dotting the I's and crossing the T's, is, I am sure, long overdue. Finally, although I have sketched in very roughly three distinguishable courses, it is obvious that there is also a good deal of unexplored territory between each and that combination and shifts of emphasis would be possible.

September 30, 1960   A.D.P.H.

Index